THE OPPOSITE MIRRORS

Law and Philosophy Library

VOLUME 22

The titles published in this series are listed at the end of this volume.

EERIK LAGERSPETZ
University of Jyväskylä, Finland
and
University of Turku, Finland

THE OPPOSITE MIRRORS

An Essay on the Conventionalist Theory of Institutions

KLUWER ACADEMIC PUBLISHERS
DORDRECHT / BOSTON / LONDON

A C.I.P. Catalogue record for this book is available from the Library of Congress.

ISBN 0-7923-3325-X

Published by Kluwer Academic Publishers,
P.O. Box 17, 3300 AA Dordrecht, The Netherlands.

Kluwer Academic Publishers incorporates
the publishing programmes of
D. Reidel, Martinus Nijhoff, Dr W. Junk and MTP Press.

Sold and distributed in the U.S.A. and Canada
by Kluwer Academic Publishers,
101 Philip Drive, Norwell, MA 02061, U.S.A.

In all other countries, sold and distributed
by Kluwer Academic Publishers Group,
P.O. Box 322, 3300 AH Dordrecht, The Netherlands.

Printed on acid-free paper

Printed in the Netherlands

A LEENA

toujours pour la première fois

TABLE OF CONTENTS

ACKNOWLEDGEMENTS

This book is about institutions, about their existence and about the roles they play in our lives. Thus it is a book on the metaphysics of certain elements of our social world. Legal institutions occupy a central place in it, but it also contains chapters which are intended to be relevant for economists, sociologists, political scientists, and for students of human societies in general. It is, however, written by a professional philosopher who has only a limited and fragemented knowledge of these disciplines. My only excuse for these digressions is that my worthy colleagues in the departments of Social Sciences and of Law have no inhibitions about doing philosophy when they see a need for it. I have greatly benefited from their efforts, and, by this book, I would like to reciprocate their contributions.

This work has not grown as a tree grows. Rather it has developed and spread like ivy: different branches have grown separately, yet ultimately, I hope, to form a kind of unity. An earlier version appeared in *Acta Philosophica Fennica*, published by the Finnish Philosophical Society, and was presented as a Ph.D. thesis in the University of Turku. I have expanded some chapters, and made minor corrections in all, but the basic structure and the important arguments are the same. After completing this new version, I became acquainted with Dick Ruiter's new book *Institutional Legal Facts* (Dordrecht: Kluwer 1993). Ruiter's book is clearly relevant for my project, and I should have taken it into account. Finally, I decided not to comment it, hoping that I shall have an opportunity to discuss on Ruiter's important theory in some future work.

Numerous people have helped me, in various ways. My teachers, Juhani Pietarinen, Risto Hilpinen and Hannu Nurmi have taught me most of what I know about philosophy. They have also encouraged in the moments of hesitation. The year I spent at Oxford was decisive for the development of this work. I was fortunate in having an excellent supervisor, Joseph Raz, who is not only a good philosopher, but also a most lovable person. Without my friends, I would never have written this work. Of those many people who have been important for me, I shall single out only three: Simo Vihjanen, Matti Wiberg and Jari Talja. From Oxford, I want to mention the people in the little informal discussion group who frequented the Ryle Room. Leslie Green acted as the examiner of my thesis. He performed his role in a most judicious way, and his comments were extremely helpful. Govert den Hartogh is the man who has always understood what I have tried to say and has, then, explained it to me. I have profited from the comments to the first version made by Aulis Aarnio, Raimo Tuomela, Ilkka Niiniluoto and by many others. Mikko Heiniö, the musicologist, and Heikki Patomäki, the specialist on International Relations, have borrowed some of my concepts and applied them in a critical way to new areas. None of these people shares all my ideas. Of course, all the mistakes, etc. etc. George Maude corrected my English, with great patience. He also made some useful substantial remarks on the manuscript. Valtteri Arstila prepared the Index and provided technical assistance.

I want to express my deep gratitude to all. There is one person left, one who has helped me through this sometimes difficult process of writing, and with whom I have started a project much more important and challenging than this book. To her, I dedicated the first version. So, there is at least one line in that book which needs no revision.

CHAPTER 1

METHODOLOGICAL REMARKS

1.1. Conventional facts

Terms which are used to refer to institutions are in some sense like theoretical terms. The word 'State', for example, does not refer to anything directly observable. We say that 'the state' has some properties, or even that it does something. But all we can perceive are just people and their doings (plus certain physical objects). 'State' seems to have something in common with, say, 'electron' or 'eco-system', which are theoretical terms having a meaning only as parts of scientific theories. However, it is not only political scientists or legal theorists who use terms like 'State'. Ordinary people have to deal with the State almost daily, and when referring to it, they do not usually suppose the truth of any scientific theory. As institutions form a part of our everyday life, the terms referring to them belong to our everyday vocabulary. Neither can these terms be removed from our vocabulary. A scientist could claim that the extension of an established theoretical term is empty. There was no thing corresponding to the term 'phlogiston'. But 'State' is clearly different. The State as an institution could perhaps whither away, but it cannot be proved to be non-existent.

These terms – I will call them institutional terms – have another interesting property. Somehow they are connected with norms and rules. When we refer to something as 'a legislature', we suppose that its existence as a legislature is based on some norms which make it what it is: a legislature is not just a group of people having the habit of gathering together in a big building. These norms form a part of a larger normative structure, and the actions of a legislature and even the fact that some actions are ascribed to it can be understood only by grasping the content of this structure.

Besides entities, some acts and properties seem to have this inherently normative nature, too. 'Cashing a cheque' or 'having a legal right' are understandable only in a pre-existing normative context. In this sense they have something in common with expressions like 'wrongdoing' or 'having a moral right'. These are meaningful only in a context of a presupposed system of moral norms. But nevertheless, it seems that we can speak about institutions or institutionally defined properties and acts without committing ourselves to any substantial moral position.

Hence, there seems to be something mysterious in the existence of institutions. Heidegger, for example, was puzzled by it:

> A state – is. By virtue of the fact that the state police arrest a suspect, or that so–and–so–many typewriters are clattering in a government building, taking down the words of ministers and state secretaries? Or "is" the state in a conversation between the chancellor and the British foreign minister? The state is But where is being situated? Is it situated anywhere at all? (Heidegger 1959, 35)

The following intuitions seem to be widely shared:
(1) Institutional terms refer to real things: there *are* states and legal rights, for example.
(2) Nevertheless, when we try to *explain* the properties and actions of institutions, we are ultimately able to find only individual people, their properties, beliefs, actions and interactions.
(3) Statements about institutions and institutionally defined actions and properties are not statements about people's mental states or physical movements. They have something to do with norms and rules which are not physical things.
(4) It is possible to speak about institutions without committing oneself to the acceptance of a system of norms or rules.

I take it for granted that scientists as well as laymen often have these intuitions. I also think that properly interpreted, these intuitions are mutually compatible and correct. The main reason why one or the other member of the pairs (1), (2) and (3), (4) is sometimes rejected is that the members of the pairs do not look compatible at first sight. Thus, I do not believe that the solution I will provide is self–evident. Although the solutions to the apparent dilemmas created by the pairs are not logically dependent on each other, certain types of solutions often run together. We could take examples from social sciences – but the apparent dilemmas are equally relevant in legal theory.

For example, Karl Olivecrona – as a representative of the Scandinavian school of jurisprudential realism – firmly rejects both (1) and (3). The resulting theory is strictly nominalistic and non–normativistic; for example:

> Duty has no place in the actual world, but only in the imagination of men. What really exists is certain feelings of duty with which the idea of an imaginary bond is connected. (Olivecrona 1939, 75)

For Olivecrona, "the actual world" is "the world of space and time", and therefore all things referred to in legal language are but "fictional" or "imaginary", and all institutional actions are "magical". A right, for example, is "an empty word" referring to "an imaginary power", which nevertheless is "apt to engender a feeling of power".

The difficulties arising from the rejection of (1) are clearly visible in the early works of such theorists as Olivecrona or his compatriot and fellow realist Lundstedt. On the one hand, they try to deny the reality of all institutional objects and properties; on other hand, they have immense difficulties in saying anything informative about their subject, law, without using these terms which are supposed to be void of meaning. Lundstedt puts terms like 'right' in inverted commas, thus trying to avoid the ontological commitment by a typographical trick. These difficulties reflect the nature of institutional terms mentioned at the beginning of this chapter: they cannot simply be removed from our language any more than, say, colour terms, merely by inventing a new theory. (Louis Althusser, being an extreme opponent of (2), puts terms like 'subject' in inverted commas.)

If we try to find theories which take the opposite course and deny the intuition (2), we easily find several dead horses: theories of organic states, collective personalities or national spirits. But there are also more modern and plausible–looking versions. For example, N.E. Simmonds explains that questions of the validity of constitutional norms cannot be merely about officials' actions and intentions, for

> if the question about the nature of a practice *were* a question about what officials *thought* then the content of their thought could not be a thought about the nature of the practice.

> What is needed at this point in a legal theory is a notion of meaning that is not restricted to the subjective intentions and valuations of individual actors. (...) The essential point to grasp here is that intersubjective meaning is not only shared subjective meaning, it is what makes shared subjective meaning possible. (Simmonds 1984, 104)

Simmonds seems to suppose it would be circular to maintain that individuals try to form beliefs about the nature of a practice and to follow it, and, at the same time, claim that the practice simply consists of these beliefs and actions. But can intersubjective meaning exist independently of these beliefs and actions? Can it exist even if it has no effect at all on individual intentions and beliefs? Did it exist before people – officials, for example – recognized it? If not, it seems that shared subjective meaning is equally necessary for the existence of intersubjective meaning. So, why give a preferred status to the intersubjective meaning?

In an earlier version of this book, I characterized my attempt to preserve the intuition (2) as a commitment to a form of methodological individualism. After a more cautious reflection on the holism–individualism dispute, I have decided to reject the label. I am not requiring that theories of institutions should be reduced to theories of individuals, or that statements about institutions should or could be translated into an individualistic language. Intuition (2) is not about language, but about the explanatory primacy of certain things and properties. The corresponding methodological requirement is the following: when we try to explain or describe something in institutional terms, we should *also* try to develop a *model* which is formulated in individualistic terms, and which could help us to know the typical actions, attitudes and properties of the individuals which make the institutional description possible. Thus, if we say that the State does something, we should, as social theorists, try to understand the nature of and motives behind the actions performed by individuals who are occupying the relevant positions in the state machinery. It seems that this idea of corresponding models at the 'micro–' and 'macro–' levels is not dissimilar from the relations between the levels of description in the natural sciences. There, too, reductions or theoretical replacements in the strict logical sense are untypical.

My position does not exclude the possibility that individual actions and properties, are in turn, explained by institutional terms. This is a chicken–and–egg problem: my theory just reminds us that in order to have chickens there must always be eggs. Then, it might be asked, why should we give any kind of primacy to individuals in our explanations? My answer is the following. Because individuals are, among other things, *agents* and therefore able to make free choices, their actions have, at least sometimes, aspects which cannot be fully explained by pointing to the institutional setting of the actions. In regard to institutions, there is no comparable explanatory residual. Then, of course, arises the further question: why should we describe individuals as agents? In the chapter 2.1. I try to show why we have to describe individuals (most importantly, ourselves) as free agents. Generally, I would leave open the question whether a theory of this type should be characterized as a form of methodological individualism or not.

If problems of this kind are usually more familiar to social scientists (although my examples were from legal theory) , the problem created by the pair (3), (4) usually appears in the context of legal science. Indeed, a great part of the ever–recurring dispute between Positivism and Natural Law seems to be about this issue. However, we can find interesting instances of the problem in other areas. One of the most influential theories denying the validity of the intuition (4) is John Searle's theory of brute and institutional facts.

Searle defines *brute facts* as follows:

> One might say that they share the feature that the concepts which make up the knowledge are essentially physical, or in its dualistic version, either physical or mental. The model for systematic knowledge of this kind is the natural sciences, and the basis for all knowledge is generally supposed to be empirical observation recording sense experiences. (Searle 1974, 50)

Searle's brute facts are obviously the stuff of which Olivecrona's "actual world" is made of. *Institutional facts* are different:

> They are indeed facts; but their existence, unlike the existence of brute facts, presupposes the existence of certain human institutions. (...) These 'institutions' are systems of constitutive rules. Every institutional fact is underlain by (a system of) rule(s) of the form 'X counts as Y in context C'. (Searle 1974, 51–2)

This characterization of institutional facts has inspired many social and legal theorists (including MacCormick and Weinberger 1986). The distinction between institutional and brute facts is, I think, sufficiently clear. Institutional facts: 'X cashes a cheque', 'Y has a legal right', 'Z makes a move in chess' – are inherently dependent on rules which exist in some community. *But what kind of fact, then, is the fact that these rules do exist in relevant communities?* Obviously, a fact about the existence of a rule cannot be a brute fact in Searle's sense: it is not a fact on the furniture of the physical world, neither are the statements expressing it subjects of direct perceptual control. If Searle's classification is meant to be an exhaustive one, *facts about rules must themselves be institutional facts.* Therefore, they are inherently dependent on the existence of further rules: something is a rule only if there is a rule with the effect that it is counted as a rule. We are in an infinite regress. This might be called as the logical regress of rules.

Searle believes that institutional facts have an irreducible normative aspect; otherwise his famous derivation from 'is' to 'ought' wouldn't go through. But he admits that we cannot put people under full moral requirements simply by inventing a new institution and trapping outsiders in it. The moral force of institutions is ultimately derived from the acceptance of people participating into these institutions. But where does this ultimate acceptance get its moral force? Is it based on a rule that certain acts are counted as expressions of acceptance in certain contexts and therefore create obligations to follow other rules? This is a more familiar version of infinite regress: it is like Prichard's problem of the promise to keep promises. (It should be added that in a more recent article, Searle developes a notion of social fact which is very near to my own. See Searle (1991).)

My solution to these problems is to develop a notion of non–brute fact which is not inherently rule–dependent. The basic idea behind the solution is the following: *There are things which exist and facts which hold only if the relevant individuals believe that they exist or hold and act according to these beliefs.* What we call as institutions and institutional facts fall under this description.

Descriptions of these things and facts are implicitly circular or self–referential, but the circle in question is not a vicious one. In the descriptions, institutional terms reappear only in the scopes of propositional operators describing the attitudes of relevant individuals. Moreover, the existence of the related beliefs is only a necessary condition for the things being there. Here are some examples:

> What the international community accepts as a state is a state. (van Maarseveen and van der Tung 1978, 234)

> Money is whatever is generally accepted in exchange. (Dornbusch and Fischer 1978, 209)

> A nation exists when a significant number of people in a community consider themselves to form a nation, or behave as if they formed one. (Seton–Watson 1977, 5)

> A work of art is an artifact of a kind created to be presented to an artworld public. (Dickie 1984, 80)

> A social class is a quasi–group of people whose links are that they *think* they have similar interests, and who share common *beliefs* about the system of social class, their own position in that system, and similar dispositions as to their behaviour appropriate to their position in that system. (Jarvie 1972, 120)

I am not claiming that these descriptions are necessarily correct: only that they are of the right type (the fourth one becomes more transparent when we try to describe "an artworld public"). All the descriptions are *functional* in the sense that *any* object which can be a subject of the relevant attitudes and actions may satisfy them. There are functional limitations. Items which are accepted as money must be distinguishable, relatively durable, relatively scarce, not too difficult to use etc. But inside these constraints anything, including cows, furs, shells, and bits of information in a computer can be used as money. And almost anything can work as an artwork. In this sense, these terms behave like, say, 'weapon'. Anything used or intended to be used as a weapon satisfies the term. But unlike the existence of a weapon, the existence of money, or a state, or art is a social or conventional and not a private matter. Private money is as impossible as private language. Money is something existing in a community. Neither is it enough that members of a community just happen to believe that some objects are money: they must also know that this belief is generally shared by other members. Moreover, the attitudes must be shared by *relevant* individuals. And lastly, these attitudes must be related to actions. They must appear as (at least partial) reasons for the members of the respective societies to do certain things. If something is money, it is generally used as a means of exchange and as a measure and store of value. The shared belief is a necessary but not a sufficient condition for the existence of institutional entities and properties. (Cf. Searle 1991, 339)

The idea that institutions and institutional facts exist by the virtue of shared beliefs in their existence is called here conventionalism. Institutional terms are normally used in expressions which can be analysed in this conventionalist way. Such statements express conventional facts.

As my examples show, there is nothing new in this idea. However, there might be some new elements in my attempt to explicate the idea in a more precise way and to connect it to other theories and issues.

One claim which has been made against the idea of conventionality of social facts is that it is just an instance of conceptual relativism or subjectivism. For example, Alexander Peczenik argues against Tore Strömholm's conventionalist theory of law in the following way:

> Strömholm... claims that the concept "valid law" does not refer to anything extant. The reason is that valid legal rules would disappear had people not thought about legal rules. However, cannot one say about material things? The fact that one now and here sees a forest depends not only on the forest but also on the eyes and mind of the observer. (...) Had people not interpreted the "data" as a forest, the forest would disappear, precisely as valid law. *All* concepts are conventional. Yet, it is absurd to claim that *no* concepts refer to anything extant. (Peczenik, 1989, 262)

According to my version of conventionalism, the concept "valid law" refers to something extant, namely to conventional entities of certain kind. These entities do exist, in their own peculiar way. Nevertheless, it is true that they would necessarily disappear if people ceased to use the concept, and *in this sense they are not like forests.* The claim is not that our *concepts* are just conventionally agreed ways of classifying our perceptual world. The claim is that the entities themselves may have a merely conventional existence. This claim is neutral in respect of the ontological realism–antirealism issue. A realist would say that there were forests before humans entered the scene, and, hopefully, there may be some forests left when they leave it. But there were no valid laws before the emergence of human societies. Here, I do not take any stand on the question of realism. I admit, however, that my theory may provide certain resources for the use of critical realists, for it may provide a neutral interpretation of some seemingly anti–realist intuitions we have.

1.2. Mutual beliefs

What makes propositional attitudes so intriguing is their capability for self–reference and for cross–reference. We can have beliefs about other people's beliefs, while they have at the same time beliefs about our beliefs. This gives rise to the phenomenon called mutual or shared belief, or common or mutual knowledge (the terminology is not well established). For example, according to *The Economist* (29. 12. 1979) "...the Russians know the Americans believe the Russians think the Soviets could win a first strike nuclear war." Suppose that this is true, and also that the Americans, by reading *The Economist*, learn this and the Russians learn that they have learned it. The epistemic situation between the super–powers would then be the following:

(1) The Russians believe that they can win.
(2) The Americans believe (1).
(3) The Russians believe (2).
(4) The Americans believe (3).
(5) The Russians believe (4); or, they believe that the Americans believe that the Russians believe that the Americans believe that the Russians believe that they can win.

Obviously, these reiterated beliefs can be of extreme practical importance. Uncertainty at some level may affect the behaviour of the parties. For this reason the parties not only engage in intelligence activities in order to find out each other's beliefs, they also try to find methods to convince the other side. But reiterated beliefs appear also in less exciting contexts. Here is a nice list of possible examples: "Shaking hands is an everyday example, and so is rowing a boat, speaking and listening, driving down a highway, signalling a Morse code, walking in a crowd of people, meeting, and dancing". (Clark and Carlson 1982, 2) In all the cases certain beliefs are normally shared by the participants. People become more conscious of these beliefs when there is some room for uncertainty, when it is not self–evident that all participants of an activity master the same rules of language, traffic or dancing. Sociologists have coined phrases like "taking the role of the generalized other" (Mead), "interpenetration of perspectives" (Dewey) or "reciprocity of perspectives" (Schutz), but it seems that they all are talking about situations in which we not only believe something but also expect others to have the same beliefs, including this belief about others' beliefs (Bach 1975, 191). Consider, for example, Schutz' analysis of the face–to–face relationship:

> as I watch you, I shall see that you are oriented to me, that you are seeking the subjective meaning of my words, my actions, and what I have in mind insofar as you are concerned. And I will in turn take account of the fact that you are thus oriented to me, and this will influence both my intentions with respect to you and how I act toward you. This again you will see, I will see that you have seen it, and so on. This interlocking of glances, this thousand–faceted mirroring of each other, is one of the unique features of the face–to–face situation. (Schutz 1967, 170. See also the fascinating examples in Lacan 1966, 11–61, 197–213.)

The standard notion of mutual belief includes a series of reiterated beliefs like (1)–(5) ascending to infinity. The first analysis is then:

(MB) It is mutually believed in a population S that p iff
  (1) everyone in S believes that p;
  (2) everyone in S believes that everyone in S believes that p;
  and so on ad infinitum.

This analysis supposes that human beings can have infinite sets of beliefs in their minds. However, the human mind seems to be an apparatus with a limited capacity.

The defenders of (MB) can argue in the following way. Although people can possess only a finite number of propositions as contents of their minds at any one time, they can have an access to infinite sets of propositions: they can believe them in a dispositional or potential sense. For example, I could work out the truth, and form the respective beliefs, of an infinite number of arithmetical propositions , if I only had enough time. Similarly, if I know the syntactical rules of English, I can in principle form an infinite number of judgements on the grammaticality of different expressions (on this defence, see Tuomela 1984, 210). Schutz may mean something like that when he says that in a face–to–face relationship the mirror images are not grasped reflectively but lived through (Schutz 1967, 170).

Jane Heal (1978) has shown two flaws in this defence. Firstly, we are interested in mutual beliefs that have an effect in interaction situations. These beliefs are able to guide people's actions. A belief with, say 10^{30} iterations ("I believe that she believes that I believe...") cannot possibly occur in my practical reasoning under any circumstances (Heal 1978, 119–20). The supposition that I "dispositionally" have this kind of belief has no explanatory role whatsoever. Secondly, the analogy with arithmetic or syntax does not hold. I can "dispositionally" have an infinite number of beliefs about the truths of arithmetical propositions in the sense that I know the rules of arithmetic and can apply them recursively. But my beliefs about the beliefs of some other person are empirical. I cannot mechanically infer the contents of anybody's mind (Heal 1978, 121). And in any case, it is not clear what it means to have dispositions which cannot actualize themselves in any physically possible circumstances.

Another solution would simply be to cut off the regress. Thus, Kent Bach (1975, 192) proposes that only the first two iterations are needed; we get an adequate definition simply by deleting the *ad infinitum* clause from (MB). But this proposal seems to be ad hoc. Even if beliefs of a higher order are unusual, they certainly can exist (witness spy stories and some of the psychological analyses of R.D. Laing).

Clark and Carlson (1982) remark that in order to form a mutual belief, people need not have separate pieces of evidence for all component beliefs: they can make inductive inferences from a single or a few pieces. This idea is already in Schiffer (1972, 32–6). In the acquisition of mutual beliefs, this claim is relevant. The super powers in our case cannot safely infer that beliefs are distributed symmetrically between the parties, but normally we can make such inferences. We form new mutual beliefs by using the earlier ones as premises. As members of the human species, and as members of various human communities, we already believe that individuals being in an interaction with us have similar inductive, practical, linguistic, perceptual, etc. capacities, and that they also share with us some background beliefs and standards. From this we can infer that certain properties of a situation are generally taken as evidence for certain beliefs, and therefore we can in such a situation relatively safely make inferences about other people's beliefs, including their beliefs about our beliefs. Thus, if I see you looking at me while I am sitting at a table, I have evidence that you know that there is a table, that you know that I know that there is a table and that you know that I know that you know that there is a table... Only under special circumstances (e. g. I recognize that you are heavily intoxicated) are there reasons not to make such an inference automatically.

The question is how these beliefs should be represented in a formal definition. Although we do not have infinite sets of propositions as contents of our minds, we have beliefs about infinite sets. We believe in generalizations, generalizations about all arithmetical propositions for example. The infinity condition in the definition of mutual belief is most naturally represented as a generalization over higher– order beliefs:

(MB') It is mutually believed in a population S that p iff

(1) everyone in S believes that p;

(2) everyone in S believes that everyone in S believes that p;

and so on i times, when i is the number of reiterations needed to describe the beliefs of the members in S ($2 \leq i < \infty$);

(i+1) everyone in S believes that no one in S has any such beliefs of a higher order (>i) about the beliefs of the members of S which would have an effect on the behaviour of any member.

Thus, there can be just two reiterations, or arbitrarily many. Some members of S can be more sophisticated in their beliefs than others. Mutual beliefs make understanding and interaction possible, and (i+1) guarantees that there is no uncertainty inhibiting this. When agents have – dispositionally – this belief, they have no reason to worry about the beliefs of others. (i+1) also guarantees that there is no uncertainty concerning the belief (i+1) itself.

In a sense the situation is similar in the cases of a single agent. When I believe a theory, I do not believe in all its consequences. I believe that its axioms are true, that I can work out many of its consequences, and that I do not at the same time have any beliefs inconsistent with my believing the axioms. The last belief is a generalization like (i+1). It can be untrue. I can test it by working out some of the consequences, as I can test the generalization that there are no higher order beliefs creating uncertainty among the people I am interacting with.

In personal correspondence, Raimo Tuomela criticized my suggestion (MB'). According to him, the requirement of a positive belief on the nonexistence of "disturbing" beliefs (i+1) is too demanding. I suggested an amended version:

(MB") (1)–(i) as in (MB')
(i'+1) no one in S believes that it is possible that anyone in S has any such beliefs of a higher- order (>i) about the beliefs of the members of S which would have an effect on the behaviour of any member.

Instead of speaking about a positive belief prevailing in S, (i'+1) speaks about the absence of beliefs of a certain kind. This condition is weaker than (i+1): the latter entails the former but not vice versa. As Tuomela remarked, there are many possible suggestions for a definition, among which there is not much to choose.

Mutual beliefs, however defined, form the basis of what I have called conventional facts. We may recall that there are certain facts which hold because relevant individuals believe that they hold. This belief must be mutual in the relevant group. Let us give an example. Suppose that the relevant population S consists of all the inhabitants of a certain village – S–ville. From time immemorial, the S–villeans have held their meetings under a tree growing near the village. It is a mutual belief among S–villeans that there is a meeting place under the tree. That there is a meeting–place under the tree is a conventional fact in S. The definition of a *conventional fact* is the following:

(CF) 'a is F' expresses a conventional fact iff it is a necessary and a sufficient condition for a's being F that
(1) it is a mutual belief in the relevant population S that a is F, and
(2) in the situations of the relevant type, (1) is at least a partial reason for the members of S to perform actions which are meaningful because a is F.

For example, because the S–villeans believe that meetings are held under the tree, and because they believe that the others believe it, too, they have a reason to go under the tree, provided that they want to attend the meetings. For those S–villeans wanting to avoid the meetings it is a reason not to go there; for a woodcutter it is a reason not to cut that particular tree down, and so on.

It is a peculiar property of conventional facts that propositions expressing them cannot be false if they are generally believed to be true and if this belief plays a relevant role in the behaviour of relevant persons. The sentence "There is a meeting–place under the tree near S--ville" cannot be true if the S–villeans do not believe it. But if they do, the sentence is true simply by virtue of the mutual belief. While any individual S–villean can be mistaken in his beliefs (and act inappropriately), *collectively* the S–villeans cannot be wrong in their belief: their meeting–place is there if they say so. Similarly, any individual speaker of a language can have mistaken beliefs about the grammaticality of a sentence. But the whole linguistic community cannot collectively be mistaken. Beliefs about conventional facts are collectively non–corrigible. This belief–dependency makes conventional facts quite extraordinary. Nevertheless, I cannot see any reason to deny that they are indeed facts. They form an important part of our environment. The fact that shops close their doors at eight is a conventional fact in my society. As a fact, it is at least as reliable and as important for me as the natural fact that the darkness will fall at eight this time of the year, and it equally constrains my actions. From my point of view, it could as well be a law of nature. Conventional facts are like natural facts in the sense that they are not dependent on the beliefs and actions of any particular individual. They are unlike natural facts in the sense that they are dependent on the beliefs and actions of all relevant individuals.

We must, of course, allow some exceptions to the universality requirements in (MB') and (CF). It is enough that sufficiently many S–villeans believe that the conventional fact holds. We ascribe mutual beliefs to populations in the same way we generally ascribe beliefs to groups. If we say that the Finns believe in a personal God, we express a statistical generalization about the reactions of Finns in certain situations. Some Finns do not believe in a personal God; most of them go on most of their time without thinking about the matter at all. If they were questioned about their faith, most of them would affirm that they believe in God. The claim that there is a mutual belief in some S is made in a similar way.

(CF) says that conventional facts exist by virtue of beliefs of "relevant populations". How is the relevancy to be determined? Intuitively, if the S–villeans generally believe that some place is their meeting–place, it is their meeting–place, while if the R–villeans believe that some other place is the meeting–place of S–villeans, that place is not necessarily a meeting–place. But if we want to test the statement that some place is the meeting– place of the S–villeans, we have to determine which people are S–villeans and which are not.

Populations relevant to the existence of conventional facts can normally be identified by other conventional facts. If, for example, something is a conventional fact in the Finnish society, the relevant population is defined by the legal facts which define the territory of Finland and set the criteria of citizenship – and these legal facts are based on explicit conventions. In the case of S–ville the matter may be more complicated. Perhaps there are no explicit rules defining the borders of S–ville. There may be some disagreement on whether some person really is an S–villean or not. But there are criteria, however inexact, and these criteria exist because they are used by the S–villeans themselves. Thus, "relevant populations" define themselves. Human beings live and act in groups, and these groups – families, clubs, neighbourhoods, communities, tribes, churches, parties, nations and alliances – define themselves by referring some criteria of membership. Quite often, these criteria are recognized by outsiders, by the State, for example. Sometimes this outside recognition is fundamental. The statelets ("bantustans") created by the South African government are not states because the international community has not recognized them as states.

There is still one problem in my notion of conventionality. Suppose that the S–villeans themselves believe in my theory of conventional facts. Suppose, moreover, that they are epistemically rational in the sense that they form only justified and true beliefs. It seems that they cannot create any new conventional facts. For how can the relevant beliefs get started? Suppose the S–villeans are considering whether a certain place has become their meeting–place or not. Before an individual S–villean can form an opinion about the matter, he has to learn whether a sufficient number of other S–villeans have formed an opinion about the matter. Being conventionalists, they believe that the truth of the matter is settled only when they have formed an opinion. Thus, none of them can believe that there is a meeting–place until most of the others have formed that belief. Then, of course, they cannot form that belief and the conventional fact does not hold.

In some cases the problem is solved by a *fiat*, by an instant creation of a conventional fact. Suppose that there is a general meeting of S–villeans, but no established practice of having meetings. The question of having some commonly agreed meeting–place arises in discussion. Somebody proposes loudly "Let this place be our meeting–place in the future". If no one protests, and if the need of having a meeting–place is generally shared, the mutual belief and the related conventional fact are created. The participants simply decide to accept it, and with that decision they simultaneously form the relevant higher–order beliefs.

But what if there is a time lag? How can a conventional fact emerge gradually, except by virtue of at least some false beliefs? Some people may, for some reason, start to believe that certain place is a meeting–place, and behave accordingly. If the belief becomes widely spread, it also becomes true. But, so runs the argument, it can get started only if some individuals originally have false beliefs. If all members of the population are epistemically rational, i.e. do not accept false beliefs, the conventional fact cannot arise.

This counter–argument is indeed valid, but only in an ideal case. Suppose that there is a community consisting of two members, Ms. A and Mr. B. A and B are (i) epistemically rational, accepting only justified true beliefs, and (ii) *epistemically transparent to each other* in the sense that whenever A (B) believes something, B (A) immediately knows that. In such a community, no conventional fact can arise. For A believes that a conventional fact holds only if she believes that B believes it, and vice versa.

Compare this with a less ideal case in which (ii) does not hold. A and B have no direct access to each other's minds. Instead, they accept beliefs when there are reasonable grounds for acceptance. They are considering the question of whether a certain place actually is their common meeting–place or not. If they share an interest in having a meeting–place, if the place they are considering satisfies that interest and if there is no obvious alternative to that place, A and B may have reasonable grounds for accepting the belief that the place in question is their meeting–place, and for behaving accordingly. Then, it becomes their meeting–place. William James recognized this phenomenon in his famous lecture 'The Will to Believe':

> wherever a desired result is achieved by the co–operation of many independent persons, its existence is a pure consequence of the precursive faith in one another of those immediately concerned. A government, an army, a commercial system, a ship, a college, an athletic team, all exist on this condition, without which not only is nothing achieved, but nothing is ever attempted. (...) There are, then, cases where a fact cannot come at all unless a preliminary faith exists in its coming.

The conclusion is that conventional facts can arise only among people who are not epistemically transparent. Far from being a problem, it is an essential part of my theory. In chapter 2., I shall try to show that general epistemic transparency is an impossibility: our knowledge about the beliefs and actions of others is always a subject of substantial uncertainty. *The role of conventions in human life is to diminish this uncertainty.*

What kinds of facts are conventional in my sense? The paradigmatic cases I have in my mind are (1) cases in which a is a rule or norm or practice in S and (2) cases in which a is F because there is a rule, norm or practice in S that a should be counted as F. Both rules and instances or applications of rules can be treated as conventional facts. But two things should be noticed. Firstly, this is not intended to be a linguistic analysis covering all the possible meanings of the words 'rule' or 'norm'. For example, technical rules are not conventional: we have a reason to follow them even if they are not generally recognized or followed, if they are useful for our purposes. The norms of personal or critical morality are not conventional either. If I believe that eating meat is wrong, I have a reason to follow the rule never to eat meat even if I am the only person having that conviction. The contrast with the rules of grammar, etiquette or (some parts of) law is obvious. (Theorists having a conventionalist view of morality may disagree here.)

A second important point is that the notion of conventional fact is not inherently tied to the existence of rules. It is possible that some a is F simply because the relevant mutual belief is there: this cuts off the regress appearing in Searle's account. We can sometimes create new conventional (or, as Searle calls them, social) facts without a reference to a pre–existing practice. I can sometimes communicate meanings without relying on rules which would give my expressions or actions that meaning; I can give authoritative commands without a rule authorizing me (as in Weber's case of charismatic authority) and so on. Some convention–creating acts can have their intended effects simply because they are believed to have these effects. Ultimately, every chain of rules has to originate from convention–creating acts.

There are several classifications of rules in the literature. Searle's distinction between regulative and constitutive rules is important because it reminds us of the fact that rules do not only regulate actions by prescribing and prohibiting: they also make it possible for us to do new things, by defining something as something. However, these classes are not mutually exclusive. It seems that every rule called "regulative" by Searle has a constitutive aspect. A rule which forbids stealing creates new types of actions: stealing and refraining from stealing. Any regulative rule makes it possible to re–describe actions as instances of following or breaking that rule. On the other hand, not all constitutive rules have a regulative effect. But many do. A constitutive rule of football says that players have to kick the ball, not to throw it with hands. If this rule is not generally observed in a game, the game in question is not football but a different game. Nevertheless, an individual player can break the rule and suffer a penalty. We could either say that the general observance of a regulative rule constitutes the practice, or that the constitutive rules of the practice have a regulative effect in individual cases. These descriptions are equivalent.

My first analysis of rules is the following:

(R) R is a regulative rule in S if
- (1) the members of S generally comply with R;
- (2) there is a mutual belief in S that R is a regulative rule in S,and
- (3) (2) is at least partly a reason for (1).

(DR) R is a definition rule in S if
- (1) the members of S generally count a's as F's;
- (2) it is a mutual belief in S that there is a definition rule R in S which defines a's as F's, and
- (3) (2) is at least partly a reason for (1).

These analyses cannot be the whole story. Sometimes it is possible to say that there are rules, for example, legal rules, which are not generally followed by the members of a particular society. Therefore (R) and (DR) give only sufficient conditions for the existence of rules. Rules can also exist by virtue of belonging to systems of rules, systems which by and large are effectively accepted and followed. Another condition for the existence of rules is the following:

(RR) R is a rule in S if there is a rule R' which defines R as a rule in S.

(R) and (RR) are special cases of my description of conventional facts. (RR), however, shows how the existence of a rule is not necessarily a conventional fact. A rule can exist because it is defined as a rule by another rule. But because the chain produced by the reapplications of (RR) cannot go on indefinitely, the ultimate rules which define other rules must exist conventionally. The conjunction of (R), (DR) and (RR) gives the necessary and sufficient conditions for something's being a conventionally existing rule in S.

This account of rules leaves many questions unanswered. For example the question of how, how the belief that R is a rule for the community can work as a reason for the members of that community to comply with it? The fact that it is recognized as a rule is a necessary condition for conscious (and not merely epiphenomenal) compliance, but it is not a sufficient condition for that. There is no simple answer, for rules affect on individuals' practical reasoning in different ways. Some answers are provided in the later parts of this book.

Institutions are systems of existing, interlocked rules. By giving a conventionalist analysis for rules, it is possible to build up a theory of such basic institutions as law, money or language which satisfies our pre–theoretical intuitions mentioned before. Notice that the term 'institution' is used in a wide sense. Usually, we do not call language an institution. Here, this use is adopted in order to indicate the common nature of rule–governed practices. A more restricted use of the term presupposes that 'social institutions' are only those practices which are related to *authority* and *power*. In chapters 4.– 9. the term 'institution' is mainly used in this, more restricted sense.

1.3. Methodological individualism and non–individualism

Because methodological individualism is a hotly disputed issue, some further remarks might be useful. Firstly, it is important to notice that not all statements about social entities or properties are analysable with the help of conventional facts. My analysis applies only to such concepts (or their roughly translatable equivalents) which are themselves used in the relevant societies. Many concepts used in social theory are constructions produced by the theorists themselves. The methodological desiderata adopted here recommends that for explanations using concepts of that kind, we should try to formulate corresponding individualist explanations; but the conventionalist machinery is not necessarily of any help in that search. The militant defenders of individualism (Popper, Watkins and Hayek) are certainly wrong if they claim that when we do not have an individualistic explanation which corresponds to a proposed explanation referring to social wholes, we should reject the holistic explanation. For we may be able to find it only in a (perhaps distant) future. The situation is the same in the natural sciences: Mendelian genetics, for example, was a great step forward in spite of the fact that its underlying molecular mechanisms were discovered much later.

Secondly, a general reduction to individualistic theories is not on my agenda. A reduction is a logical relation between theories. An obvious problem in the social sciences is that we do not have generally accepted theories on either side of the relation. Some theories may be reducible to some other theories: in any case, it is a contingent fact.

In order to make the methodological claim more explicit, we can distinguish the following levels of description:

(A) the level of neurophysiological descriptions and descriptions of theoretical psychology;

(B) the level of agency descriptions, (such as actions, intentions, and deliberations);

(C) the level of institutional descriptions;

(D) the level of theoretical social constructs (such as social systems, socio–economic classes, or stages of development).

In social theory, level (B) is the fundamental one. It is fundamental because we necessarily conceive ourselves as agents, and we can understand others as we understand ourselves, by supposing that they, too, are agents. We form descriptions at the (C)–level by understanding the meaning of described institutions for the agents living under those institutions. The theory presented here is mainly about the relationships between the (B)– and (C)– levels. In respect of the possibilities of descriptions at the (A)– and (D)–levels, I am neither denying their importance, nor trying to explain their relations with the (B) and (C)– descriptions. Indeed, the descriptions used in this text, while concerning the relationships between the (B)– and (C)–levels, are themselves at the (D)–level. Notions like that of conventional fact are theoretical constructs.

Both the (C)– and (D)– level descriptions include descriptions of "social wholes". They are, however, wholes of different kinds. What is essential for the (D) –descriptions is that they are constructs made by social theorists, not explications of the notions used by the agents living in the relevant societies. Sometimes they can be adopted by the agents themselves (the alleged truths of various social sciences have become absorbed into commonsense of the modern societies). Sometimes they cannot be adopted without changing the described phenomena – if people generally adopted the economists' theory of the money illusion, or the Marxist view on ideology, or the psychoanalytic idea of rationalization, or the structuralist interpretation of gift–giving as a form of exchange, the phenomena themselves would disappear or at least change their appearance. These descriptions are correct – if they are correct – not because people believe in them but rather because they are not aware of them. Theoretical descriptions at the (D) -level can have either self–supporting or self–refuting effects.

After making these reservations, I will comment on the most plausible defence of non–individualism in contemporary literature: the work of David–Hillel Ruben (1985). His work is interesting for two reasons: he uses a very sophisticated analytical machinery to defend non–individualism, and moreover, his analysis on the basis of what he calls "social properties" is almost exactly like my notion of conventional facts (Ruben 1985, 114–15).

Ruben claims that a reductive or "non–reductive illuminative" identification of social entities or social properties with individual entities or properties is impossible. This is an ontological thesis. He also claims that individualistic explanations do not enjoy any priority over non–individualistic ones: this is his methodological thesis. In respect to the ontological thesis, I may profess agnosticism. I have already accepted an ontological thesis shared by Ruben, namely that institutions do really exist (the intuition (1) above). The intuition (2) which I also accepted, was about methodology. However, I am not unwilling to accept the possibility of reductive or "non–reductive illuminative" identification of institutional entities or properties with the related attitudes and actions, in spite of Ruben's contrary claims.

Why does Ruben think that irreducible social entities exist? His example of such an entity is France. It seems that we ascribe several properties to the entity called 'France', and that there is no set of individual facts and entities which would be identical with that social entity. Only the last of the candidates rejected by him, "reduction of France to beliefs and attitudes" (p. 30), is relevant here. His counter–argument is this: The set of relevant beliefs can be described only if the name 'France' itself appear inside the scope of belief–operators. But if somebody has an intelligible singular belief about an entity, then the entity must exist. In that case the identification of France with beliefs about France becomes circular:

> A necessary condition for there to be persons with singular beliefs about France is that France exists. (...) Nor, for that matter could the identity be even non–reductive but illuminative, since the circularity is so obvious. (Ruben 1985,

35–6)

His argument in respect to the identification of social properties with systems of beliefs is just the same:

> Whatever the properties are, if there is an intelligible belief that x is P, there must be the property of being P. (ibid. p. 124)

Now, the problem, admitted by Ruben himself, is that the argument implies that fictional entities like Zeus, Santa Claus or the alleged planet Vulcanus also exist (cf. Ruben 1985, 35). And the same holds with fictional properties, like 'having a magical power'. An individualist is not likely to be much afraid of a theory which claims that social entities or properties have the same ontological status as Santa Claus has. The basic disagreement between Ruben and me is, however, on the issue of circularity. Ruben believes that the circularity, obvious in my definition of conventional facts (CF), makes the analysis completely trivial, while I find it illuminating. For me, the circularity is simply a matter of fact. *A* may believe that certain objects have the property of being money. He may be wrong in his belief. But if his belief is generally shared, it is necessarily correct. If the conventionalistic analysis of money is generally accepted in the community, everybody also believes that money is only money because it is the object of a general belief that it is money. The analysis is circular, or reflexive, because the things referred to in the analysans, beliefs, are themselves reflexive.

Suppose that we can analyse Ruben's example entity, France, in this way. More exactly, suppose that the nation of France is identical (reductively or non–reductively) with a system of attitudes concerning the nation of France. This analysis is illuminative, for numerous attempts to identify the nation with some racial, linguistic, cultural, metaphysical, etc. properties or entities are inconsistent with it. Indeed, if the conventionalist analysis is accepted, a substantial part of the ideology of modern nationalism has to be rejected. According to the conventionalist analysis, a nation comes into existence just when sufficiently many people, for some reason or other, do form the relevant shared attitudes. Ruben cannot accept this, but he fails to tell us what the real status of entities like France is. Notice that it does not follow from my analysis that nations like France are somehow irreal or "merely fictional". They are as real as their constituting parts: beliefs, intentions and actions.

The ontological arguments of Ruben do not threaten my position. As he remarks, a *methodological* individualist could well admit that there are irreducible social properties (Ruben 1985, 154). But he also denies that social facts could be *explained* in terms of individual beliefs, attitudes and actions. His argument is basically the same as before:

> In the case of rationally held true belief, we don't explain the social facts by means of agents' beliefs about social facts: we explain the beliefs about social facts in part by the social facts. (Ruben 1985, 168)

Thus, he accuses individualists of reversing the correct order of explanation. In normal cases, a fact is part of the explanation of the belief about the fact, not the other way round.

I think that beliefs about social facts can be partially explained by these facts. If we ask:"Why does A believe that certain objects are money?", the natural answer seems to be: "They are money in the society in which he lives". This answer refers to a social fact which exists independently of any particular beliefs about the fact. But how has A learned this fact? Well, the others – B,C,D, and so on – have told him that the objects are money, and he has seen that B,C,D, etc. behave in a way which becomes understandable by supposing that the objects are money. B,C,D etc. have formed their similar beliefs in the same way: by learning from others, A among them. The continual existence of the belief is partially explained by mutual reinforcement: the beliefs of individuals support each other. Every individual sees the behaviour of all others as a part of his environment with which he or she has to cope. From individuals' point of view, the fact is just there: others use certain objects as money. My thesis is that this situation itself constitutes the social fact – the fact that the referred objects are money. If we want a further explanation, it must be a historical one. How did the members of the society originally form their beliefs? The explanation is likely to be complex: there are the practical constraints (only some kinds of objects can function as money); there are psychological factors, including memories of the past, and conscious selection, which make some conventions more likely to arise than others. These factors may be partially explained by a general theory of human perception. But conventions are partially arbitrary: pure chance may play an important role in their formation.

This theory is, indeed, circular. The mutual belief about the existence of a social fact is a kind of self–fulfilling prophecy which necessarily makes itself true. The only alternative seems to be that social facts exist independently and before the beliefs. That is implied by Ruben's account. He does not, however, tell us *how* they exist. The claim that there is an objective natural law existing independently of human–made laws *might* be interpreted in this way (Simmonds' argument, cited in pp. 3–4 is basically the same as Ruben's). Perhaps the classical objectivistic theory of economic value also implies something like that. Both theories have led to serious metaphysical difficulties.

Compare again the status of social facts with the status of such facts as a's being a weapon. If I take a stick with the intention of using it as a weapon, the stick *is* a weapon. It is possible for me to form such an intention only because I have learned the concept of weapon, or at least I have some kind of corresponding idea in my mind. Somehow, the idea or concept exists. But I don't think that this implies any of the following positions: (a) that the concept exists independently of human minds and activities, or (b) that even if it exists, that particular object was a weapon before I formed that intention, or (c) that my intention–formation should be explained by some kind of causal effect the concept had on my mind. We cannot explain why a stick is a weapon by referring either to its physical properties or to the general concept. It is necessary to refer to my propositional attitudes: I need a weapon and I believe that this particular stick is a suitable object to be used as a weapon. Thus, my propositional attitudes are used to explain an external fact and not the other way round. There seems to be nothing odd in this.

Conventional facts and properties are different mainly because they require mutual attitudes in order to be realized. *I* can make something a weapon, but only *we* can make something money. If there is no collective consciousness or World Spirit operating behind our backs, the fact that something becomes money has, ultimately, to be explained in terms of our individual actions and beliefs.

After commenting on what seems to me the most plausible theory of anti–individualism, I should perhaps say something about the theory which is historically the most influential one. In his famous *Les règles de la méthode sociologique*, Émile Durkheim defends his "scandalous" position that social facts are things, existing independently of individual minds. This seems to be a denial of any form of methodological individualism, and clearly in contradiction with my account. But what are Durkheim's reasons for holding such a position?

In Chapter 1. of *Les règles*, he makes clear why social facts should be considered as things. Like physical objects, social facts are there whether I like it or not, and I cannot change them at will:

> Le système des signes dont je me sers pour exprimer ma pensée, le système de monnaies que j'emploie pour payer mes dettes, les instruments de crédit que j'utilise dans mes relations commerciales, les pratiques suivies dans ma profession etc. etc., fonctionnent indépendamment des usages que j'en fais. Qu'on prenne les uns après les autres tous les membres dont est composée la société, ce qui précède pourra etre répété a propos de chacun d'eux. (Durkheim 1927, 6)

Moreover, these independently existing social facts can effectively *constrain* my actions. If I try to ignore them, I will be frustrated in my actions; and the same again is equally true of all other members of my society:

> Je ne suis pas obligé de parler français avec mes compatriotes, ni d'employer les monnais légales; mais il est impossible que je fasse autrement. Si j'essayais d'échapper a cette nécessité, ma tentative échourait misérablement. (ibid., 7)

The fundamental reason for the postulation of social facts as things is this property. Social facts are, like physical objects and natural regularities, constraints on individual action. Durkheim's definition of social facts shows that the constraining nature of social facts is fundamental for him:

> Il est fait social toute manière de faire, fixée ou non, susceptible d'exercer sur l'individu une contrainte extérieure.(ibid., 19)

Now many social scientists hold a position which seems to be the opposite to that of Durkheim. They want to say, with Johan Galtung, and with many Marxists and other radicals, that everything in society is man–made; and what man has done, man can change (Galtung 1977, ch. 3). There are no unbreakable regularities in social life. How is my conventionalist theory of institutions related to these two apparently inconsistent positions? *Prima facie* it seems that I have already affirmed both of them. I have said that people have (in an epistemic sense) a free will; I have also said that some social facts possess a constraining power comparable to that of the laws of nature.

I shall argue that we can find a way between Durkheim's social determinism and complete voluntarism. What we need is a theory about how institutions (and the social facts in the first and second quotations from Durkheim are about institutions) make individuals act in one way rather than another. Firstly, there are acts which are possible for any one individual without being possible for all individuals. An individual may withdraw his deposit from a bank, or break the law, or the rules of football, without causing the change or collapse of the institutions concerned. Such an action would not be possible for *all* individuals acting as a collective. Conversely, there are acts which are possible only for all individuals, but not for any single individual. Changing, creating, maintaining or destroying institutions are examples of this. In institutional contexts, all individuals, taken as a collective, can be free, while the possible actions of any one individual are strictly constrained. Only groups and communities can establish or change laws, monies or symbol systems. The fact that the options open for any individual are not the same as the options open for all individuals is not a contingent matter; rather, it follows conceptually from the nature of institutions.

Secondly, individuals act on the basis of reasons. Here many social theorists do disagree with me. They want to see individual actions as conditioned, instinctual, or socially programmed. Now, I admit the possibility that for a reason–based, rationalistic explanation of an action there might an alternative non–rationalistic (perhaps neurophysiological) explanation which is equally plausible. What I deny is that we could ever get rid of the idea that human beings are also agents, acting from reasons. Human beings can perhaps be automata, or instinct–driven animals, or social constructs, or products of discourses, but they are *also* agents, and any of the former descriptions can be correct only if they can be made compatible with the latter. All this can be made compatible with the thesis that agency, both at the individual and at the general level, has its historical, social and biological roots. There can be interesting non–metaphysical answers to the question how human agency is possible. What is most important, the theory presented here is compatible with the idea that human beings can develop to agents only in a society. I am not committed to the implausible claim that all human powers can be realized in total isolation.

The capacity that institutions have for constraining human actions is not a metaphysical force. It is simply a capacity that provides reasons for individuals to act a certain way. Think of the examples given by Durkheim. I have a reason to use a language as far I believe that the others will understand that language. I have a reason to use and accept money as far as I believe that the others will also use it. Generally: for most individuals for most of the time there is a strong reason to conform to the rules of the institutions of their society if and only if they have a reason to believe that most individuals for most of the time will conform to the same rules.

Usually there are further reasons for believing that the others will conform, most importantly the fact that we can see them conforming. There is then a reason for conforming, and the resulting behaviour provides a new reason for others to believe that conformity is general. General conformity arises from reasons, not from an unreflective instinct to conform. If conformity becomes habitual and quasi–automatic, it does not necessarily mean that individuals cannot rationally justify their actions; it only means that they do not have a need to go through their justifications in every singular case of conformity. The fundamental point is that free, rational agents can intentionally or unintentionally create social facts which provide them with reasons to reproduce these same facts.

In a sense, the Marxian–inspired idea that the seemingly thing–like existence of institutions is an expression of fetishism, is correct. Institutions are man–made, although they may look like natural necessities from an individual's point of view. But the inference that human beings *can* therefore change the institutions is true only in respect of some senses of 'can'. Perhaps there is no law–like regularity preventing for making a change. It can still be true that there is no way of convincing them that they should join the concerted action which is necessary for the change. *If we know beforehand that there is a way to persuade or coerce them to change the institutions, there should at least be some unbreakable social regularities, namely those on which our knowledge of this possibility is based.* Institutions can be changed in the sense that they will necessarily change if sufficiently many individuals try to change them. At the same time, it is possible that they cannot be changed because the individuals never *want* to do that.

This is the root of necessity in the social world. A community can deliberately change some linguistic habits, say replace some Swedish nouns with purposely invented Finnish equivalents. But it is practically impossible for a large community just to switch to Esperanto. All social necessities (except those which follow from our biological makeup or from the laws of ecology) are of this nature. Ceteris paribus, a plurality voting system with one–seat constituencies creates a two–party system. This is a social "law" (the so–called "Duverger's Law"). But it holds because, in a given institutional setting, people generally want to act in a certain way. We may give an interpretation for Durkheim's postulation of social facts as things in conventionalistic terms. We may agree with him that social facts exist independently of any individual mind, although they are not independent of all individual minds. What is needed is a more exact picture of the nature of individual reasons and their interconnections in institutional settings.

CHAPTER 2

GAME THEORY AND MUTUAL BELIEFS

2.1. The role of games

Conventional facts are based on mutual beliefs which work as reasons for actions. The question remaining is: How can other peoples' beliefs in something, which leads them to act accordingly, be a reason for someone else acting in a similar way? What is the compelling force of conventional facts noticed by Durkheim?

I will follow the example of many other theorists by trying to connect the notion of convention with elementary game theory. There is, however, no definitional connection between my concept of conventional fact and game theoretical concepts. The latter are used mainly as an illustrative device.

Formal theories are not philosophically neutral. The use of game theory, for example, commits us to a certain theory of rationality and of human action. That view is itself controversial. The most important claims presupposed by the theory are that agents have, at least in some contexts, rational preferences and are able to act according to those preferences.

At the same time, it is important to recognize what is *not* presupposed by the theory. (1) It is not necessary to suppose that "rationality" means simply ability to act according to consistent preferences. There may be many other requirements for rationality. (2) The players can be groups and organizations as well as individuals. Game theory is generally seen as a natural ally of "methodological individualism" and "economic imperialism" in social theory. Against this, it should be noted that many (perhaps most) applications of the theory treat social wholes – firms, nations, trade unions and parties – as agents. (3) The players are not supposed to be self–interested; their preferences can reflect altruistic or moral considerations. (4) A cardinal or interpersonally comparable measure of values is not needed. (5) The actions that players take are not necessarily actual, conscious choices. The descriptions can be "as if" descriptions, counterfactual descriptions (how agents of a certain type would choose) or normative descriptions (how agents should choose when certain goals and beliefs are given).

What, then, is presupposed by game theory? At least the following suppositions are philosophically important. (6) We have to suppose a framework in which actions and outcomes can be described. Such a framework is not naturally given. It can be institutionally defined in certain contexts: in a voting game, "Aye", "No" and abstention can be the only meaningfully distinguishable actions. But in most interactions, the alternatives available for an agent can be described in different, non–equivalent ways. (7) Contrary to a common assumption, game theory and other related rationalistic theories are, at least in one important sense, holistic theories (cf. (3) above). Agents, firms or states as well as individuals, are supposed to possess consistent sets of beliefs and valuations. This excludes the possibility that they consist of multiple "selves", tendencies or powers driving them to different directions at the same moment – although games between separate, internally consistent "selves" are conceivable. This is problematic in respect with human individuals; it is much more problematic in respect with organizations.

(8) Stability of values is a usually unstated assumption related to the unity of agency. Rationalistic approaches take values or preferences of agents as givens. This is meaningful only if the values or preferences are relatively stable. If they change constantly in an exogenous and unpredictable way, they lose their descriptive value. (9) Game theory has to suppose a distinction between the rules of the game and the strategies adopted by the agents. "Rules" include all constant constraints. The laws of nature are obviously constants. Technological constraints can often be taken as constants, although this supposition limits the use of the models in an obvious way: quite often, especially in economically or militarily competitive situations, the most rational strategy is to pursue new technological inventions which expand the ranges of options available to the agents. Social constraints, such as norms, are the most problematic ones. If a businessman refrains from making illegal transactions, should we describe this as a strategic choice from a set which includes illegal options, or should we restrict the description to those options permitted by law? Is it the subjective attitude of the businessman which determines the description? As William Riker has emphasized, in the long run all social constraints are variables.

It seems, however, that *something* analogous to suppositions (6), (7) and (9) is required by any social theory. Some framework for the description of actions has to be supposed. Some things ought to be taken as causes rather than as effects. Some constraints ought to be considered as constants rather than as action variables. These selections are based on theoretical decisions. Any particular application of game theory lays itself open for a substantiated criticism of its choice of basic suppositions. So does any other social theory.

One possibility is that rationalistic methods like game theory are suitable only for an ideal description of a certain classes of social situations. Their basic preconditions, often presented as parts of universal human nature (ordinal rationality, unity of agency, stability of values, rigidity of constraints) are actually variables. Rationalistic models are useful and meaningful only when these variables are given certain values. Only certain aspects of human interaction can be explained by rationalistic means. This does not mean that their applicability is necessarily limited to some pre–defined areas of human life (say, the economy). For example, we usually think that means–ends rationality characteristic of game models does not determine our choices concerning marriage or religious convictions. But for a seventeeth–century prince these might have been matters of political expediency.

When game models are used in this work, the basic assumptions of game theory are not questioned. Game models are used as a heuristic device – to construct ideal types of human interaction situations. The only variable which is problematized here is the knowledge available for agents in games. My reason for this is that the knowledge factor is often neglected and many interesting things can be done simply by relaxing the assumptions concerning the agents' knowledge. But there is a deeper reason. The heuristic value of game models derives from the fact that they, unlike many other models in social sciences, treat human beings as agents potentially able to choose between different options. But some widely used assumptions on the knowledge are actually inconsistent with the notion of agency. In the following section I try to prove that *we are, at least in certain circumstances, bound to describe human beings as free agents.*

What is a game in the standard sense? *An ordinal game in normal form* is normally defined by the following components:

(i) a specified set of n players;
(ii) n sets of strategies,one for every player;
(iii) n sets of rational preference orderings, one for every player.

(R) *The Rationality assumption* means that the players make their choice according to their preference orderings.
(I) *The Full information assumption* means that (i)–(iii) and (R) are common knowledge for the players (i.e. mutually believed by them in the sense of (MB) – with the *ad infinitum* –clause). Therefore, they can predict each others' actions. It is this assumption which now calls for our attention.

2.2. The unpredictability of human action

I believe that there are good epistemological reasons for denying that human beings can, even in principle, become fully predictable for each others. There can also be good metaphysical reasons for the same conclusion; in this treatment, however, the latter are ignored. The epistemological reasons are presented here in the form of theses; none of them is my own invention.

Thesis (1): I cannot always predict my own decisions (and, consequently, my actions). Suppose that, at time t, I try to predict my decision made at some future time, t'. That prediction, if it is more than a guess, has to be based on the information I have about myself and about my environment. But it is also the information about myself and about my environment which is used in the making of the predicted decision. However, the information I use in making the prediction at t cannot include all the information I have at t', because at t' I shall also have the information that (i) I have tried to make a prediction at t, and (ii) the content of that prediction. That information is a new "causal" factor which can have an effect on my decision at t', either a self–fulfilling or a self–destroying one. Thus, I cannot have all potentially relevant information needed for predicting my own decisions, and thus I cannot predict my decisions. Q.E.D.

This thesis is sometimes used against the predictivist versions of Legal Realism. The content of legal statements cannot be a prediction concerning the decisions made by the officials, because an individual judge, when making a legal statement in court, is not predicting his own future decision.

Thesis (1) is not incompatible with metaphysical determinism. It does not exclude the possibility that I am just an automaton. It does not exclude the possibility that another person could in his predictions take into account the effect of my prediction at time t and predict my decision correctly. Or, suppose that I know at t that before t' I shall suffer a partial amnesia which makes me to forget my prediction. Then the prediction cannot have an effect on my decision at t', and self–prediction is not excluded, at least not for that reason.

Thesis (2): I cannot always predict the decisions (and actions) of an agent who is in interaction with me. There are two reasons. Firstly, from the Thesis (1) it follows that I cannot predict my future decisions, and they can have an effect on have the decisions of the other person. (Hence, I cannot unconditionally predict the future course of my natural environment, either.) Secondly, the other person can learn or anticipate the content of the prediction I made, and change his behaviour accordingly. I can try to take that into account when formulating my prediction, but, again, he may learn or anticipate that move, too. If the other person is able to anticipate or learn the content of my prediction, and if he has an interest in making them untrue, I cannot predict correctly the actions taken by him. Q.E.D.

The following game illustrates the paradoxical nature of mutual predictability:

(Matrix 1.)

		Player 2	
		C	D
Player 1	C	1,0	0,1
	D	0,1	1,0

Suppose that Player 1 is able to predict how Player 2 will choose (Random choices are prohibited). Obviously, his predictions must be based on some information he has about Player 2. If this information becomes available Player 2, she is able to predict the content of Player

1's prediction. As a rational agent, she will frustrate the prediction by choosing differently – if, for example, Player 1 predicts that Player 2 will choose C, Player 2 will choose D. Suppose that Player 1 can also anticipate that Player 2 will predict the content of his prediction. Then he can change his prediction accordingly – but if Player 2 can predict that mental move of Player 1, she will, again, revise her plan of conduct. The conclusion is that in this game a prediction cannot simultaneously be correct and common knowledge for the players.

One application of Thesis (2) with actual importance is the Rational Expectation hypothesis in economics. According to the hypothesis, the Keynesian hypothesis that governments can buy more employment by an inflationary policy holds only when other economic agents (firms, unions) cannot predict the actions of the government and their consequences, while the government can predict how the others will react. When the other agents learn the government's model of the economy, and base their expectations and decisions on that knowledge, the relationship between inflation and employment disappears.

Thesis (3): I cannot base my decisions on the assumption that my decisions are always predictable to some other agent. Suppose that I believe that whatever I decide, another agent can predict the content of my decision in advance. Then, the other agent has to have some information on which she bases her predictions. But she is in the same situation in respect with me as I am in respect to her. She cannot exclude the possibility that I could learn or anticipate the content of her predictions. This is Thesis (2) reversed.

One much–discussed example of this is Newcomb's Problem, which becomes a problem because a decision–maker has to suppose that another agent (symptomatically, a Demon) can predict his decisions, and make decisions on that basis. In such a situation, rational decision rules seem to conflict. Andrew Schotter has shown that the Rational Expectation hypothesis leads into such a situation. The government which believes that the extreme form of the Rational Expectations hypothesis is true, i.e. that the other economic agents can always anticipate its actions correctly has no rational course to choose, if its interests diverge from those of the other agents. (Schotter 1985, ch. 7.) The lesson to be learned from the Problem is that no decision–maker should believe in the existence of the Newcombian Demons.

As I said, the Theses (1)–(3) do not imply metaphysical

indeterminism. What is implied is (to put it in Kantian terms) that the possibility of unpredictability is a necessary postulate of practical reason. Nevertheless, the methodological and political consequences are important. One consequence is that no predictive, universally valid statements describing the laws of social behaviour of rational agents can be formulated. All intended law–statements (or statements about structures, patterns, trends etc.) are potentially predictive in the sense that in relevant conditions we could use them for making predictions. But in the relevant conditions, the agents who are supposed to be subjects of those laws can also learn them and make the predictions based on them come untrue. (All this holds also in respect to probabilistic laws.) Thus, even in a deterministic universum a deterministic theory of human behaviour is inaccessible for human beings because no formulation of such a theory can predict it own effects. From this, it also follows that there cannot be any "scientific" policy or praxis based on universally valid laws.

Another consequence relevant for social theory is that theories based on the postulate that agents are always fully informed about each other are inconsistent. This is a more important consequence, for it implies that many economic models, and also the game theory in its standard form, are inadequate. Again, this has been noticed in several particular cases. Here are some examples. There can be no generally predictive theory for stock markets, for

> if such a rule were found and followed, those following it would invalidate it by incorporating whatever the rule contained in the price of stocks. Once the information was incorporated in the price of stocks, the rule would cease to work, not because it was wrong, but because it had mined of its informational value until rendered exhausted and worthless. (Thurow 1983, 153)

The same is true in collective decision–making. Consider the possibility of manipulating voting by using the knowledge of the preferences of others. Universally, such a practice would be impossible:

> for successful manipulation of a voting procedure, an individual participant needs complete information about the preferences which the other voters are going to announce. But if such omniscience were indeed present, manipulation would become virtually impossible since everybody would then know the sincere preferences of everybody else. (de Bruin 1987, 45)

In spite of all this, we can often predict the actions taken by other individuals. Indeed, predictability is a central presupposition of social life. As T.W. Hutchinson (1977) remarks: "Virtually any economic or social life or co–operation, other than the most 'nasty, brutish and short', would be impossible if all human behaviour, individually and in aggregates, was completely unpredictable". There is no deep difference between scientific and everyday predictions. Everyday predictions can be used and are actually used by social scientists; especially in the modern society, scientific predictions are used by laymen. How is successful predicting possible?

Firstly, we can sometimes predict actions because the agents in question are not fully rational (in the wide sense of the term). They may act instinctively, or may be compelled, or may act out of habit, as we all sometimes do. Secondly, some agents are less well informed than those who want to predict their actions: they do not know that we are trying to predict their actions, or are not aware of the content of our predictions, or do not understand them, or do care about them even when they should. Hence, stock markets and political meetings can be manipulated. These cases cover a large part of our everyday predictions, and of the predictions made by professional social theorists. If we can be sure that one or more of these conditions hold, the Theses (1)–(3) can be ignored. Perhaps we can even formulate our predictions as if they were instances of general laws. However, for a sincere social theorist it would be a rather dismal idea for his or her theories hold only because his or her situation was informationally superior to that of his or her research subjects, that the theories hold just because those who are concerned either do not understand them or ignore them. In this way the methodological problem also has an ethical aspect.

There is, however, a large class of social situations in which the possibility of making predictions does not presuppose irrationality or compulsion or asymmmetric knowledge. That is the class of situations in which there exists a unique equilibrium (in the game theoretical sense: the agents do not have either the power or the motive to change their predicted courses of action). In such a situation the expectations of the agents in respect of the actions of each other converge into a single solution. A new piece of information, including information provided by a social scientist, cannot have any self–destroying effects, even if it is believed and taken into account. Conversely, when there is no equilibrium (e.g. in Matrix 1.) rationality itself does not determine any outcome, and no rational prediction is possible. (Strictly speaking, this presentation is slightly inaccurate, for some equilibria are not self–enforcing in this sense.)

But what if there are several equilibria? In the cases of several equilibria, people have an interest to make themselves predictable for us. They want us to predict that they will make certain choices, so that we would make certain choices and they could then safely make the choices we predict them to make. *Institutions* are means for people to make predictable choices.

Economists believe that material scarcity is a fundamental part of the human condition. There is a long line of argument from Hobbes to James Buchanan which makes material scarcity *the* reason for having institutions. But scarcity is a function of both the amount of material resources and of human wants. Therefore, it is possible to claim – with Rousseau and Marx – that material scarcity is a part of the modern condition only, and that in The Stone Age (see Sahlins 1974) the was no material scarcity, or that in the communist society of the future it will disappear. According to my belief, scarcity of information is a more fundamental fact, and the most important and the most permanent cause of this scarcity is the unpredictable nature of human action. Perhaps there are no limits to our ability to predict and manipulate external nature, but we have seen that there are definite limits to our ability to predict the behaviour of others. Even in a superabundant society, human beings are somehow dependent on each other; even in a society of angels there is no pre–established harmony of beliefs. Because we cannot become fully transparent to each other (to continue the metaphor, if society were fully transparent, there would be nothing to be seen), we need *institutions*. Institutions are artificial islands of predictability in the stormy sea of unpredictability. Institutions create predictability in two ways. Firstly, they shape our preferences by educating, manipulating, coercing and rewarding us – by exercising power over us. Secondly, they resolve ambiguities by providing us with *conventional solutions*.

Thus, institutions are functional. There is, however, no magical force creating institutions whenever they are needed. Human beings create their institutions, sometimes in long and painful ways. Some institutions are created by existing institutions; some others emerge gradually in human interaction; some are established by explicit agreements.

2.3. Prisoners' Dilemma

In disequilibrium situations described above, agents are supposed to know the relevant preferences, but they cannot predict each others' actions. But there are other forms of uncertainty. Leaving aside the most radical cases of information imperfection, people do not often know what the preferences of others are, or, they do not know whether the others know their preferences. I will discuss the role of knowledge in some familiar 2 x 2 games.

The Prisoners' Dilemma game (PD for short) is one of the most discussed games. The standard 2 x 2 game matrix is the following:

(Matrix 2.)

		Player 2	
		C	D
Player 1	C	3,3	1,4
	D	4,1	2,2

(In this game 4 is the best outcome for a player, 3 the second best, etc.; C is the cooperative and D the non–cooperative choice.)

This game has enjoyed an enormous popularity among political scientists and moral philosophers. One important reason for this is that it seems to reflect common and often felt incongruities between the individual and the general interest, or between self–interest and morality. Thus, it seems to explain the social role of moral norms, sanctioned laws and the state. Following Parfit (1984, 62–6) we may distinguish *political* and *psychological* solutions to practical problems with a PD–structure. Political solutions are external changes in the players' situation which either make noncooperative choices impossible, or add a sanction or some other discouraging effect to non–cooperative choices, or add an extra reward to cooperative choices. These solutions are based on power. Among possible psychological solutions to the practical problem, moral solutions are the most important. The players may internalize a moral norm which prescribes cooperating. Of course, these are not solutions in the game–theoretical sense; they "solve" the game by changing it.

Because PD is less important from my point of view, I will only make some critical remarks (but see ch. 9.4.). It is important to notice that the usual moral interpretation of PD (morality vs. self–interest) is not dictated by the game itself. We may easily invent another story. Suppose that the players are highly moral agents choosing on behalf of others (say, the groups they altruistically want to benefit). Moreover, they may both believe that they have a moral *right* for their favoured ((D,C) or (C,D)) outcome and that, when choosing D, they are only acting in accordance with their conviction. Nothing in the logic of the game itself is changed by this new reading. But we can no longer say that the problem illustrated by the game is solved when the players learn to be moral or altruistic: the problem is there just because the players *are* morally motivated. In the real world, this version of PD may well be as common as the standard one. Indeed, in many standard applications of the PD–game the players are collectives, e.g. nations or political parties. In those cases, it may well be that operative decision–makers are acting on behalf of the interests of their collectives rather than for their own personal interests.

Another relevant point is made by J.W.N. Watkins (1974; 1985). A moral solution to PD implies that players accept moral reasons which change their evaluations in respect of the outcomes. Parfit (1984, 64) gives several possible examples. The players may become reluctant to be "free riders": if each believes that many others will play cooperatively, he prefers to do his share (this is the Rawlsian norm of fairness). They may become Kantians and would then do only what they could rationally will everyone to do. And so on. But a reasonable morally motivated person is still not a complete altruist. Moral players would consider both (C,D) and (D,C) outcomes as unfair. The matrices for reasonably moral players would be as follows:

(Matrix 3.)

		Player 2	
		C	D
Player 1	C	4,4	1,2
	D	2,1	3,3

(Matrix 4.)

		Player 2	
		C	D
Player 1	C	4,4	1,3
	D	3,1	2,2

The latter game is known as the Assurance Game (AG). These games are not "dilemmatic" in the sense of PD. There is no incompatibility between the common interest and particular interests. For players satisfying the information assumption (I) cooperation is unproblematic in these games. The problem perceived by Watkins is that if the players are less than fully informed, they can still fail to cooperate. Suppose that the preferences of Player 1 are of the form described in Matrix 3. (or 4.). In Watkins' terminology, he is a Moralist. However, he is not sure whether the preferences of Player 2 are of the same form (she is a fellow Moralist) or whether they are of the PD–form (she is an Egoist). Then Player 1 plays sure and does not cooperate. Or, suppose that he believes that Player 2 is a Moralist who believes that Player 1 is an Egoist (or at least it remains unsure whether Player 1 is a moralist or not). Again he will not cooperate, for he reasons that Player 2 will reason as he himself did in the first case. Watkins (1984, 70) supposes that two Moralists will cooperate when they are convinced that the other is a Moralist who knows that the other is a Moralist. However, Segerberg (1979) shows that two iterations are not enough; actually, no finite amount of iterations is enough to assure cooperation. What is needed, is common knowledge, or assumption (I) above. Segerberg's reaction is that this result is intuitively absurd: "...surely cooperation must be possible between two rational Moralists who play the game" (Segerberg 1979, 371). Watkins solves this by assuming that a Moralist player is always *hoping* that he is free to play cooperatively. A Moralist has an initial bias in favour of C, and he reflects that, because the symmetry of situations, a fellow Moralist player has a similar bias. This reflection strengthens his own bias by diminishing the fear that the other would play D. Thus, they will eventually end up in cooperation. (Watkins 1985, 66) But the "initial bias" supposed in Watkins' solution is a psychological assumption which violates the standard rationality postulate (R), which says that the players act according to their preferences, period.

Kreps et al. (1982) have shown how cooperation can emerge in one version of PD –games. The game in question is not a one–shot game; the players play PD several times, and can, therefore "punish" each other for noncooperation. Because the series of plays is a finite one, the standard theory prescribes non–cooperation even here. This surprising prescription follows from the simple reasoning: It is common knowledge that the last game is like a one–shot game and that the other player is going to play non–cooperatively, so let us ignore the last game. Then, the next–last game is like a one–shot game... (The prescription is almost never followed by subjects in experimental settings.) The rationality and/or the payoffs of the players are not, however, common knowledge among the players. The players believe that there is at least a small probability that the other shall co–operate. Under these suppositions, mutual cooperation is an equilibrium in the game. Notice how the simple amendments to the model increase its realism. For, when modelling a social situation, we can use the one–shot PD–setting only when it is absolutely sure that the outcome has no effect on future interactions. It has to be like a confrontation between strangers who pass each other in the desert, never meeting again. Even a game appearing in a series of interactions may be modelled as a one–shot game, if the players do not care about the future; the point is that we have to show it.

Actually there is no dilemma involved in the standard one–shot PD. For the game–theoretic reasoning unambiguously prescribes non–cooperative choices for both players. Why, then, have so many people had the intuition that games like PD can illustrate the role of moral and other norms in real life? It seems that, when using PD as a model of interaction, they have implicitly rejected some assumption of the standard presentation of the game. There is no "dilemma of cooperation" in one–shot PD–games. There is no dilemma simply because in such situation the players do not cooperate. The real dilemma is this: why and how actors who are involved in a situation which *prima facie* looks like a standard one–shot PD may avoid the trap? In other words, why is the situation in question not, in spite of all appearances, an instance of the standard PD? In this sense, PD models can be potentially important for sociologists, economists and students of International Relations. However, it is not *the* problem of social life or interaction.

2.4. Games and conventions

David Lewis' seminal book (Lewis 1969) has drawn attention to an important class of games called *games of coordination*. The following matrix exemplifies a simple game of coordination:

(Matrix 5.)

		Player 2	
		C	D
Player 1	C	2,2	1,1
	D	1,1	2,2

In this game, combinations (C,C) and (D,D) are *coordination equilibria*. Players 1 and 2 are indifferent as between them, but they have a common interest in establishing some equilibrium: Player 1 would choose C (or D) if and only if Player 2 chooses C (or D), and *vice versa*. A coordination equilibrium is a combination of choices in which no agent would have been better off had any one agent alone acted otherwise, either himself or someone else. The problematic aspect in this game is that there is more than one equilibrium. Even if there is no interest conflict as in PD, there is a problem. For the players' knowledge about the game does not provide any solution to the ambiguity.

Like PD's, these games seem to provide an intuitively plausible model for several kinds of social interaction situations. Lewis calls such situations coordination problems. Coordination problems

> are situations of interdependent decision by two or more agents in which coincidence of interests predominates and in which there are two or more proper coordination equilibria. (Lewis 1969, 24)

Lewis gives examples like that two persons wanting to meet each other, two persons who are cut off during a telephone discussion, Hume's two men rowing a boat, drivers who have to drive either on the left or on the right, oligopolists trying to set a common price, traders wanting to use a common currency and people who have to agree on a common language. All these situations can ideally be described as coordination games. In these situations, the agents involved share a common interest in finding *some* commonly agreed solution and are usually content to follow any course of action (within limits set by practical considerations) as long as they know that it will be followed by others.

Such common practices are, according to Lewis, conventions. A more exact definition of convention is the following:

> A regularity R in the behaviour of members of a population S when they are agents in a recurrent situation C is a *convention* if and only if it is true that, and it is common knowledge in S that, in almost any instance of C among members of S,
>
> (1) almost everyone conforms to R;
> (2) almost everyone expects almost everyone else to conform to R;
> (3) almost everyone has approximately the same preferences regarding all possible combinations of actions;
> (4) almost everyone prefers that any one more conform to R, on the condition that almost everyone conform to R;
> (5) almost everyone would prefer that any one more conform to R', on condition that almost everyone conform to R';
>
> where R' is some possible regularity in the behaviour of members of S in C, such that almost no one in almost any instance of C among members of S could conform both to R' and to R. (Lewis 1969, 78)

The similarity between Lewis' definition and my definition of conventional facts is obvious. Conventional facts, however, are not necessarily rules (or, as Lewis says, regularities). In the definition of conventional fact, one essential component missing from Lewis' definition was that the relevant agents share a common conception of the nature of fact. This component is important because the role of the notion of a conventional fact is to explain how social entities and properties (including rules and systems of rules) can exist. This ontological dimension is absent in Lewis' notion.

The idea that conventions are means for solving coordination problems is important because it shows how the fact that other agents are likely to act in a certain way is a reason for an individual agent to act in a similar way. Conventions are practices which are followed mainly because there is the mutual belief that they are generally followed. Thus they can possess the compelling force which was Durkheim's main reason for postulating the existence of social facts which are completely independent of attitudes and actions of individuals. But coordination games also explain why this conformity to conventions is, at least sometimes, *rational* and not due to an irrational conformism or traditionalism.

In one sense, however, Lewis' notion of coordination situations is too restrictive. As we saw, he made the predominance of the coincidence of interests a part of the definition of a coordination situation: that is

> the differences between different agents' payoffs in any square (perhaps after suitable linear rescaling) are small compared to some of the differences between payoffs in different squares. (Lewis 1969, 14)

In the presentation of the relevant games, I have tried to avoid the use of the cardinal utilities needed in Lewis' definition. But let us adopt them for arguments' sake. In the following game, Lewis' supposition of the coincidence of interests does not hold:

(Matrix 6)

		Player 2	
		C	D
Player 1	C	100,2	0,0
	D	0,0	2,100

The conflict of interests reflected by the utilities in the squares is enormous. Nevertheless (C,C) and (D,D) are coordination equilibria in the sense that in these combinations "no one would have been better off had any one agent alone acted otherwise, either himself or somebody else" (Lewis 1969, 14).

Matrix 6 is an instance of a class of games called "The Battle of Sexes" –games. The ordinal version is this:

(Matrix 7)

		Player 2	
		C	D
Player 1	C	2,3	1,1
	D	1,1	3,2

Taking games of this type into consideration makes it possible to treat a large class of rules and practices as conventional. For example, constitutions, property laws, rules of organizations or international agreements seem to differ radically from Lewis' examples. Unlike languages, or practices regulating rowing, meeting, or discussions on the telephone, rules of this kind do regulate conflicts of interest. The relevant agents may greatly prefer some other alternative to the current practice, and they may be under a temptation to try to change the practice, and consequently to take the risk of a failure of coordination. The stability of conventions in these situations is partly dependent on the normative force of conventions. This presupposes that the conventions are perceived as normative. But the inclusion of these situations into the class of coordination situations shows how a convention regulating a coordination situation can – when considered from the critical moral point of view – be *unfair* or *oppressive*. For example, conventional rules regulating the division of labour between the sexes in a society can simultaneously be mutually useful (in the sense that it is, for example, generally good that *someone* takes care of children) and unfair for women. Indeed, in most real–life conventions conflicts of some kind are at least occasionally involved.

Another restrictive supposition in Lewis' definition is its clause (4). This makes it a necessary part of the notion of convention that there should always be a *conventional alternative* (R') for any conventional practice. However, the alternative for a practice may be that there is no practice regulating the actions of the agents. Matrices 3. and 4. are possible descriptions of the underlying interaction situations. Squares (D,D) are situations in which a "state of nature" prevails and no practice exists; squares (C,C) are situations in which a practice exists. In these games, uncertainty is not due to indifference, as in Matrix 5. but to the possible lack of information on the beliefs of the other players. In such games, a practice, once established, has the same self–enforcing character as Lewisian conventions: it is followed as long as there prevails a mutual belief that others will follow it.

As Lewis says, coordination can be achieved with the aid of concordant mutual expectations about the agents' actions, preferences, and rationality. These expectations can be created by an agreement. Agents may promise each other to follow some mutually acceptable course in their future interactions. The fact that some have promised is a reason for an agent to expect that they will act according to their promise, and therefore a reason for the agent himself to act according to his promise. But although promising is a paradigmatic way of creating mutual expectations, not all conventions result from explicit promises, and the practice of promising itself presupposes conventions. Another ground for coordination is *salience*. Among possible coordination equilibria, some may stand out from the rest as unique in some sense.

However, an agent in a coordination problem does not try to find the alternative which appears to be salient for him; he is searching for the alternative which would be perceived as salient by others. Thus the search for salient alternatives is itself based on mutual beliefs concerning the perceptions of others. Ultimately it may be that our biological similarity guarantees that some alternatives will naturally appear to be salient for all of us. (The Chomskian hypothesis of the existence of internal grammars is an interesting attempt to proceed in that direction. See D'Agostino 1986) The most important thing is that when entering into a new coordination situation we already share many beliefs. We are already participants in common practices, and these practices make some alternatives salient in new situations by providing precedents. Existing practices and rules have an informative role: they give us information on how others are likely to act in new situations. This leads to a corrected notion of rational action:

(R) Agents act according to their preferences, and, when confronted with an uncertainty situation, try to utilize the information encapsulated in the existing conventions in an optimal way.

Thus, conventions are partially derived from earlier conventions, etc. The problem of "the first convention" remains. However, it is an instance of a problem shared by all social theories: how to explain the emergence of social properties in the human evolution? It is partly an empirical question, with an obvious philosophical significance.

The general and vague principle of rationality, (R), can be seen as a response to a critique of Lewis provided by Margaret Gilbert (1989). Gilbert tries to show that the salience of an alternative does not, as such, provide a reason for rational agents to choose that alternative. In her criticism, Gilbert focuses on a single–play coordination situation. Consider a situation of the type described in the Matrix 5. The agents are confronted with the situation for the first time, so there are no precedents. The action combinations (C,C) and (D,D) are equally good. Now, suppose that the combination (C,C) is perceived as salient by both players. Why should this fact create a reason for player A to choose the alternative C? He has a reason to choose C only if he thinks that B shall also choose C. But B shall choose C only if she has a reason to think that A is going to choose C, and A knows that. For agents who are rational in the narrow, game theoretical sense, and *who do not possess any background knowledge* (i.e. do not know any precedents), cannot end up in choosing (C,C) by replicating each others' reasoning.

If there is some background knowledge available for the agents, why should we suppose that it always provides a reason for choosing the salient alternative (C,C)? What if the agents, are or believe that the other agent is (etc.), "salient–shy" in the sense that they generally tend to choose the alternative which is non–salient? In a sense, the fact that the alternative (C,C) has some specific property P which makes it salient means that the alternative (D,D) also has a specific property, namely that it does not have the property P. Why is the presence of that property more important than its absence?

Seamus Miller (1991) has, I think, produced a conclusive answer to Gilbert's criticism. Firstly, he admits that Gilbert's point is valid under the specific circumstances presented in her example. If a coordination problem is a single–play case, if there are just two equally good alternatives, and if there is no relevant background knowledge, the players have no reason to choose (C,C), even if it is salient. But such a situation is very unusual, as we shall see.

Suppose that there is a situation in which there are 100 alternatives, of which only one is commonly perceived as salient. Thus, the agents have only one salient strategy, and 99 "salient–shy" (pure) strategies. Clearly, there is a rational reason for choosing the salient strategy at least in such situations.

Again, suppose that the situation is a two–alternative pure coordination situation, but contrary to in Gilbert's example, the agents have been confronted with it before. Suppose that they have, by accident perhaps, chosen (C,C). They share the background information that a certain choice has been successful before. Such background knowledge provides a precedent: they have a reason to use the same strategy.

If agents have been in situations in which the salient strategy is the most rational one, they necessarily possess some background knowledge. It is a crucial piece of the general background knowledge of human beings that precedents are sometimes useful. It is unrealistic to suppose that human agents can be entirely without any background knowledge. There exists, so to speak, the general precedent that precedents are to be followed. In other words: the real coordination games are almost never single play games, for human beings try, by using analogy, to find precedents. This means that they try to construct the situations they are faced with as recurrent games. Then, they have a rational reason to use salient strategies even in situations which, *prima facie* may appear as single–play coordination games – that is the impact of the (R)–principle.

Neverthless, I agree with Gilbert (and with Miller) that the notion of rationality used here is not the same as used in the standard game theory. Rather, it belongs to the attempt, initiated by Thomas Schelling, to reorientate game theory. Basically, it is a Humean notion. Uncertainty is an all–pervasive problem; it is custom, rather than reason, which provides a solution, but custom is not blind.

I will focus on three kinds of rule–based systems: *language, money,* and *law*. They can all be seen as means for solving problems of human interaction in large communities. They are all systems in a dynamic sense: they are based on conventions which can be used to create new conventions in new situations (by defining new symbols by means of old ones, by fixing values of new things or by creating new laws). This dynamic aspect can be interpreted in terms of salient precedents. The idea that language, money, and law are paradigmatic types of institutions is shared e.g. by Talcott Parsons (1967), by Jürgen Habermas, and by Neo–Austrian economists (strange company indeed!). The conventionalist theory of language has already been developed by Lewis and by others. Therefore, my main interest will be the analysis of law and legal authority. I will try to show that a conventionalist interpretation is compatible with some existing ideas on legal authority. The discussion on money in the next chapter will serve as an example of the application of the theory.

CHAPTER 3

AN EXAMPLE: MONEY

The institution of money, like that of language, or that of the State, has often been seen to be based on some kind of contractual agreement. Aristotle describes the nature of money as follows:

> Money has become by convention a sort of representative of demand; and that is why it has the name 'money' (nómisma) because it exists not by nature but by law (nómos) and it is in our power to change it and make it useless. (Ethica Nicomachea, V.5.II33a)

The word *nómos* is ambiguous: in another translation of Ethica it has been translated as "custom". This ambiguity reflects a theoretical problem in the classical social theory: money has been seen either as a result of an act of will of the legislator, or as a contract or convention based on voluntary agreement between economic agents. Roman jurisprudence and medieval political thinkers considered that the sovereign had an unlimited power over monetary institutions, including the power to determine the real value of money. This was the opinion supported by e.g. Thomas Aquinas, who in his commentaries translated Aristotle's *nómos* as "lex" (Monroe 1923, 27).

The contract theory of money formed a natural part of the general contractualist outlook on society in the works of such thinkers as Pufendorf or Locke. They saw monetary institutions as based on an *explicit* social contract. The views of the Physiocrat economists were mostly similar to those expressed by contractarian thinkers (Tallqvist 1920). Probably the changes in the monetary system itself, especially the emergence of paper money, made the contract theory more appealing than before.

The last great philosophical controversy on the nature of money in which the classical positions were still represented appeared among the German economists and sociologists before the First World War. The German version of the sovereign–based doctrine was the "staatliche Theorie des Geldes" as presented by G.F. Knapp (Ellis 1934).

According to Knapp, the "validity" of money was derived from the will of the State. By this formulation, Knapp did not mean that a State could arbitrarily determine the purchasing power of money, nor was this a reference to the commonplace fact that a modern State decides on the nominal values of bills and coins. Rather he was stressing the "acceptance" of the State as a necessary condition for the adequate working of monetary systems in modern societies. Ellis (1934) summarizes the Knappian theses on the "validity" of money as follows:

> (1) Money comes into being when the State selects a certain unit of value, describes its physical embodiments (coins and notes) carefully, gives it a name, and proclaims its validity in terms of the historically preceding unit.
>
> (2) The proclaimed validity is secured in trade by a State's accepting all its money at face value; legal tender in private trade is a complementary measure, not a universal one. The State makes its money a standard by forcing it out in payments to private persons. (Ellis 1934, 21)

There is some resemblance between the concept of "validity" of money and the concept of validity of law as used in legal positivism. According to positivism, a norm is legally valid if and only if it has been accepted by the organs of the State; the validity of a norm is not dependent on its actual efficacy.

Both the classical contractual theory of money, and the Statist theory in its traditional and modern guises have stressed the role of intentional planning in the explanation of the institution of money. This view was strongly opposed by Carl Menger, the founder of the Austrian school of economics. According to Menger, money, like other social institutions, should be explained in terms of the actions and interests of individual agents. But the coordination of individual actions which is a necessary condition for the existence and growth of social institutions is usually not a result of an explicit agreement among the agents. More often, it is a product of an invisible hand, an un–intentional result of numerous individually rational and intentional acts performed by agents. Menger's explanation of the emergence of money in individualistic and evolutionary terms is parallel to the earlier critiques of the social contract explanation of the State as presented by e.g. Hume.

Menger considered the individualistic explanation of the institution of money as at first sight a paradoxical one:

> That in a market anyone who offers goods for sale is ready to turn these over for another definite item, that is, according to varying conditions, for cattle, cocoa beans, certain amounts of weight of copper and silver, even when he has no direct use for these goods or has completely satisfied his possible need for them, while he nevertheless rejects certain other goods under the same presupposition – this is a paradoxical procedure. (Menger 1963, 152)

The paradoxicality is, of course, not due to any paradox in the logical sense. The paradox is simply this: why is a disinterested agent ready to participate in a common practice without an explicit agreement? It is basically the same problem which all the contractualist accounts of money, State or language purported to solve. Menger puts the general problem in this way:

> How can it be that institutions which serve the common welfare and are extremely significant for its development come into being without a *common will* directed toward establishing them? (Menger 1963, 146)

The essential part of the solution of the problem of the emergence of money is the mutual belief among the agents that some goods are generally in demand. If an agent cannot exchange his goods immediately for other goods which would satisfy his needs, he will exchange them for any goods which are easily transportable and durable, provided that he has good reasons to expect that he will be able to exchange these goods again in the future. No kind of explicit acknowledgement of the goods as money is necessary (Menger 1963, 154). Moreover, when the practice is established, it is self–enforcing. The more widely a product of a certain type is used as a means of exchange, the more certain is that it has demand in the future.

The definition of money following from Menger's theory is therefore functional in its nature: money is whatever is accepted as money. However, according to Olivecrona (1957, 11) this kind of functional definition of money moves in a vicious circle. Olivecrona goes through several proposed definitions of money, and then, being faithful to his nominalistic programme (see ch.1.1.) declares that money is a fiction:

> We have the idea the word denotes something, though we are unable to say what. This idea, however, makes it psychologically possible to count numbers of monetary units. But in reality, the something is nothing. There is only the

> word itself in conjunction with the idea that it denotes something. (Olivecrona 1957, 11)

Modern textbooks of economics use precisely the kind of definitions condemned by Olivecrona as circular:

> Money is whatever is generally accepted in exchange (...). The only reason why money is accepted in payment is that the recipient belives that it can be accepted at a later time. There is thus an inherent circularity in the acceptance of money. (Dornbush and Fischer 1978, 209–10)

Textbooks do recognize the role of mutual beliefs:

> You trust money because I do, and I trust money because you do... As long as the convention holds and the money is generally acceptable to everyone, it retains its usefulness. (Stonier and Hague 1973, 405)

It is relatively easy to see how these definitions can be interpreted in the light of the theory of conventional facts presented in earlier chapters. The circularity recognized by Olivecrona reflects the circular nature of the belief necessary for the existence of the institution of money. Something is money if and only if there is a mutual belief in the relevant community that it is money, and if this belief constitutes a reason for the members of the community to use it as money (as a means of exchange). Money can then serve us as an example of the explanatory strategy of conventionalism. The remaining question is: what is the interaction problem solved by adopting the convention to use money? Applying the conceptual instruments introduced in ch. 2., the question can be reformulated: what is the game description of the underlying interaction situation? (It is interesting to note that monetary systems – like languages or legal systems – are sometimes compared with games in the ordinary, informal sense. See Olivecrona (1957, 137))

Firstly, the existence of a common means of exchange could, as the existence of a working legal system (see ch. 9.), be considered as a public good. Ordinary public goods are defined as goods with jointness of supply and non–excludability in consumption. In modern societies, typical public goods like military defence, police protection, roads and so on, are provided by States and financed by compulsory taxation. In all these respects, money is like a public good. On the other hand, money is *not* like most public goods because it does not impose any apparent costs for individuals, and its continuous existence is not dependent on sanctions against free riders. Moreover, its breakdown (e.g. through hyperinflation) has its own special characteristics.

Public goods, including legal systems, are often related to PD–games. In these games, the interaction problem arises from the fact that for each player, the rational strategy is to play non–cooperatively (not to participate in the production of the good) regardless of the strategies adopted by the other players; but the resulting outcome of general non–cooperation is suboptimal. The standard non–analytic solution is to transform the game into a cooperative game by introducing an additional motive: sanctions for non–cooperation or rewards for cooperation.

The classical theories of social contract are often interpreted as informal descriptions of PD–situations (see further discussion in ch.9.). The social contract "solves" the dilemma by establishing an obligation which is enforceable. This cooperative result produced by a contract is not self–enforcing: it is dependent on the severity of related sanctions and/or the internalization of the contractual obligations as a moral duty. The cooperative result is, therefore, unstable. Various political crises can be described as failures in enforcing contracts in situations which have the structure of a PD–game.

The other interesting type of games is games of pure coordination. In these games, there is always a coordination equilibrium, a combination of choices in which no player would be better off had any player (or coalition) acted otherwise. The fundamental difference between PD– and pure coordination games is the absence of temptation to deviate from a cooperative solution in the latter type of games. Pure coordination games are self–enforcing. The interaction problem arises only from the possibility that the situations are ambiguous. The paradigmatic application of pure coordination games to institutions is Lewis' interpretation of language. Natural language is a spontaneously formed convention; artificial symbol systems like the system of traffic signs or Morse code are authorized conventions.

The State–centred as well as the explicit contract theories of money are mostly naturally interpreted in the context of PD–games. This is the interpretation proposed by Hillel Steiner (1978). The "paradox" of money noticed by Menger is then the collective action problem appearing in PD–games. The public good properties of monetary institutions do conform to this analysis. However, the other properties mentioned above tell against such an interpretation. Most notably, the acceptance of money is not dependent on the existence of sanctions. There is no need to enforce the cooperative solution (mutual acceptance of certain objects as a means of exchange), for there is no *temptation* to deviate from it. The practice is self–enforcing. (Usually there are regulatory norms *related* to the institution of money, e.g. norms which forbid the counterfeiting of money. These norms are often enforced by sanctions. The existence of these norms does not imply that the institution itself is based on social obligations. The prohibition of lying is a social obligation, but the rules of language which make lying possible are essentially coordinative.) Moreover, dramatic breakdowns of monetary institutions, like those in Germany after both World Wars, are not caused by failures to control "free riding".

According to Menger and modern textbooks, mutual expectations among the transacting agents are necessary for the existence of monetary institutions. This is typical of the pure coordination games discussed by Lewis. But it should be noticed that monetary institutions *can* break down. They are not completely self–enforcing. (Symbol systems analysed by Lewis have not had any serious breakdowns since the affair of the Tower of Babel. In purely coordinative cases the agents have no reason to expect widespread deviation from the convention. Consequently they have no reason to deviate.) Following an unconditional acceptance strategy, e.g. keeping savings in cash, can produce serious losses for individuals under the conditions in which a monetary system is really breaking down. An agent acts rationally when accepting money as a payment for goods if and only if he has a reason to expect that he could buy new goods with it, goods which would give him at least as much satisfaction as those he exchanged. Briefly, using money presupposes *trust* between transacting agents. The preference ordering of any single agent is the following:

(a) the agent accepts money, and others accept it too;
(b) the agent does not accept money, nor do the others;
(c) the agent does not accept money, but the others do;
(d) the agent accepts, but the others do not.

This preference ordering is that of what was earlier called as Assurance Game. It is less "dilemmatic" than the PD–game: it does not include a conflict of interests, and enforceable contracts are not necessary for a cooperative solution. However,if there is no trust it still creates an interaction problem for the agents. An individual is likely to cooperate only if he has reasons for believing that others are likely to cooperate. A lack of a mutual belief in general cooperation can upset the convention.

An enforcing agent can have a role in AG–games. The modern State with its monetary institutions, like central banks, tries to uphold trust in the money game by committing itself to acceptance, e.g. by convertability of national currency. Because the State is the strongest player, it has more resources than any other player and its commitment to a cooperative strategy is likely to further the mutual belief among other players that it is rational to accept money payments.

Several things could be learned from this example. It shows that there are goods which are neither private goods nor public goods in the economist's sense. But there is a further notion of good: the *common* good of Aristotle and his followers. This notion is alien to economists, although they should, perhaps, know it. The difference between a public good and a common good is brilliantly exposed by John Finnis (1980, ch. vi). A public road, for example, is a public good in the standard sense. It has the defining properties of the jointness of supply and non–excludability of consumption. Neverthless, it is like a private good in the sense that it is used individually and the welfare created by it is a subject of individuation and aggregation. The usefulness of a road to A is not *conceptually* dependent on its usefulness to B. Moreover, the value of the road to A is neither increased nor decreased by the fact that it has some value for B, too. From the social point of view, its usefulness increases when it has more than one user, but this does not affect to the self–interested judgements of the users. This creates the PD–structure characteristic of public goods.

A common good in the classical sense does not have these characteristics. A common good is something which is valued by A partially because it is valued by B and vice versa. This relationship is a conceptual rather than a contingent one. Friendship (the classical example used by Aristotle and Finnis), love, solidarity and religious community are examples of such relationships. It is important that in these examples, the values are really shared and cannot, for example be analysed in terms of interdependent utility functions. Like the goods produced by coordination, common goods are based on mutual trust. Common goods may have an instrumental value, but they have to be pursued for their own sake: a novelist may write better novels when she falls in love, but she cannot decide to fall in love in order to write better novels.

It is obvious that the value of goods gained by coordination is typically not that of common goods. Communication systems or systems of means of exchange are valuable for people who do not share any substantial ends. Nevertheless, we have seen that they are not just ordinary public goods. For although the gains of individuals using them are not conceptually interdependent, their usefulness for any particular individual conceptually presupposes their usefulness for other individuals. Unlike a road, a monetary system or a communication system is useful for A if and only if it is useful for some B, too. Their value is of an instrumental nature, but nevertheless dependent on the fact that they are valuable for others.

In the case of common goods, their interdependence generally excludes conflicts of interest. In the case of normal public goods, their public nature is the very source of such conflicts. In the case of goods produced by coordination, conflicts may or may not be present. Both the existence of some common language and the existence of some common means of exchange are in the interests of those who use them. This does not necessarily mean that they are indifferent in respect to all possible alternatives. The availability of different alternatives may create conflicts, it may occasionally disrupt the interaction between the parties, and it may establish permanent asymmetric power relationships.

The status of the dollar as a privileged means of exchange in international trade, and the status of the English language as the *lingua franca* in international cooperation enforce the dominant position of the United States in the international community. They are sources of power as well as products of it. Although other nations sometimes complain, they continue to accept the existing practices because they are generally accepted, and because it is more important to have some common practice than no practice at all. In reality, there are very few *pure* coordination situations; some amount of disagreement is always present in complex cases of coordination.

The extension of the Lewisian analysis to monetary systems illumines several things. It gives us an example of the gains of coordination, of the underlying interaction situation and of their role of established institutions in such situations. My next task is to apply the analysis to areas more familiar to the legal and political theorist.

CHAPTER 4

THE CONCEPT OF AUTHORITY

4.1. Authority and legitimacy

There is a general agreement that the concept of practical authority can be analysed as a right to impose obligations or commands on its subject and that this right is correlated with a duty to obey. Usually it is also implied that these rights and duties are mutually recognized. Thus authority is considered as a consensus–based notion. But it is important to notice that political authorities can have other functions, too. They can change the normative positions of their subjects by permitting, authorizing, delegating, exercising a veto, by declaring acts valid or invalid, etc. They can create and change definition rules, e.g. determine the values of units of payment. They are often authorized to speak on behalf of a group or organization and to express shared beliefs, opinions or intentions. They may be entitled to interpret, comment and criticize rules made by others and to suggest new rules without having the final say. None of these functions can be reduced to the command–obedience model.

Only persons, or groups of persons, can be authorities. They can exercise their authority only by making decisions which are authoritative. Rules, norms, and practices can be authoritative even if they do not originate from decisions made by an authority. Like decisions, they are intended to be and are generally understood as binding reasons for action. What then is fundamental to my idea of authority is that it always has an action–guiding role. Typically, political authorities have other important characteristics. They are often surrounded by symbols designating their authoritative positions, and often they are not only obeyed but praised and respected. These properties, however, are not necessary; what is conceptually necessary for someone's being in authority is that his or her decisions have the required role in people's practical reasoning. *The decisions are followed at least partly because they are his or her decisions*. This formula, however, bears several interpretations as we shall see.

As I noticed, not all authoritative acts can be reduced to commanding. Consequently, recognition of an authority cannot be reduced to obedience. The role of authoritative decisions in practical deliberation is a more complex one. Authoritative decisions are taken into account, and they are taken into account partly because they are recognized as deriving from an authoritative source. They establish salient ways of doing things (e.g. of making contracts, marrying, electing officials, playing a game, driving a car, fighting a battle) and even when people finally decide not to follow the established pattern, they are expected to present acceptable justifications for their deviations.

Authoritative acts and authoritative rules can possess the specific property of validity. Validity means that (1) acts are performed and the rules enacted under those institutionally defined conditions which are necessary to give them the normative meaning intended by the acting authorities, and (2) their content is consistent with the institutionally defined limitations of authority. Public statements with declarative contents can also be valid or invalid. If an authority is authorized to express the official opinion of a nation, an organization, etc., then his public statement about the matter, given under appropriate conditions, *is* the opinion of the nation or the organization.

If practical authority is always accompanied by a right to be obeyed, does it mean that the right, and the corresponding duty, are enforceable by coercive means? Or, is it rather that "the use of coercion is the sign of a lack of authority", as John T. Sanders (1983, 545) has it? The modern State claims both supreme authority and the supreme right to coerce. It is easy to generalize from this important example and conclude either that all practical authority is related to coercion or that the modern State lacks authority just because it uses coercion.

I disagree with both conclusions. Practical authorities exists in different social contexts (e.g. in families, private enterprises and voluntary communities); the State is a special case only. Some, but not all, of these authorities are backed by additional rights to coerce. More generally, the right associated with all practical authority does indeed create a social obligation (see ch. 7.) among the people who accept it. This implies that in that group disobedience is generally conceived as a sufficient reason for critical reactions. Critical reactions can involve anything from verbal criticism to capital punishment. We cannot say that something is accepted as a duty in a group if transgressions do never rouse reactions of any kind. The existence of an obligation to obey may justify coercion as an extreme form of critical reaction. But this does not mean that the authority itself has an additional right to enforce its decisions or even criticize a disobedient subject. The enforcement of decisions is often left to the members of the group in general, or to some outside power. As Leslie Green says, coercion secures authority but does not constitute it (Green 1988, 75). This securing role of coercion will be discussed later (chapter 9.).

This discussion, however, shows that the recognition of an authority does not mean anything like complete unanimity about, or automatic acceptance of every single decision. The notion of recognition has to allow the possibility that someone can be an effective authority even if his or her decisions are occasionally disobeyed, or obeyed for reasons not related to their authoritative nature. If complete unanimity or consensus were a necessary condition for authority, there would be no need for coercive or non–coercive social pressure.

Authority is often divided into subclasses. One important distinction is drawn between practical and theoretical (or epistemic) authority, political authority being a sub–subclass of practical authority. Another popular distinction is that between *de jure* or legitimate and *de facto* or (merely) effective authority. The latter distinction is troubled with a further complication: the notion of legitimacy is itself ambiguous. In the classical social theory (in Rousseau, for example) it means "being justified by the right principles". However, especially after the contributions of Max Weber sociologists have started to use it as a purely descriptive notion. In this use, authority is characterized as legitimate if, as a matter of fact, subjects believe that it is legitimate. Authority, unlike some other forms of power, is dependent on its recognition.

Sometimes legitimacy is equated simply with a ruler's ability to rule. To take an influential example, David Easton wants to broaden the term "legitimacy" "to cover all command–obedience relationships, discriminating further in each case by reference to the reasons why the exercise of the power or authority is effective" (Easton, 1979, 208). This may be called the purely external notion of legitimacy. The following (tentative) definition shows us the conceptual relationships between the various notions of legitimacy:

A is a legitimate authority iff

(1) A claims authority;

(2) A's decisions are generally obeyed;

(3) (2) is true partly because the claim in (1) is generally accepted;

(4) the claim in (1) ought to be accepted because it is supported by good reasons.

The conditions (1) and (2) constitute the purely external notion of legitimacy. In this use of the term no difference is made between the various sources of power: the decisions of a government may be obeyed because it has a sufficient control over some other sources of power, and authority as such may explain only a small portion of the general obedience. Conditions (1)–(3) define the descriptive or Weberian notion of legitimacy. It is an internal notion in the sense that it is based on acceptance (the distinction between internal and external notions is elaborated in ch. 7.). All conditions (1)–(4) together define the full normative notion of legitimacy.

What are the relationships between legitimate and *de facto authority*? In his account Raz (1983, 5–11) claims that the notion of justified or legitimate authority enjoys a conceptual primacy in regard to the notion of *de facto* or effective authority and that the legitimacy of an authority does not imply its effectiveness. It seems that the first claim is, for him, the main reason for accepting the second. He gives examples of authorities which are legitimate but not effective:

> It seems clear that scientific genius can go unrecognized and that a man who is in fact the greatest authority in a certain field may have very little influence over people's research or their beliefs on issues within his competence. Parents have authority over their children regardless of whether their children actually acknowledge their authority. (Raz 1983, 8)

The notion of legitimacy used here is a version of the normative notion. If an authority is legitimate in this sense, then it is justified by good reasons. It requires that conditions (1) and (4) above are fulfilled.

Raz' first example is about theoretical authority. He wants to minimize the differences between theoretical and practical authority, for "there are practical authorities whose authority is based entirely on their being theoretical authorities" (p. 8). This is certainly correct.

However, there seem to be certain undeniable differences between theoretical and practical authorities. It is not clear, for example, what being an effective or *de facto* theoretical authority means. A political authority is effective when the people within its sphere of validity actually take its pronouncements as authoritative reasons for acting. But a theoretical authority does not have a sphere of validity. Its authority is expressed by theoretical statements which are accompanied with universal acceptability claims: any person who tries to form an informed opinion about the matter should accept these theoretical statements. It is possible that the statements of a scientific genius are generally accepted by that small group of scientists who have specialized in the subject, while people in general do not believe in them. Is this form of authority effective or not?

It seems that there is a difference between theoretical and practical (or at least political) authorities. We may say that somebody is a theoretical authority in his field, implying that his statements should be believed, although people do not actually believe them. But a nameless prisoner who, like Dumas' Man in the Iron Mask, actually is the legitimate heir of a former king is not a political authority, even if, according to the justified political principles, he should be one.

What about Raz' second example of parental authority? Although individual parents may not have effective authority over their children, the authority of parents is based on a practice which is generally effective in our society. There may be societies in which the corresponding authority is possessed, not by the biological parents of a child but by somebody else, say, the heads of clans. According to the conventionalist approach, parents in these societies have no kind of authority, although it might still be true that if our practices are morally preferable, they should have it.

Thus legitimate authority (in the normative sense of the term) does not mean that someone should be an authority according to the proper principles. It means that somebody is an authority, and that he or she should be one. The relations between *de facto* and legitimate authority are the following:

(i) A is a legitimate authority only if A is a *de facto* authority.
(ii) A is a *de facto* authority only if A is generally believed to be a legitimate authority by the relevant population, or A is defined as an authority by a *de facto* authoritative practice.

Principle (ii) implies that the authority of a person (or a group) is like the validity of a norm. A norm can be said to be valid either because it is generally recognized as such, or because it is a part of a system (see ch. 7.). Normative legitimacy in the sense meant by Raz is a (contingent) property of authorities, and authority is a "success" notion: it is always effective. Therefore, contrary to Raz, legitimacy presupposes effectiveness. But it is still true that legitimate authority has, in a sense, a conceptual primacy over *de facto* authority. For only acceptance, or the belief in legitimacy, can make someone a *de facto* authority.

Several authors have criticized the Weberian practice of using the term "legitimacy" in a *de facto* sense. Thus, R. Grafstein writes that

> the concept should properly signify a normative evaluation of a political regime: the correctness of its procedures, the justification for its decisions, and the fairness with which it treats its subjects. In Weber's hands, however, legitimacy no longer represents an evaluation of a regime; indeed, it no longer refers directly to the regime itself. Rather, it is defined as the *belief* of citizens that the regime, to speak in circles, legitimate. Legitimacy becomes, for Weber, simply a matter of fact, the fact that citizens hold a certain belief. (Grafstein 1981, 456)

Thus, Grafstein sees the normative use of the concept (criteria (1)–(4) all fulfilled) as the only correct one.

However, an important instrument of social analysis would be missing if the descriptive notion of legitimacy were ruled out. We may, for example, believe that only a democratic government is worth being called "legitimate" in the normative sense. Nevertheless, we have to admit that non–democratic governments may sometimes enjoy a widespread acceptance, and do not base their stability on coercion only. This observation has both a theoretical and a moral significance. We must be able to understand authority systems which are radically different from ours. On other hand, it is important to see that even our legitimate authorities are authorities (and not only claimants to authority) partly because we accept them. These observations may open the road to normative relativism (which rejects the applicability of the criterion (4)), but it is not necessary to follow that road to the end.

In his recent study on legitimacy, David Beetham (1991) criticizes the Weberian account of descriptive legitimacy, and introduces an alternative account. His criticism is interesting, because it differs from that presented by Grafstein. Beetham also produces an important criticism of the Weberian ideal types of legitimacy, as well as an interesting account of the legitimation crises emerging in different political systems. I shall not discuss on those parts of his work; my counter–criticism is directed against his treatment of the general Weberian notion of legitimacy.

Beetham is not saying that the Weberian notion of legitimacy is inadequate simply because it uses people's own beliefs rather than our critical morality as the yardstick of legitimacy. Rather, the fault of the Weberian notion is that it equates legitimacy with people's beliefs on the legitimacy of a particular authority without taking into account the totality of their beliefs and actions. Beetham defines legitimacy as a product of three components:

> Power is said to be legitimate to the extent that
> (i) it conforms to established rules
> (ii) the rules can be justified by reference to beliefs shared by both dominant and subordinate, and
> (iii) there is evidence of consent by the subordinate to the particular power relation. (Beetham 1991, 15–16)

Thus, it is possible for a social scientist to make the judgement that a *de facto* authority is actually illegitimate without substituting his own moral view for that of the subjects. For a social scientist can show that there exists a contradiction between the beliefs generally shared in some community and the belief in the legitimacy of some particular authority or rule temporarily accepted in the same community. The following example produced by Beetham is especially illuminative:

> It is argued that the British electoral system, with its first–past–the–post rules determining who shall be elected in each constituency, is losing its legitimacy, and to an extent therefore also weakening that of the government elected under it. This is not because of any shift in people's beliefs, but because the rules have increasingly delivered results that diverge, both regionally and nationally, from the proportion of votes cast, and hence from accepted notions about the representative purpose of elections in a democracy. It is the increasingly unrepresentative character of the electoral system, and its consequent vulnerability to attack in a society that believes in representation, that is the basis for the weakening legitimacy of governments appointed under it. The vulnerability was there before it was exploited, and the weakening of legitimacy took place before people publicly acknowledged it. It may have taken the

> poll–tax legislation to bring the issue to the forefront of public attention. But the potential for doing so was already present in the growing discrepancy between the rules and the beliefs or values underpinning them. It is this discrepancy that is important to an analysis of legitimacy; what has occurred cannot made intelligible in terms of a shift in people's beliefs about legitimacy or 'belief in legitimacy'. (Beetham 1991, 11–12)

Now, the British electoral rules form, in any international comparison, one of the oldest and best–established electoral systems. It may still be true that they had recently lost some of their legitimacy because they produce results which are incompatible with the belief in representative government. Of course, they always had the potentiality of producing such results. This fact does not, as such, entail the judgement that those rules could not be justified in a community which believes in representative form of government. For it is a property of any legal or social rule that it can under some conceivable circumstances produce results which are inconsistent with some accepted values. This is especially clear in the case of power conferring rules: the legitimate heir of the throne can be a madman, a democratically constituted parliament can choose a dictator, etc. But if those particular circumstances are never manifested, these possibilities need not affect the legitimacy of the rules. We cannot say that because the British electoral system could produce illegitimate results, it was illegitimate from the start, for then any electoral system would be illegitimate at any moment. For example, systems of proportional representation are often blamed for the crises of legitimacy which occurred in the Weimar Republic and in the Fourth Republic of France; but e.g. in Scandinavia they have not produced similar effects. Legal and political systems can, unlike scientific theories, tolerate possible contradictions. In formal terms, they can tolerate the conjunction of Op, Oq and (p & r) –> –q, as long as the state of affairs denoted by 'r' is not likely to emerge.

A social scientist can infer that if an accepted rule is likely to produce results which are incompatible with accepted values or other rules, troubles will be forthcoming. The contradiction may even create a legitimacy crisis, because it may force people to modify their beliefs in the acceptability of institutions which use the rule and simultaneously appeal to the incompatible values. The resulting changes of beliefs can lead in different directions. The British may, for example, reject or change their electoral system, or their traditional notion of representative government. A prediction that a crisis of legitimacy is likely to arise is not, however, the same thing as an actual crisis. Sometimes, such a prediction can become a factor in producing an actual crisis. The widespread pessimism in the twenties about the viability of democracies contributed to the actual collapse of many democracies in the thirties. Neverthless, it was the actual disbelief in the legitimacy which constituted the crisis. We should make the distinction between a disposition and its realization.

All this constitutes a criticism of clause (ii) in Beetham's definition. Clause (iii) in his definition requires that the subjects of a legitimate authority give their consent. I think that this is too demanding, unless consent is equated with any form of acceptance whatsoever. Beetham is probably right when insisting (pp. 18–19) that institutionalized expressions of consent to authorities are widely used even in pre–modern and non–Western societies. But his discussion on the subject makes it clear that his notion of 'consent' is not what modern moral theorists would count as binding consent. Ritual oaths of allegiance underline the role of acceptance, but do not constitute consent in the moral sense. There need not be an alternative for giving them, and they can be given on behalf of others without consulting them. Binding consent is neither necessary nor a sufficient ground for the existence of an authority relationship in the descriptive sense.

Clause (i) in Beetham's definition makes all authority dependent on the existence of rules. This is the least controversial part of his definition; I shall try to show that even that part of it should, in the end, be rejected.

Richard Flathman (1980) has divided theories of political authority into two groups. Theories called "substantive–purposive" by Flathman try to merge political authority with theoretical authority. Flathman's characterization of substantive–purposive theories is the following. Firstly, an authority issues statements to be believed. Secondly, authority is an attribute of a person or persons. Thirdly, authority cannot be understood without understanding the substance and purpose of those rules and statements that constitute and express it. Fourthly, authority presupposes inequality – basically inequality in knowledge and skills.(pp. 14–15) The consensus behind authority defined in the substantial–purposive way is a consensus on certain values and beliefs. A person is an authority because he or she possesses supreme knowledge and understanding of those values and beliefs.

As Raz noted, theoretical authority is sometimes used as a justification for political authority. A member of a Supreme Court, a top manager, or an influential official are generally believed to be authorities because they possess special theoretical knowledge. Another basis for political authority is "local knowledge". Delegates representing a group in negotiations may be considered as authorities in their groups, not because this is a part of their formal position, but because they have had an opportunity to acquire knowledge about the situation which is not available or even communicable to other members of the group. However, the fact that theoretical authority is a possible justification for practical authority shows that they are distinct concepts. It is not inconsistent to complain that persons in authoritative positions are ill informed, uneducated or simply stupid, and, at the same time, recognize that their decisions are binding. As MacIver says:

> The man who commands may be no wiser, no abler, may be in no sense better than the average of his fellows; sometimes, by any intrinsic standard he is inferior to them. Here is the magic of government. (MacIver 1947, 13)

For this very reason, some supporters of substantive–purposive theories reject the notion of political authority. The everyday practices of political authorities cannot be made compatible with a substantive–purposive explanation of authority (cf. Sanders 1983).

The second class described by Flathman, the "formal–procedural" theories, can easily explain this. The essential idea behind these theories is that "authority can be correctly predicated of A only if there are established rules by virtue of which A has authority" (Flathman 1980, 35). Authorities are established by rules and they themselves establish rules. Authority is a property of roles, not of persons *simpliciter*. David Beetham's theory, discussed above, clearly belongs here.

To take a better–known example, Peter Winch (1967) tries to explain authority in terms of rule–governed activity. Firstly, he states that *all* human activity is rule–governed: "All characteristically human activities involve a reference to an established way of doing things". Secondly, "to participate in rule–governed activities *is* a certain way to accept authority" (p. 99). Thirdly, authority can be understood only in the context of rules.

Winch's third thesis seems to follow directly from the first: if all forms of human activity presuppose rules, so does of course, authority. However, Winch claims more than that. He accepts something like Flathman's essential idea of formal–procedural theories as quoted above. This is clearly revealed by Winch's discussion of Weber's notion of charismatic authority. Charismatic authority, as described by Weber, is by definition inconsistent with Flathman's description of formal–procedural theories:

> Where in charismatic authority the leader generates norms, in traditional authority, the norms generate the leader... Charismatic authority is substantially unbounded by norms. (Spencer 1970, 125)

Winch tries to show that Weber's types of authority are not conceptually distinct, for his "charismatic authority" is equally dependent on rules. Winch takes as examples the charismatic authority of Jesus, which is "completely unintelligible apart from the Jewish religious tradition", and the authority of William Webb Ellis, the inventor of the game called rugby, whose rule–creating authority is understandable only in relation to the pre–existing rules of football.

Given thesis one, namely that all human activity is understandable only against the background of rules, it is certainly true that the existence of rules is necessary for authority. Human action may be meaningful only in contexts governed by some rules. But, contrary to Winch, this does not imply that Weber's notion of charismatic authority is empty. For Weber's point is that authority of this type is not based on specific rules *authorizing* the authorities; a widespread belief (of the right kind) that someone is the authority is sufficient to make him an authority, even when this belief is not supported by a pre–existing rule. These situations can be distinguished from the situations in which an authorizing rule (a constitution, a tradition) exists.

Winch's second thesis – that participating in rule–governed activities amounts to accepting their authority – is also problematic. For people can follow rules for different reasons, e.g. in order to avoid sanctions. Persons following a rule only for this reason cannot be said to accept the authority of the rule. The rule is for them a reason for acting, but it is a reason of a wrong type. It may still be true that they can follow the rule only if they understand what it is to take it as authoritative.

Against the formal–procedural theories, I hold that not all authority is dependent on authorizing rules. Although Weber's notion of charismatic authority may have other theoretical defects (and here it is used only as an example of a notion of authority which does not presuppose authorizing rules), it is not unintelligible. Ultimately, it seems that the formal–procedural theories cannot avoid infinite regress. Ronald Dworkin, for example, claims that

> a rule can never be binding just because some person with physical power wants it to be so. He must have authority to issue the rule, or it is no rule, and such authority can only come from another rule which is already binding on those to whom he speaks. (Dworkin 1978, 20)

The starting point is certainly correct: authority neither equals nor is derivable from physical power. But if a binding rule must get its authority from another binding rule, how can this "binding quality" ever come into existence? If a self–justifying authority were an impossibility, the emergence of authority would remain mysterious. Suppose, for example, that a person called the Prophet were a charismatic authority in the Weberian sense. This would mean simply that the relevant population obeys the Prophet because it believes that, due to some extraordinary personal qualities, the Prophet is an authority. We *may* describe this by saying that there is a rule that the Prophet must be obeyed. But this rule emerges and disappears with the authority of the Prophet. Unlike a constitution defining the Prophet as the possessor of authority, this rule neither explains nor justifies his authority. It has to be formulated so that it refers to the authority of a particular individual, "the Prophet". It lacks the property which gives rules their justificatory and explanatory power, namely generality.

The conclusion of my discussion is, that neither the substantial–purposive nor the formal–procedural theories of authority are fully correct. Theories of the latter type are nearer the truth because they recognize the specific institutional nature of many authorities. They are, however, wrong when claiming that all authority can be fully explained in terms of rules.

4.2. Authority and power

Political authority is sometimes identified with political power. This, however, is a mistake which can result either from too wide a definition of authority or from too a narrow definition of power. The discussion on the nature of power is in a state of extreme confusion (for various accounts, see e.g. the anthologies edited by Barry (1976) or by Bell, Edwards and Wagner (1969)). Whatever is said about power will be contradicted by some distinguished author. For example, Parsons (1967, 331) does not count force and the use of sanctions as sources of power at all, while for Bacrach and Baratz (in Bell et al. 1969, 101–2) they are the only sources of power. The reason for this confusion is obviously that power is both an everyday concept and a theoretical concept used in explanatory social theories. An adequate definition of power cannot be reached by using our linguistic intuitions as a test.

Many theorists have made the distinction between the power to *do* things and the power to *make other people to do things*. This distinction is important for certain purposes. However, because the main subject of this chapter is authority, I shall ignore the first form of power – for authority is necessarily a relation between persons (or groups).

Raz (1983, 11–12) starts from the distinction between authority and power proposed by Lucas (1966, 16). If A has authority, then from his saying "Let X happen!" it follows that x *ought* to happen. If A has power, then it follows that X *will* happen. When A has authority, his saying is taken by the relevant persons as a reason for acting so that X is realized – authority works through reasons. This is not necessarily true of power in general. But, as we have noticed, political authority is necessarily effective, an authoritative command generally produces the effects intended by the authority. Therefore political authority is a form, or rather a source, of political power.

Authority is generally taken as a reason–based concept, while power is not. Many theorists try to analyse power in terms of causality. But causality in social contexts is at least as problematic a notion as power. In the following typology of the sources of power, some sources are classified as "causal" while others are "reason–giving".

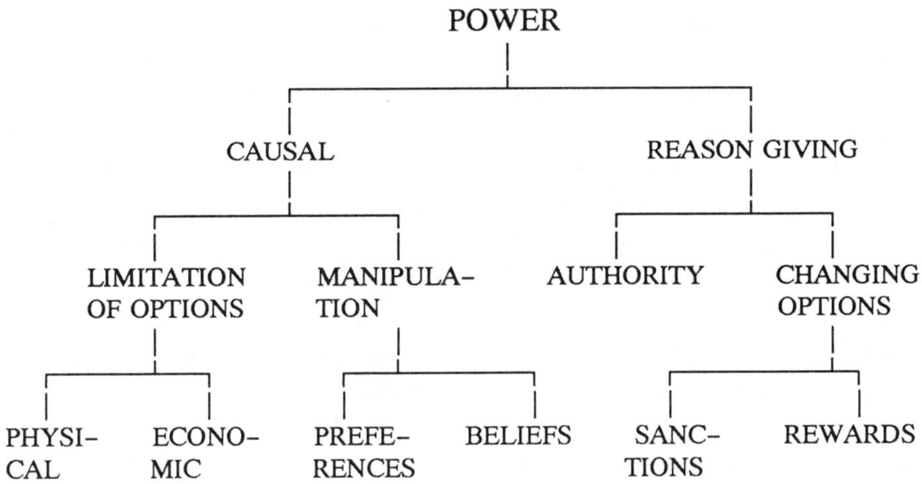

This typology is in accordance with Lucas' idea of power, which might be described as the effective–intention conception. A has power if he has effective means for realizing his intentions. In many situations, the sources of power enlisted here are alternative or complementary means for individuals and organizations to get what they want. An authoritarian government fighting against opposition may provide an example. The government may physically constrain the opposition leaders' freedom of action by locking them up. It may confiscate the property of opposition groups or prevent them from getting money for their political work. It may use subtle forms of propaganda or direct brain–washing. These exercises of power are causal in the sense that they do not leave a rational choice for the individuals who are subjects of them. The government can also threaten the members of the opposition with punishments, or it can promise bribes for those who are willing to leave the opposition. And lastly, the government can appeal to its authority. It can declare that oppositional activity is treacherous and wrong.

It is important to note that coercion, unlike the use of physical force, is a reason–giving form of power. By threatening to do something, unless the opposite side does what the government wants, the government provides a new reason for its subjects to do as it says. Coercion, like authority, presupposes that the power–holder can communicate its intentions to subjects, and that the subjects can rationally understand them and take them into account. Irrational persons can be constrained and perhaps manipulated, but not coerced.

Generally, *all forms of power, except those based on direct physical constraining, work through the practical deliberation of the subjects of power*. Hence, power phenomena cannot be explained in causal terms.

Both coercion and authority are forms of power which are effective only if they are recognized as effective by the subjects. If I have no means of convincing a person I want to coerce that I actually can coerce him, I cannot coerce him. Suppose that I have in my possession a powerful bomb which can be used to blow my enemies away. But suppose I have only one bomb, and nothing, short of using it can convince my enemies that I actually have it. Then I am able to use force against them but not to coerce them. Many of the examples of the exercise of power can be explained as attempts to convince power–subjects that those claiming power actually have power. The most convincing way of communicating that one has power is to use it. Army officers often give pointless commands in order to show that they have the power to give commands; dictatorial governments stop harmless activities because they want to show that they have the power to stop any activities they like. Even when states and organizations seem to use force indiscriminately and blindly, they usually intend to do more than bring the immediate effects: they try to warn, to make their threats credible, to "teach the lesson".

Because coercive power is partly based on beliefs, it has a conventional aspect: individuals, groups, and institutions have coercive power because there exists a mutual belief that they have it. This was already noticed by the Russian legal sociologist Nicolai Timasheff in his classic *Introduction to the Sociology of Law*. Timasheff shows how power can simultaneously be "objective" and based on the beliefs of its subjects:

> In a system of three elements, A, B, C, there are three links, AB, AC and BC, and for every member one of the links is independent of his will, is "objective", e.g., BC for A, AC for B and AB for C. Imagine that the illusion of the "chain of power" has been destroyed in one of the members, say A. The links AB and BC cease to exist, but the link BC continues to exist, and the corporate influence of B and C upon A may be strong enough to withhold A from acting in a manner corresponding to complete freedom. A learns from experience that the idea of objective links or chains of power may be an illusion, but that notwithstanding he must perforce behave as if they were real.

> Imagine now that the number of group-members is larger. With every new member the number of links which are "objective" for each increases very fast. (...) Vaguely feeling such a situation, A will, of course, be inclined to consider the power system as "objective", and of course it is transpersonal for him, as also for every other group-member, whereas it is not transpersonal for the totality. The mistake of A will therefore consist in transforming a situation which is transpersonal for him into a situation absolutely transpersonal. The mistake is intelligible and excusable. Moreover, everyone acts as if it were not a mistake but an actuality. (...) The sentiments (subjective attitudes) of others are objective facts. One has to submit even if one is disgusted and rebellious; and every group-member has to do the same. (Timasheff 1974 (1939), 186–7.)

Inadequate understanding of the nature of coercion has led to the conclusion that, for purely conceptual reasons, all permanent power relationships "rest on opinion" – ultimately social power, as distinguished from irregular acts of coercion, would be a matter of authority. The route which leads into the conclusion is simple: B may do what is required just because she is coerced by A; A may, in his turn, coerce B just because he is coerced by C etc. But the chain has to end to somewhere. The actor at the end of the chain, the "supreme coercer" cannot be just a single tyrant, except in very small groups. In any large-scale society, there has to be a considerable group which is willing to enforce the commands of the supreme rulers voluntarily. This is the famous "Praetorian Guard Argument" of Hume.

This argument is accepted by theorists as diverse as J.R. Lucas, H.L.A. Hart, Hannah Arendt and Jose Ortega y Gasset. As an empirical conjecture, it is plausible. Surely, no one wants to rule by coercive means, if it possible to rule by opinion. As Dennis Wrong says, there are psychological pressures on both sides of a power relation to make it acceptable. A rule based on pure coercion is not likely to last very long – in the long run, it either collapses or transforms itself into a mixed system of power. Neverthless, the Praetorian Guard argument is not a conceptual truth. In the passage quoted above, Timasheff shows why the "supreme coercer" is not needed. A is willing to coerce B (or, at least, is not willing to defend her) because A believes that if he disobeys, there are others who are ready to coerce him. Every individual in the society may have similar beliefs – and as long as they act according to these beliefs, they are correct. To quote Barry Barnes' formulation

> everyone knows that every else acquiesces in the regime, wherein this is known to everyone, and wherein the general knowledge of the general level of acquiescence is what sustains the acquiescence of which there is general knowledge. (Barnes 1989, 123; see also Kavka 1983)

This theory is interesting, because it explains both the forms of the political technique used in modern tyrannies (e.g. public rituals of expressing loyalty, limitation of information, seemingly arbitrary use of force, and extensive surveillance), and the way they collapse. It is unlikely that any large societies can, in the long run, be ruled by coercion only. For the structure of mutual beliefs, upholding coercive power presupposes mutual ignorance which can be removed, sometimes by a single event. The cry "Jos Ceaucescu!" – "Down with Ceaucescu!" shouted by the angry audience at the surprised dictator and broadcasted to every part of Romania was enough to bring down the most vicious tyranny of contemporary Europe. Even if the original protest–calls were made by the agents planted in the audience by the dictators' enemies, the calls were taken up by the masses, and this was the decisive factor.

There are several empirical connections between authority and coercion. The holders of coercive power often claim authority. Most notably, modern States claim both a monopoly of coercive power and supremacy in the field of political authority. For several psychological reasons, people are likely to accept these claims: otherwise powerful rulers can create their own authority. Sometimes, the existence of a coercive framework may be necessary or contributive to the maintaining of a belief in the effectiveness of authority (see ch. 9.5.), even if coercion is not a main motive for obedience. Thus, the opposite mistake is also common: authority is reduced to coercive power. It has been claimed that political authority implies a right to use coercion, although the subjects have no corresponding duty to obey. (See e.g. Ladenson 1980 or Sartorius 1981). Even if the existence of the duty is admitted, the attempt is made to explain the duty itself in terms of coercion.

An example of the difference between authority and coercion would be a government of a country fighting a defensive war. The government tries to exercise coercion against the invading enemy: this may be justified, the officials of the government may have a duty to do so and the probability that certain acts of the enemy will be punished by coercive measures may be high. Still, the government or its officials are not supposed to have authority over the enemy, they do not appeal to their supposed authority and the enemy soldiers do not recognize that they have authority over them (not even when the enemy soldiers admit that the country attacked has a right to defend itself). The same government also exercises coercion against its own citizens in order to enforce its commands: here the relation is an authoritative one.

Coercion and use of authority are similar in the sense that they are both ways of changing the kind of reasons that emerge in someone's practical reasoning. However, the reasons provided are of different kinds. Coercion changes the balance of first–order reasons by making certain options less appealing to the agents. Coercion affects peoples' interests. An exercise of authority changes the reasons by providing second–order reasons not to follow certain first–order reasons. Instead of appealing to individuals' immediate interests it (typically) gives reasons not to follow those interests.

4.3. The conventionalist notion of authority

A fully developed conventionalist definition of authority is the following:

A is an authority in S iff

(1) A claims that his decisions intended to direct the actions of the members of S should be followed by the members of S because of their authoritative nature.
(2) A claims legitimacy, i.e. he claims that (1) is justified on grounds acceptable to the members of S.
(3) The members of S generally do accept the claim expressed in (1).
(4) The members of S generally follow the decisions of A.
(5) There are mutual beliefs in S that (3) and (4) are true
(6) (5) is at least partly a reason for (4);

or

(7) while (3)–(6) are not true in respect with A, there is a further authority A' which authorizes A, and (3)–(6) are true in respect of A'

The definition does not presuppose that A's justification in (2) is actually accepted in S. As Hart and Weber have noticed, different individuals can have different reasons for accepting authority. Thus A can claim that his rule is of divine origin, while his secularized subjects may be ready to accept his rule for other reasons. The definition is compatible with both a substantial justification and a justification derived from pre–existing rules. A's authority can be related to his officially defined role or to his personal qualities. If the existence of an authority is based on conventional facts, the problem of authorizing rules is solved. Authority may be, but need not be, based on pre–existing rules. It also may be, but need not be, backed by coercive sanctions.

What is essential in this conventionalist definition is the idea of the interdependence of individual attitudes towards the authority, reflected by (6). The belief that somebody is the authority in a society implies that the members of that society generally share the same attitude and therefore generally follow the decisions of the authority. In other words, it implies a belief in the effectiveness of the authority. This idea is actually quite common. Compare it, for example, with Reinhard Bendix' description of Max Weber's theory of legal authority:

> Like other types of authority, legal domination rests upon the belief in its legitimacy, and every such belief is in a sense question–begging... Laws are legitimate if they have been enacted; and the enactment is legitimate if it has occurred in conformity with the laws prescribing the procedures to be followed. This circularity is intentional. (Bendix 1977, 418–19)

The apparent "circle" common to many classical conceptions of the validity or legitimacy of norms is the following: If a norm, decision or command is valid or legitimate, it is a reason for following it. A decision, etc. is valid or legitimate only if it belongs to a system or practice which is by and large effective. But this effectiveness is nothing but the fact that those decisions, etc. which belong to it are generally followed (See for example Aarnio 1984). The conventionalist interpretation of this "circularity" is that it reflects the interdependent nature of the attitudes of individual subjects. Thus, it is not a vicious circle as Habermas (1984, 265), among others, has claimed.

This circular structure can be used for explaining crises of legitimacy. The collapse of the autocratic regimes in Eastern Europe or in Iran, for example, were not just breakdowns of the coercive structures discussed above. At least among the ruling strata of the respective societies, these regimes certainly possessed some authority. When facing the rising tide of rebellion, the members of the ruling groups might still have considered that the claim to authority (1) of the old regime was morally or politically acceptable. What was lacking was the mutual belief (3) and (4) that it was generally accepted.

Certainly the fact that many people in my neighbourhood obey the decisions of somebody (say, of the local Mafia boss) cannot be, as such, a reason for me to obey them. Authority is, as we have seen, a power to change certain reasons used by people in their practical reasoning. The question is why *rational* people would ever grant such a power to anyone. I have argued that it is not based either on the greater wisdom or on the coercive abilities of the authorities. Authority in the full sense of the term is rationally justifiable only if it is at least sometimes reasonable to accept decisions because they are made in an authoritative way. Conventionalism should provide an alternative theory of the role of authority in societies.

CHAPTER 5

AUTHORITY AND COORDINATION

5.1. Simon's theory

There are many possible starting points for attempts to link authority with the coordination of human interactions: the most famous forerunner here is of course David Hume with his theory of justice. I will, however, start from a more recent classic. Herbert A. Simon's *Administrative Behaviour* (1945, 2nd ed. 1957) includes an important theory for the role of authority. It is an obvious sign of the lack of communication between different branches and traditions in social theory that many jurists and political theorists emphasizing the coordinative functions of authority have paid no attention to Simon's classical book.

Simon's starting point is an extensive criticism of the traditional economic notion of rational decision making. Against this notion, he stresses such factors as the imperfection of human knowledge, the incommensurability of values relevant to decisions and the interdependence of individual decisions. Although all these aspects are relevant from my point of view, the last is especially important. Simon describes how the problems it gives arise in the following way:

> ...each individual, in order to determine uniquely the consequences of his actions, must know what will be the actions of the others. This is a factor of fundamental importance for the whole process of administrative decision-making.
>
> There is really a serious circularity involved here. Before A can rationally choose his strategy, he must know which strategy B has chosen; and before B can choose his strategy, he must know A's. (...) The resulting system will be of a highly indeterminate nature, for the instability of each behaviour choices leads to the instability of the other. (Simon 1957, 71)

Simon shows that the existence of common goals or values is not enough to create stability, if the individuals do not possess sufficient knowledge about each others' future behaviour (p. 72–3). A successful coordination of individual actions is dependent on stable, mutual expectations concerning the actions of others. In the simplest situations individuals can coordinate their activities by observing each other; Simon calls this "self-coordination". However,

> under most practical conditions, self-coordination is infinitely less effective than a predetermined scheme of action that relieves each member of the group of the task of anticipating the behaviour of the others as a basis of his own (Simon 1957, 106).

For Simon, authority is the factor which creates expectations necessary for coordination in large groups. There are several interesting connections between Simon's theory of administrative authority and the theory presented here. Firstly, Simon uses the term "authority" in the same way as I have done. For him, the existence of authority is dependent on the acceptance of subordinates, and the acceptance of authority consists of permitting one's own behaviour to be guided by a decision of authority, irrespective of personal judgements on its merits. Secondly, by accepting this kind of definition Simon is able to make the correct distinction between authority and other sources of power, such as influence or sanctions (pp. 126–7, 146).

Thirdly, Simon shows why acceptance of authority can be rational in large groups. It is rational precisely because it creates the expectations necessary for the coordination of individual activities. In complex organizations (as contrasted with small self-coordinating groups), an agent

> sets himself a general rule which permits the communicated decision of another to guide his own choices (i.e. to serve as a premise of those choices) without deliberation of his own part on the expediency of those premises. (Simon 1957, 125)

Simon still subscribes to the common idea that a person accepting an authority follows authoritative decisions without forming a judgement about their merits. This idea is mistaken. In democratic societies, citizens are often supposed to have a *duty* to form an independent opinion about the correctness of major political decisions. For the acceptance of authority the essential thing is that an agent *acts* according to the decisions of the authority.

5.2. Authority and the problem of "the balance of reasons"

The problem of authority is a problem about the nature of practical reasoning. It can be put in this way: Authority, as we have seen, implies a normative right or power to change the reasons applying to some agent. The decisions of an authority are themselves reasons for an agent to do or not to do something. Now it seems to be a fundamental principle of rationality that an agent has to act according to his or her best judgement. The best judgement of an agent is a judgement which takes into account *all relevant reasons* (i.e. reasons relevant to the ends of the agent), *only* relevant reasons, and *balances* them correctly. But if an agent follows the decisions of an authority, he or she does not necessarily act according to his or her best judgement.

We can try to solve the problem by supposing that the decisions of a legitimate authority are relevant reasons. But why are they so? The fact that somebody commands us to do something is not, as such, a relevant reason to do anything. It is a relevant reason only if we have already concluded that authority matters, and that the commanding person is an authority.

The problem created by authority is not dissimilar to the problem created by rules. How can rules be reasons? The commitment to follow some rules can also be a source of a judgemental conflict.

Theories of practical reasoning belonging to the *act–teleological* type are especially problematic in this context. By this term I mean the theories which (i) take individual acts as the subjects of evaluation, (ii) evaluate them solely by reference to their total consequences, and (iii) suppose a single scale of value. The term covers both normative and descriptive theories; act–utilitarianism as well as the theory of rationality used in neo–classical economics belong to this type. These theories can accommodate rules and authorities only as far as rules or authorities can provide information about the consequences of different possible actions. An act–utilitarian or a neo–classical *homo economicus* can follow technical rules or the advices of a specialist, but cannot take them as binding reasons for action.

Another type of theories potentially inconsistent with our normal notions of authority and rule are *act–deontological* theories. These theories suppose that there are no useful inter–subjective moral standards which could be taught or applied. Rather an action is always based on an irreducibly personal moral choice. Again an authority can provide reasons for actions only by providing new information; rules can be relevant as personal maxims only. Some existentialist thinkers have a theory of this kind.

It is well known that many (but perhaps not all) forms of rule–utilitarianism collapse into act–utilitarianism. A less well–known but equally valid point is that some deontological theories of the intuitionistic variant are likely to collapse into act–deontology. In these theories, a system of prima facie –rules is supposed, and these rules are claimed to be central for the moral evaluation of actions. But if there is no ordering of these prima facie rules, or if the ordering itself is only prima facie, there is no systematic balancing. Any supposed moral rule can override any other moral rule. Again, if we, following Prichard, suppose that an act is right when the agent *thinks* it is in accordance with his or her moral duties, we seem to accept that there are no inter–subjective moral standards.

Some act–teleologists and act–deontologists have actually drawn the political consequences which seem to follow from their theories, namely that there is no justifiable form of political authority. This amounts what Robert Paul Wolff calls "philosophical anarchism". Philosophical anarchism should not be equated with political anarchism. A political anarchist challenges the state's right to exercise organized force. He or she can accept at least some forms of political authority, e.g. the authority of a majority decision made in a voluntary political organization. A philosophical anarchist could, at least in principle, accept the state's right to coerce people. What a philosophical anarchist cannot accept is its (or any de facto authority's) claim that it should be obeyed just because it says so. An example of philosophical anarchism based on act–teleological foundations is William Godwin's *Enquiry Concerning Political Justice*. A modern work on philosophical anarchism based on act–deontological premises is Wolff (1976).

Wolff's argument is based on his notion of autonomy. Every agent has an obligation to act autonomously, or, in other words:

> each of us must make himself the author of his actions and take responsibility for them by refusing to act save on the basis of reasons he can see for himself to be good. Autonomy, thus understood, is in direct opposition to obedience,

> which is submission to the will of another, irrespective of reasons. (Wolff 1969, 607)

Wolff accepts the definition that authority involves "the right to command, and correlatively, the right to be obeyed". Obedience is a matter of doing something because one is told to do so. Therefore authority is incompatible with autonomy and must be rejected. Only non–authoritative methods of decision– making can preserve individual autonomy, for

> neither majority rule nor any other method of making decisions in the absence of unanimity can be shown to preserve the autonomy of individual citizens. (Wolff 1969, 608)

Thus Wolff believes that only a consensual agreement among all agents (which he misleadingly calls unanimous direct *democracy*) is a morally acceptable way to make collective decisions.

Some authors have argued that even the consensual method proposed by Wolff is inconsistent with the requirement of autonomy, for "since consensus can require that one trades off some of one's moral convictions, unanimous consensus does not guarantee autonomy" (Nelson 1980, 64). However, this counterargument seems to be based on a misinterpretation. Even in the consensual system people are under an obligation not to give up their autonomy. If A proposes to B that they should perform a common action, but B is willing to participate only on the condition that A acts against his moral judgement, A is under an obligation to refuse. The society of A and B remains in an anarchical status quo. As Wolff says:

> since by rule of unanimity a single negative vote defeats any motion, the slighest disagreement over significant questions will bring the operations of the society to halt. It will cease to function as a political community and fall into a condition of anarchy. (Wolff 1976, 24)

Wolff's theory implies that such an outcome is also acceptable; without consensus no collective action is morally required. Moreover, this veto–right is continuous. If the decision–makers change their mind afterwards, the decision does not bind them any more. This is the difference between a consensual decision– rule (as used e.g. in some international organizations, in the old Germanic deliberative bodies, in juries, or in the Diet of the Kingdom of Poland), and Wolff's Utopia. A consensual decision rule binds the decision makers. They have to follow the unanimously agreed decisions even when, after further reflection, they come to the conclusion that all things considered, it would be better not to follow them. Thus, even consensual decision rules possess an authoritative character.

Exactly the same contrast between authority and consensual decision making appears in the works of the seventeenth–century absolutist Sir Robert Filmer. Like Wolff, Filmer claims that the only alternatives are unanimous decision making and a submission to the will of another:

> For what freedom or liberty is due to any man by the law of nature, no inferior power can alter, limit or diminish. No one man, nor a multitude can give away the natural right of another... Therefore, unless it can be proved by some law of nature that the major, or some other part, have a power to overrule the rest of the multitude, it must follow that the acts of multitudes not entire are not binding to all, but only to such as consent unto them. (Filmer 1949, 82)

> If it be true, that men are by nature free–born, and not to be governed without their own consents, and that self–preservation is to be regarded in the first place, it is not lawful for any government but self–government to be in the world, it were sin in the people to desire, or to attempt to consent to any other government. (Filmer 1949, 225)

For Filmer, this anarchistic conclusion was a *reductio ad absurdum* result, while for Wolff it is the very foundation of his theory. Still, they use similar arguments for the same purpose: all authoritative methods of decision making, most importantly democratic ones, are in contradiction to the requirement of individual liberty. Even in a democratic society, some people "are governed against their wills" (Filmer) and "those who submit to laws against which they have voted are no longer autonomous" (Wolff).

Filmer's opponents, the social contract theorists, actually ignored this part of his argument. In both *Treatises*, Locke destroys Filmer's theory of absolutism with rigorous logic and magnificient irony, but he has very little to say against the argument about the contradiction between majority rule and individual liberty. Locke's argument for majority rule, and against unanimity, is that "where the majority cannot conclude the rest, there they cannot act as one Body, and consequently will be immediately dissolved again" (Locke, *Second Treatise* ch viii.98.). This is exactly what, according to Filmer and Wolff, *should* happen if people are bound only by their own conscience and judgement.

The problem of Wolff and Filmer is especially important for the theorists of democracy. Any plausible defence of democracy has to accommodate the notions of autonomy and authority. Thus, the famous formulation of Rousseau in his *Du contrat social*, Bk.I ch. vi is still *the* problem of democracy. In Rousseau and Sieyès, this difficulty led to their idea that those in the minority actually consent to the decisions made against their will.

Can political authority be defended against Wolff? Firstly, we should notice the difficulties in his own doctrine of autonomy. The obligation of autonomy can be formulated in this way:

A ought to do X if A believes that (all things considered) X is the morally right thing to do.

Now this principle itself is an exception in Wolff's theory. The principle holds unconditionally, not only when people *believe* that the right thing to do is to act according to what they believe the right thing to do is. This means that they are not permitted to forfeit their autonomy even if they believe it to be the right thing to do in a given situation. They are not permitted voluntarily to limit their own autonomy. This reveals the fundamental ambiguity general to most theories of freedom or self–government. They are typically ambivalent in the question of whether the most perfect state of freedom includes a freedom to abdicate voluntarily one's freedom. Paradoxically, people would in one sense be more free if they were not limited by Wolff's strong requirement of autonomy. (The problem is analoguous to the traditional problem of self–limiting sovereignty, discussed in ch.6.)

Another problem is that Wolff's principle in practice generates incompatible requirements for different individuals. While A believes that morality requires him, in some situation, to do X, B may simultaneously believe that it requires her to prevent A from doing X. Then it is true that A ought to do X and B ought to prevent A from doing that. This brings us near to the fundamental problem of both act–deontological and act–teleological theories. Phrases like 'the right thing, all things considered', 'balance of reasons' etc. seem to presuppose that we can always fix the context of an agent's action, and then meaningfully ask: "What should this agent do in this context?" Human action, however, typically appears in conditions of interdependency, as illustrated by the games described in ch.2. The best choice of agent A is often determined by the choices of B, C, etc., and vice versa. There exists no best choice but only several optimal or permitted combinations of choices for all agents involved. In such situations agents may, after rational deliberation, conclude that they have overwhelming reasons not to act according to their own deliberation. Instead, they can commit themselves to a mutual adherence to a rule or an authority. By deciding to accept the decisions of an authority as binding, they treat these decisions as second-order reasons in the sense that they are not compelled to go through the deliberation process in every individual case. They cannot always give independent reasons for their actions in individual cases, but they can justify by rational arguments this submission to an authority.

Does this mean that by accepting someone else's decisions as authoritative, an agent admits that the authority is morally superior to him? Not necessarily. If a group of agents perform a collective action by co-ordinating their individual contributions according to the decisions of an authority, they are not committed to the claim that the judgements of the authority are morally superior to their own judgements. They are only committed to saying that acting according to an authority's judgements leads to a state of affairs which is likely to be morally superior to any state of affairs which would have resulted if the group had tried to use non-authoritative methods of decision-making. Every agent may still be convinced that his or her personal moral judgements are better than the judgements of the authority; unfortunately the judgements of the other members of the group might be even worse. "Self-coordination" is a morally safe option for a group only if (1) they share the same conception of morality in regard to the requirements of the situation, (2) they also share the same factual beliefs about the nature of the situation, and (3) both (1) and (2) are mutually believed in the group.

The consequences of the Wolffian position become more clear when it is recognized that his argument against authority concerns officials and executive decision-makers as well as their subjects. Consider, for example, the position of the Danish government in 1992. Both the Cabinet headed by the Prime Minister Poul Schluter and the majority in the Parliament favoured the ratification of the Maastricht Treaty. However, constitutionally the final authority in the issue was the Danish people, who rejected the ratification in a referendum. After the referendum, the task of the Prime Minister and his Cabinet was to negotiate with the European Community on Denmark's relationship with the Community. In spite of the fact that the negotiators themselves would had preferred the ratification of the original Treaty, they had to take the result of the referendum as binding, and to act in the negotiations *against the balance of the reasons accepted by them*.

This example emphasizes the fact that my defence of authority has nothing to do with "authoritarianism". All collective decisions, including such unanimously made decisions which bind the decision–makers in the future, are intended to have an authoritative character. When authority is defined in the standard way, it is often forgotten that in constitutional systems all agents are under some authority. A theory which says that authoritative commands cannot rationally limit the autonomy of a citizen also implies that laws cannot rationally limit the autonomy of the judges, constitutions cannot rationally limit the autonomy of the politicians, the decisions of elected ministers cannot rationally limit the autonomy of the generals etc. For the relations inside a politico–legal system are relations of authority. This may well be the most important consequence of the theory of philosophical anarchism. Ordinary citizens are usually faced with a great variety of reasons for complying with the existing laws. Wanting other reasons, we sometimes comply because we are coerced to do so. But the supreme decision makers are in a different position. It seems that there is no reason why a power–holder could not accept philosophical anarchism and still retain power. Such a power–holder would simply say that although his decisions have no binding power as such, he may justly coerce others to follow them because he thinks them to be morally correct decisions. If the others disagree, they may in their turn try to persuade or coerce him, but he is not going to follow any orders just because the legally determined authority structure would require it.

In modern political and moral discourse, hardly anyone has defended the thesis that supreme political decision–makers should make decisions which they consider to be best rather than those dictated by the law (The decisionist theory of Carl Schmitt may be an exception). Many legal theorists, however, have argued that judges should make such decisions. They should base their decisions on their intuitions of substantial justice, or on the particular requirements of a concrete situation, or on utilitarian considerations. This is the core of the criticism directed against rule–based legal theories. The criticism can be expressed in act–utilitarian or act–deontological terms; occasionally, it is connected with rule–scepticism which says that rules cannot play their supposed role in decision–making. Usually, it omits the question of whether the arguments which allow the judges to follow their own moral lights can be applied to other decision–makers. Both ordinary citizens and political and executive decision makers are often expected to apply and interpret the law when making decisions. Thus, the criticism of rule–based decision–making ultimately implies either judicial elitism – judges, unlike ordinary people or democratically elected leaders, are not constrained by positive rules – or philosophical anarchism. In either case, the theory is incompatible with democracy (Richard Taylor combines both elements in Taylor 1983).

These considerations show how authority can be seen as necessary for the effective collective pursuit of ends. Now I think that a great part of morality is, or presupposes, pursuit of collective ends. This claim may seem to be inconsistent with the strong individualistic emphasis typical of modern moral and political philosophy. However, the realization of individualistic programmes are equally dependent on coordinated and determined action. One obvious defect of many individualistic programmes (including Wolff's version) is that they do not tell us how to get into the proposed Utopias. But in any case, it is clear that we can neither change nor maintain a political system without collective action. This also means that consequences matter. Even if our ideal morality consists of "side–constraints" only, the moral value of actions aiming at realizing the ideal system must at least partly be judged in terms of consequential effectiveness.

Wolff actually recognizes the role of authority described here:

> Men's almost universal belief in the legitimacy of the states which rule them serves the largely positive social function of coordinating the economic and social behavior of large numbers of people in complex, functionally differentiated and integrated societies. The fact that this belief is false does not diminish the social usefulness of the belief. It is perfectly appropriate to ask: if

> men cease to believe in the authority of the state, what besides force and threats will maintain an adequate level of social coordination? (Wolff 1977, 304)

This is a surprising concession from the proponent of philosophical anarchism. Only one step further is needed in the argument presented here: People can recognize this useful function of authorities and accept it as one (perhaps the only) reason for the legitimacy. Why should Wolff insist that this belief is nevertheless false?

Thus, the coordination theory explains that fundamental intuition which is the source of the problems discussed by Wolff, namely that in some situations, it is reasonable to do x just because an authority has commanded x. In coordination situations we are not acting against a balance of reasons when following a command, for in such situations there is no balance which would be independent of the command. However, for many theorists this is not enough. According to them, the authoritative force of commands and decisions should be decisive even if there exists a balance of reasons. This is often explicated in terms of Joseph Raz' notion of an exclusionary reason. An exclusionary reason is a reason to do something, and, at the same time, a reason not to follow certain other reasons, or even not to take them into account at all. It is not just an especially weighty reason which overrides less important reasons, but a reason of a qualitatively different kind.

In the discussion on exclusionary reasons, two kind of reasons are sometimes dealt with as if they belonged to the same class. There are, I think, valid moral reasons. These reasons do possess an exclusionary force in certain situations. A businessman may argue that although there are moral reasons not give bribes, the economic reasons are sometimes so strong that they override the requirements of morality. Such a cost-benefit analysis does not treat morality in a correct way. Moral reasons are not just important, they are decisive, and can be weighed against (and excluded by) other moral reasons only.

Some reasons may by said to "exclude" other reasons in a different sense. We may have rational reasons to follow a general plan or policy instead of weighing every individual case separately. Quite often, we may have even reasons to close our ears to further information. (1) The most common and the most discussed reason is that deliberation itself may have costs. Often it takes time and effort to acquire information and to process it, and there is no guarantee that the resulting decision would be any better. Thus, rational human beings have to rely on (epistemic) authorities, intuition, traditions, and rules of thumb when making their everyday decisions. This is called by Herbert Simon "satisficing rationality".

(2) The second reason for excluding some reasons is that one does not trust one's own ability to deliberate on them. We may believe that some issue is too complex for us consider, or that our present mental state does not allow us to make the decision in a rational way. We may know that we are too tired to go through the arguments, or too weak–willed to resist a temptation.

(3) Finally, refusing even to consider certain reasons can be a necessary part of a general strategy. As game theorists like Schelling and Elster have shown, precommitment is often the most rational strategy in a situation. Precommitment, however, requires credibility in order to be effective. One way to increase the credibility of commitments is to refuse to discuss the issue.

A justification based on coordination implies that authoritative decisions can work as second–order reasons. It is rational (in the revised sense) to follow them in order to reduce the complexity of decision making. Authoritative decisions are thus related to the second–order reasons (1) and (3) (and sometimes to (2)). The coordination analysis does not imply that they possess an exclusionary force in Raz' sense. According to my view, only moral reasons can have that force. Because authority can be used as a descriptive notion, it follows that authoritative decisions are not necessarily exclusionary reasons.

Many theorists of authority are not happy with this conclusion. They claim that the binding force we associate with the decisions we take as authoritative has to be a stronger one. Consequently, either they suppose that there are exclusionary reasons which are not moral reasons, or, then, that the notion of authority is, contrary to the analysis given in ch. 4., a moral notion.

In ch. 4., I tried to show how authority can be used as a descriptive (e.g. as morally neutral) term. Thus, I reject the latter supposition. Why, then do, we often tend to think of authoritative decisions as binding, if only moral reasons can possess the strong binding property analysed by Raz?

The answer is that, contrary to the strong individualist conception which dominates a large part of the contemporary discussion, moral requirements can often be fulfilled only by collective action. Quite often, both our personal and group interests, and morality, require us to cooperate with other people and to coordinate our actions. This is true even in simple cases. We should generally follow the traffic regulation because by violating them we may risk our lives. But even a person who does not care about his personal safety has a moral reason to follow traffic rules. Even if morality permits suicides, no one has a right to risk the lives of other people. Thus, it is often true that we are under a duty to coordinate our actions, and that the required coordination can be secured only by relying on authoritative decisions. In such a situation authoritative decisions possess a moral exclusionary force. Their exclusionary character is dependent on the contingent but all–pervasive fact that we cannot fulfil our duties without coordinating our actions.

The relation is not, however, a conceptual one. Coordination may be necessary in order to execute some immoral plan. The leader of a criminal gang may be an authority in the sense that the members of the gang have a rational reason, based on the need to coordinate their criminal activities, to follow his commands. Coordination may be used for morally evil or neutral purposes. In cases of coordination on a large scale, there is usually a complex mixture of different reasons. Large coordinative institutions, such as language, money, or law work as media for numerous individuals groups to realize their different purposes and values.

Nevertheless, there can be purely moral reasons for obeying authoritative decisions, reasons which may have nothing to do with their coordinative function described above. We may personally promise to be loyal to a certain authority, or we may see our obedience to it as symbolic actions which express some higher, e.g. religious, values. Those moral reasons may bind us, if they are not excluded or overriden by other moral considerations. Even if there is no general moral obligation to obey authorities, many traditional justifications may play an important role in specific situations.

Finally, it is important to remember that many claimants of authority do not have any rational justifications for their claims. The notion of coordination is important because it reminds us that institutions are justifiable as far as they help human beings to solve their practical problems. Thus Ms. B, an orchestra conductor, may be a great artist, but she has an authority over the orchestra just because both the orchestra and the audience benefit from it. If my theory is correct, the authority of the governments, legislators and judges is justified in the same way.

5.3. Arguments against the conventionalist theory of authority

In his brilliant book on the authority of the State, Leslie Green (1988) presented a series of critical arguments against the conventionalist theory of authority. His criticism is directed against the legal theories of Raz and John Finnis. Both theorists use a conventionalist notion of authority (in a wide sense of the term). Green equates their conventionalism with the more technical use of conventions appearing in the works of Postema (1982) and Ullman–Margalit and (1977) which originates from Lewis (1969).

The technical (Lewisian) definition of a convention was the following (cf. Chapter 2.):

> A regularity in the behaviour of members of a population S when they are agents in a recurrent situation C is a *convention* if and only if it is true that, and it is common knowledge [mutual belief in my terminology, EL] in S that, in any instance of C among the members of S,
> (1) everyone conforms to R,
> (2) everyone expects everyone else to conform to R;
> (3) everyone prefers to R on condition that the others do, since C is a coordination problem and uniform conformity to R is a coordination equilibrium in C. (Lewis 1969, 58)

In this technical sense, convention is any arrangement which helps the members of S to settle coordination equilibria, i.e. such a combination of choices that no member of the group would have preferred a combination in which any agent had chosen otherwise. In their recent works, both John Finnis and Joseph Raz have tried to dissociate their own, non–technical treatments of convention and coordination problems from the technical conception of game theory (Finnis 1984; Raz 1984; both emphasized this in personal discussion). Here Green's critique may then be misguided. However, I think that Finnis and Raz are over–cautious in this question. The role of game theory in the work of Lewis is an illustrative one; his theory, including the definition above, can be reinterpreted without using game–theoretical terms. The same is true about the theory presented in this work. Still I believe that the use of games as ideal–typical descriptions of the problems of human interaction is legitimate.

Green tries to show that authority is never necessary to solve coordination problems, and even if it is sometimes sufficient, it does not have any "evolutionary advantage" over the other types of solutions. He does not explain his notion of evolutionary advantage, but his description of the disadvantages of authoritative solutions makes it plain that by the term he means simply rationality; his claim is that in any coordination equilibrium, there is always an equally rational solution which does not require any authoritative decision.

Why does Green think so? The alternative solutions (called here non–authoritative methods of decision–making) were coercion, negotiations and self–coordination (or spontaneous convention formation). Green's claim is that in coordination situations (unlike, perhaps, in other cases of the human interaction) we can always reach an equilibrium by these means:

> To achieve a co–ordination equilibrium by appealing to or creating a conventional norm, one need only act on the balance of first–order reasons. Even in the absence of existing facts, one can solve a CP [a coordination problem; EL] just by providing ordinary reasons in favour of one of the alternatives. One could suggest, advise, persuade or threaten the others to follow it. Each would act rationally in weighing the likelihood of the rest following that option, O_1, as opposed to any O_2,...O_n. When there is no existing reason to choose any of them over the others, and the first–order reason is then given for choosing O_1, it follows that there is some reason to choose O_1 and no reason to choose O_2,...,O_n. If all other options are outweighed, then O_1 will enjoy general compliance. Hence, equilibrium can be secured without authority. (Green 1988, 114)

The essence of Green's argument is that authoritative decisions cannot be exclusionary second–order reasons, because in coordination situations there are no reasons that would be excluded: agents are, by definition, indifferent as to choice between alternative options leading to an equilibrium:

> A conventionalist might, however, further object that while the existence of a CP always provides some reason for conformity it may not be an overriding reason. Each may still have preferences among the possible outcomes such that authoritative requirements are needed to single out a particular one. But this

> plays fast and loose with the description of the problem. If contrary preferences are strong enough to outweigh preferences for conformity, then there is no common interest strong enough to create a CP and the problem will instead be one of bargaining or arbitration, the outcome of which depends on threat advantage or considerations of fairness. Neither of these provides a conventionalist justification of authority. If, on the other hand, conflict of interest is less than the interest in conformity, the problem remains one of coordination, but the above arguments against the necessity of authority hold. (Green 1988, 115)

Green argues in the following way: The coordination situation discussed in the conventionalist theories must be a Lewisian CP. The Lewisian CP presupposes an approximate similarity of interests among the agents. But then any property marking out one combination of possible choices as salient will do; it will create the mutual belief required for coordination.

I have already remarked that a conventionalist is not necessarily committed to accept the Lewisian notions of coordination and convention. But even if we do accept it, authority can have its advantages. Suppose that a situation is a pure CP in the sense that the players are motivated merely by the interest in finding a common solution among several alternatives. As Green says, they can solve the problem by "suggesting, advising, persuading or threatening". But which one of them should do that? And what if several agents try to make suggestions, etc. at the same time? Agents are again in a CP. Which one of the several messages trying to mark out one alternative as salient will have a decisive effect on the other agents? One specific advantage of authoritative practices is that they can limit the range of relevant sources of information. So in order to find out the content of the existing rules of traffic, I have to consult law–books, or the decisions of courts, but not the opinion of all the people I meet on the streets. While doing so, I can rely on the belief that the others have consulted the same sources and expect that I have done the same.

Now, it may be objected that the coordination problem remains. For then arises the question who should be the authority. Why should I consult the decisions of courts rather than some other claimant of authority? Why are these decisions, rather than some other decisions, salient?

Ultimately, this question is the same as the question of the rationality of saliency considerations in general, the question raised by

Margaret Gilbert and discussed in the chapter 2. 2. of this book. The decision of a court is salient in a particular case because of the general saliency of official decisions in our society. Official decisions are salient in our society because they are authorized by our legal system, which can be seen as a salient solution to the general coordination problem created by social interaction. Our legal system – any legal system – provides a solution because human beings have developed the practice of relying on salient solutions, and they have developed such a practice because it is by and large more effective than e.g. a practice of never relying on salient solutions.

What is more important, Green is wrong in supposing that all agents need to have the same or approximately similar interests in Lewisian coordination situations, so that there is no room for bargaining or considerations of justice. Actually it is a logically sufficient condition for the existence of a CP that all agents will prefer any equilibrium outcome to every non–equilibrium outcome. There can still be room for an intense conflict of interests concerning different equilibria.

Some defenders of the conventionalist view have made the same mistaken supposition. For example, William S. Boardman (1987) sees, correctly, that for the conventionalist setting it is essential that "everyone would surely prefer to live in a society which observed some... set of rules than in one which did not". From this, it does not follow that "the marginal benefits of one set [of rules] over another pale in comparison to the benefits of having any one set established rather than none at all" (Boardman 1987, 551; the same mistake appears also in McMahon's critique of Raz in McMahon 1987, 326, n.24). It is possible that an existing system of rules is perceived by some of its subjects as better than having no system at all, and, at the same time, as *much* worse than some other conceivable system. Intensive conflicts are not excluded. It should be remembered that any plausible measure of the intensity of a conflict has to be a function of two things: the configuration of preferences and the intensity of preferences. A card game played between friends is formally a zero–sum game. A war between two hostile nations is not necessary a zero–sum game: both may, for example, have an interest in preventing the intervention of a third party. Although the conventionalist theory of authority is consensual in one sense, it is not based of a consensus–view on society (cf. Chapter 9.).

Let us take a simple example of coordination. Suppose that a group of teachers' has to fix the times and places of their lectures for the next term. They clearly have a coordination problem in the Lewisian sense: there are several possible options and a common interest in finding a solution. At the same time, they may have strong and partly conflicting preferences about different solutions. As a method of finding a solution, pure self–coordination is excluded, for the task is probably too complex to be solved by a pure trial–and–error method. The agents could negotiate and try to settle a unanimously accepted solution. But negotiations are often boring and they take time; the teachers may have more important things to do. Instead of negotiating, they may delegate the task to some individual – let's call her Miss A. Miss A has now a delegated power to make a schedule which will bind all the members of the group. In other words, she has authority. When the schedule is completed, it may turn out that some members are more satisfied by their lot than others, but anyhow, the problem is solved and no one has any interest in not following the schedule, as far as they can expect the others to follow it. In spite of the supposed conflicts of interest, the schedule fulfils the Lewisian conditions of a convention. Most importantly, it creates a coordination equilibrium: there is no agent who would prefer some agents not to follow the schedule (here I am supposing that the normal academic condition of scarcity of time and lecture rooms holds).

The authority is not free to decide whatever she wishes. Firstly, she is expected to consult the preferences of others: her plan should at least be minimally effective in the sense of Pareto–optimality. For example, if Friday evenings are especially unpopular, this common preference should be reflected in the schedule. Some members may have special claims which are generally considered as legitimate: for example, the preferences of a teacher who has family responsibilities may take precedence over the preferences of an unmarried teacher. Secondly, the authority is not expected to decide according to her own personal preferences. She is not expected to favour her friends or to accept benefits. In other words, she is expected to be *impartial*. Although these requirements, impartiality and effectiveness, are not necessary for her to be a *de facto* authority, her claim to authority is made under the supposition that she will honestly try to fulfil the requirements.

The formal game corresponding to the above–described situation is a n–person Battle of Sexes game. A two–person ordinal matrix of the game is the following

		Player 2	
		C	D
Player 1	C	1,2	0,0
	D	0,0	2,1

This is a coordination situation in the Lewisian sense. There are two coordination equilibria – (C,C) and (D,D) – but the players are not indifferent as to the choice between them.

The players can either rely on non–authoritative decision making methods or submit their decision to an authority. Now suppose that players 1 and 2 have a mutual belief that (1) their bargaining (and/or threatening) resources are approximately equal, that (2) bargaining (and/or threatening) is not costless, and that (3) there is a possible authority which is expected to be effective and impartial in its decisions. More formally, suppose that 1 and 2 are able to make judgements about the values of the outcomes in cardinal numbers, for example:

		Player 2	
		C	D
Player 1	C	5,10	0,0
	D	0,0	10,5

If P_B is the subjective probability estimate of a player that he is able to persuade, bribe or threaten the other party to accept the solution preferred by him, P_A is the probability that the authority will choose the same solution, and C_i is the value of the expected negotiating costs for the player, it is rational, or at least not irrational, for him to submit the decision to the authority, if

$$P_A\ 10+(1-P_A)\ 5 \geq (P_B\ 10+(1-P_B)\ 5)-C_i.$$

If the players have no probability estimates, the authoritative solution is dominant as far as $0 \leq C_i$. In the real world, agents usually have only qualitative estimates about costs, gains and probabilities. If both authoritative decision–making and negotiating are equally uncertain methods, the fact that the latter method is expected to be more expensive is often a decisive argument in favour of the authoritative solution.

Several comments are needed here. Firstly, what are the negotiation costs? In some cases, they may consist of 'real–valued' compensations or payments paid by the parties favoured by the solution. In cases like our example, the costs are psychological or organizational: losses of time, costs of personal effort, stress and so on. Factors affecting the costs are the existence of a time–limit for negotiations, the complexity of the issues and the size of the negotiating group. The last factor can be illustrated by the following example. Suppose that the costs of negotiating are simply a function of the total amount of messages needed to be exchanged between the negotiating parties. For example, every member of a group has to communicate his preferences to every other member in order to make an agreement. In a group with n members, $n \cdot (n-1)$ messages have to be exchanged. On the other hand, suppose that there is an authority. Every member has to communicate his or her preferences to the authority, and the authority has to communicate the decision to every member. In this case, only $2 \cdot (n-1)$ messages are needed. This, of course, is only a simple thought experiment, but nevertheless it shows how the size of a group is likely to make non–authoritative decision–making more costly.

Secondly, in my approach, the impartiality or fairness of authoritative decisions is connected with probability calculations. It seems that this reflects an important intuition. Impartiality in an authority is essentially the lack of an internal bias in decision–making. A judge is impartial if he or she is not prejudiced against some specific group, a voting system is impartial if it is not designed to favour some political opinions, a competition is impartial if all the participants start at the same line. These judgements are, in a sense, judgements about probabilities. But a trial can be impartial even if the decision is predictable beforehand, an election can be impartial even when opinion measurements show that one party will certainly win, and a competition can be impartial even if one contestant is likely to be the winner.

One way of expressing the probabilistic nature of the impartiality judgements is the following. There are two mutually exclusive sets of properties: the set of relevant properties, R, and the set of irrelevant properties, R'. A procedure is impartial, if, for any possible decision outcome, o_i, $p(R \mid o_i) = p(R,r'_j \mid o_j)$ for any r'_j R'.

Even when an agent expects that a decision made by an authority is likely to be unfavourable to him in a single case, the agent can still expect to be better off in the long run by committing himself to the decisions of an authority, if the authority is not known to be systematically biased against him. Another way of describing the situation is to formulate it as a Rawls–like contractual argument. Rational agents are behind a veil of ignorance: they know only their irrelevant properties R'. They can unanimously accept only an authority which is expected to be impartial in respect of these properties. This argument is more modest and realistic than Rawls' original argument, for the veil of ignorance is 'thinner'. The argument can be applied to real situations. In respect of future cases, we are behind a veil of ignorance. Let us take an example of an authority which explicitly bases its authority on acceptance: The International Court. A country can accept an unfavourable decision of the Court because it believes that it is in its general interests to support the existence of an international arbitration mechanism.

Thirdly, like all contractualist arguments, this argument tries to combine morality with rationality. It tries to show that in certain circumstances agents have a rational reason to accept an authority which is expected to be impartial and effective. These properties are also normal justifications for authority.

Raz (1985) formulates two justificatory theses for authority. Firstly,

> the normal and primary way to establish that a person should be acknowledged to have authority over another person involves showing that the alleged subject is likely better to comply with reasons which apply to him (other than the alleged authoritative directives) if he accepts the directives of the alleged authority as authoritatively binding and tries to follow them, rather than by

> trying to follow the reasons which apply to him directly. (Raz 1985, 18–19)

Secondly,

> all authoritative directives should be based, in the main, on reasons which already independently apply to the subjects of the directives and are relevant to their action in the circumstances covered by the directive. (Raz 1985, 14)

In my presentation, I have tried to show how the first justificatory thesis holds if the subject faces a coordination problem, and if there are extra costs involved in the non–authoritative ways of solving it. I have also tried to show why the second thesis is important. It can be divided into two parts: (1) *All* reasons which are relevant should be taken into account. This is a wider requirement than the requirement of Pareto–optimality used here. However, when all the relevant reasons can be incorporated into subjects' preferences, Pareto–optimality is an explanation of the all reasons –requirement. If it is not satisfied, the parties could gain more by using other methods. Rational subjects would not, for example, accept the authority of a tyrant who usually resolves disputes by (impartially) cutting off the heads of both parties. (2) *Only* relevant reasons are taken into account. This requirement was formulated in probabilistic terms.

The reasoning presented above is just a thought–experiment. Its purpose is to show how authority can be a rational way of solving problems of human interaction under certain (idealized) conditions. If rational agents regularily find themselves in such conditions authoritative ways of solving the problems are likely to emerge in communities of rational agents. They would, contrary to Green's opinion, enjoy an evolutionary advantage.

Green's discussion on the supposed *disadvantages* of authority is illuminating. He claims that commitments to authoritative decisions may introduce pointless rigidities and that ordinary (self–coordinating) conventions are more responsive to environmental changes. Sometimes this is certainly true. But it depends on circumstances; Green's own example illustrates this better than any example I could invent. "A country which drives on the left may begin to drive on the right when its neighbour does and if there is increased traffic between them."(Green 1988, 115) How would it work in the modern world? When the Channel Tunnel is opened, will the drivers in the surroundings of Dover begin to drive on the right? Will this new habit then gradually be diffused to the other parts of Britain? The absurdity of such a spontaneous change of conventions shows how important authorities can be. A spontaneous convention does change only through individual, converging trial–and–error –processes. Those processes can work smoothly only when occasional failures of coordination do not impose too heavy costs on individuals. This is true even when the interest for a change of convention is general.

As Green correctly notices, laws often seek to replace spontaneous conventions with authoritative ones preferred on the grounds of efficacy or justice. This function of law is not incompatible with the thesis that legal authority is conventional. An authoritatively–imposed convention is still a convention, and efficiency and justice may be among the relevant reasons considered by authorities.

Green also claims that conventionalism is unable to explain the normative nature of law:

> Conventionalism presupposes that conformity with convention is always conditional: each should conform if and only if he expects others to do the same. When he does this he has no reason to do anything else. It is part of the concept of authority, however, that it is binding. One who is bound to a standard of behaviour conforms to it unconditially (though perhaps within limits). Common to all forms of practical commitment is their capacity to insulate agents from conditional, calculating allegiances. If the only value of the state's authority were attributable to useful conventions, this would never validly claim allegiance of this form. (Green 1988, 121)

However, most great legal theorists, from Hobbes to Hart, have agreed that our legal obligations *are* indeed conditional: they are binding only if the legal system is efficacious, i.e. generally accepted and obeyed. Even natural law theorists accept this in respect of man–made (instituted) law. This can be generalized to cover other types of practical authority. I may believe that the orders of the Commander are binding, but if the whole army has already escaped from the battlefield in disorder, I have no obligation to remain and try to hold the line alone. Unlike the categorical requirements of critical morality, authoritative decisions have their specific status as reasons for action only in the context of an efficacious normative order. This is the "circle of efficacy" discussed before (ch. 4.3.). The force of conventionalism is lies precisely in its ability to explain this difference between moral or technical rules and authoritative decisions.

Green has remarked (in personal communication) that legal obligations themselves purport to be unconditional rather than conditional; their logical form is "Do X", not "Do X, provided that the legal system is efficacious". This is certainly true. Obviously, law cannot say anything about situations in which it has ceased to be in force. But this does not change the fact that the allegiance we owe to a particular legal system stands and falls with the efficacy of the system.

As the discussion on the "balance of reasons" models and philosophical anarchism shows, the conventionalist approach does not suppose that agents continually calculate their conditional allegiances. What they are considering are different strategic commitments in recurrent interaction situations. The expected values of different strategies often reflect the moral and social values accepted by the agents. For a conventionalist, authoritative institutions are mutually beneficial arrangements, but the benefits they produce can be moral ones. However, Green is correct when claiming that, according to my analysis, authoritative rules or decisions are not exclusionary reasons as such. They gain their exclusionary force only in those cases in which the benefits of coordination are of moral nature.

The scope of the thesis defended in this chapter is a limited one. The justification of political authority by coordination is not meant to by a justification of all the activities of the modern State. It is not a theory of political obligation. On the one hand, the State is not the only possible center of political authority. Even in the modern world, international organizations, churches, trade unions and local communities, for example, possess political authority, and the theory is applicable to them, too. On the other hand, not all activities undertaken by the modern State are related to coordination. Some might be justified by other means, e.g. by direct appeal to morality. Some other of its activities are perhaps not justifiable at all, and should instead be left to other authorities, or to individuals.

Nevertheless, the thesis that practical authority can be rationally justified under certain circumstances can be used as a premiss in a more specific thesis according to which, under certain circumstances we have to recognize the authority of the law. But the rejection of philosophical anarchism presented here is compatible with the anarchism of the more traditional kind. Theoretically it is possible that, in the case of the modern State, the justificatory conditions of authority are not fulfilled. If that were true, we should reject the State and use other authoritative solutions. In the following chapters, I shall try to incorporate the conventionalist theory into the theory which deals the normative aspects of the modern State, the legal theory. But although I am not an anarchist, no full–blown defence of the modern State is offered here. There may be several unexamined paths between the full acceptance of the modern State and outright political anarchism.

CHAPTER 6

THE FOUNDATIONS OF LEGAL SYSTEMS

The most important institution claiming political authority in modern societies is the State and its legal system. Both in legal and in political theory the questions which are traditionally held to be the most fundamental are centered around this claim.

(1) *What are the identification criteria for rules belonging to a legal system?* Can they be traced back either to the decisions of a supreme authority, or to a supreme norm? If the former holds, what is the locus of the authority in a particular system? How it can be identified? Can the supreme authority be identified in legal terms without moving in a circle? If not, how can the decisions of an authority identified in a non–legal way acquire their legal force? If, on the other hand, the ultimate criterion of identification is a supreme norm, how is it itself identified – by legal or by nonlegal criteria? Is the supreme norm itself an element of the system?

(2) *Can the authority of the supreme legal organs be limited by legal rules?* What are the identification criteria of those limiting rules – can they be traced back to the decisions of the same authorities? Can they traced back to non–legal facts? To International Law? How these can limitations be interpreted and enforced?

(3) *If there are supreme norms or norms defining the supreme authority in a system, can these norms be changed by legal means?* Can the authorities themselves change them? How can extra–legal changes, e.g. revolutions or conquests create new legal facts? Do these extra–legal changes change the entire system? When does a legal system cease to exist?

(4) *What are the normative reasons for obedience to the law? What are the limits of such obedience?* Can law itself provide the limits – can there be a legal right to resistance? If so, how are those limits interpreted and enforced? Are there similar limits in respect of the obedience of the supreme legal organs to the supreme norms – may these organs also overstep their legal limits e.g. in emergency cases?

This list, I think, comprises the central problems of classical political and legal theories. Roughly, we can classify the theories provided as answers to these questions into two different groups. Theories which conceive legal–political systems as systems of norms or rules are called here *normativistic* theories. Theories which conceptualize legal–political systems as systems of power and as relations of authority prevailing between individuals and groups are called *decisionistic*. This classification cuts across the traditional divisions in legal theory. Hans Kelsen, the brilliant Austrian legal positivist, was a normativist; so were most of the classical theorists of Natural Law. Carl Schmitt, the German critic of legal positivism, was a decisionist. Most representatives of the sociology of law have been decisionists; but Max Weber, perhaps the greatest among them, was a normativist. In this chapter, I shall try to present a short and selective history of the questions and of the various theories purporting to provide answers to them.

6.1. Hobbes' problem

An adequate account of the ultimate foundations should provide an answer to the following questions: (1) What are the identification criteria for rules belonging to a legal system? (2) When does a legal system exist? (3) What makes the rules belonging to a system binding? The answers to these questions must be found outside the system itself. A legal system can, of course, include norms which provide identification criteria for other norms, or criteria for the existence of the system itself, or prescriptions concerning the normative force of the rules belonging to it. But we cannot answer these questions simply by pointing to these norms, for these norms themselves are parts of a system. In order to answer the questions we must move into the meta–level. The analogy between the question of the ultimate foundations in jurisprudence and the distinction between object–languages and meta–languages in logic has been noted by Ivory Wilks (in Stankiewicz 1969, 197–205) and by Julian Freund (1965, 119–20).

Thomas Hobbes was one of the first theorists who clearly saw the problem of the ultimate foundations, and from his treatment of it there is a direct route to H.L.A. Hart, whose theory is discussed in the next chapter. I will start by presenting a logical reconstruction of Hobbes' influential solution; then, I shall try to show how other theories in jurisprudence can be seen as attempts to solve the dilemmas arising from Hobbes' classical solution. My reconstruction is in the spirit of Hobbes' general approach: it is well known that Hobbes believed that the proper method of political philosophy is "geometrical", i.e. deductive. The argument itself is not Hobbes' invention: the earliest version I am acquainted with appears in Dante's *De monarchia*.

Hobbes defines all laws as commands:

> ...Law in general, is not Counsell, but command; nor a Command of any man to any man; but only of him, whose command is addressed to one formerly obliged to obey him. (Hobbes, 1973 ch. xxvi, p. 40)

More specifically, civil law is

> to every Subject, those Rules, which the Common–wealth hath commanded him, by word or writing, or other sufficient sign of the Will, to make use of, for the distinction of Right, and Wrong, that is to say what is contrary, and what is not contrary, to the Rule. (Hobbes 1973, ch. xxvi, 140)

Therefore we can define the situation as follows:

(1) N is a valid norm for x –> there is some y whom x ought to obey and y has commanded N.

Hobbes' analysis is based on the pragmatics of commanding. Commands are addressed by a superior to a subject; therefore the following principles are natural:

(2) x ought to obey y –> it is not true that y ought to obey x.

(3) No one ought to obey himself.

(4) x ought to obey y and y ought to obey z –> x ought to obey z.

These principles express the *asymmetry*, *irreflexivity* and *transitivity* conditions for authority relations. The first two conditions are explicitly stated in *De Cive*:

> Neither can the city be obliged to her citizen, because, if he will, he can free her from her obligation; and he will, as oft as she wills... the city therefore is free when she pleaseth, that is she is now actually free. (Hobbes 1972, ch. vi, 80)

> Nor can he be obliged to himself, for the same part being both the obliged and the obliger, and the obliger having the power to release the obliged, it were merely in vain for a man to be obliged for himself, because he can release himself at his own plesure; and he who can do this, is actually free. (Hobbes 1972, ch. vi, 79)

In the Leviathan (p. 140) Hobbes explicitly deduces the irreflexivity and asymmetry conditions from the command notion of law. Then he applies the latter principle to the question of the role of Parliament:

> That the Common Law, hath no Controuler but the Parlament; which is true onely where a Parlament has the sovereign power, and cannot be assembled nor dissolved, but by their own discretion. For if there be a right in any else to dissolve them there is a right also to controule them, and consequently to controule their controulings. (Hobbes 1973, xxvi, 142)

Other authorities ought to be obeyed because they are authorized by a sovereign; the authority of the sovereign, on the contrary, is not based on positive norms (commands) but on the social contract and natural law. Therefore, our obligation to obey a sovereign is prior to any specific legal obligations:

> For since our obligation to civil obedience, by virtue whereof the civil laws are valid, is before all civil law, and the sin of treason is naturally nothing else but the breach of that obligation, it follows, that by the sin of treason, that law is broken which precedes the civil law, to wit, the natural, which forbids us to violate the covenants and betrothed faith. But if some sovereign prince should set forth a law on this manner, thou shalt not rebel, he would just effect nothing. For except subjects were before obliged to obedience, that is to say, not to rebel, all law is of no force. Now the obligation which obligeth to what we were before obliged to, is superfluous. (Hobbes 1972, xiv, 170)

Then, we can define the concept of sovereignty as follows:

(S) y is the sovereign for x –> x ought to obey y, and there is no valid norm that x ought to obey y.

If there are any valid norms, there must also be a sovereign, satisfying the definition. Suppose that for every y who must be obeyed by some x there were to be a valid authorizing norm with that effect. Because of (1), even an authorizing norm must be a command issued by some authority z. If this z were identical with y, the norm would be superfluous, as Hobbes says. If z were somebody else, the question about the source of authority would reappear. And because infinite regress is obviously excluded, there must be an ultimate authority which satisfies the definition (S).

According to Hobbes, sovereign power is *illimitable*. This follows from the postulate (1) that all valid norms are commands, and from the supposition that power can be limited only by norms:

(L) Some possible commands of y are not valid norms for x -> there is a valid norm N for y that some of his possible commands are not valid norms for x.

If some of the possible commands of y are not valid norms, we say that y's authority is limited. Now let us make the counter–assumption: For every y, the authority of y is limited. By (L), the limitation is always based on some valid norm N, which, by (1), is a command of some z of whom y ought to obey. Because of irreflexivity, z cannot be identical with y, and because of asymmetry, it is not so that z, in turn, must obey y; there cannot be any "loops" in the chain of commands. But according to our counter–assumption there must then be a further authority w who sets limits for z, etc. The counter–assumption leads into infinite regress, and therefore:

(5) There exists an authority y such that all its possible commands are valid norms (or, its power is illimited).

Clearly such a y is a sovereign in the sense expressed by (S). All its commands are binding; thus all other authorities in the system base their power on its commands, and therefore there cannot be a separate authority authorizing it. Hobbes himself formulates the argument in this way:

> For if his power were limited, that limitation must necessarily proceed from some greater power. For he that prescribes limits, must have greater power than he who is confined by them. Now that confining power is either without limit,

all is again restrained by some other greater than itself, and so we shall at length arrive to a power which hath no other limit, but which is *terminus ultimus* of the forces of all citizens together.(Hobbes 1972, vi, 84)

Hobbes' conclusion can also be supported by his theory of interpretation. It is an essential part of his general doctrine that the monopoly to interpret the Scriptures is preserved in the hands of the sovereign power. This is important, because the power to interpret a norm is actually a power to command the norm subjects. Interestingly, the infinite regress argument reappears here: every interpretation creates new interpretations "without any end" (Hobbes 1983, 233–34); hence, we are forced to accept the authority of some "Canonicall Interpreter" in order to avoid confusion. His doctrine of legal interpretation is similar:

And therefore the Interpretation of all Lawes dependenth on the Authority Soveraign; and the Interpreters can be none but those, which the Soveraign (to whom only the Subject oweth obedience) shall appoint. For else, by the craft of an Interpreter, the Law may be made to beare a sense, contrary to that of the Soveraign; by which means the Interpreter becomes a Legislator. (Hobbes 1973, xxvi, 146)

This doctrine can be formulated as a principle:

(6) x ought to obey norm N and y has the power to interpret N -> x ought to obey y.

Now if there are norms constraining the power of a sovereign, and if for every norm there must be someone with the power to interpret it, we are back in the regress. From (6) and from the irreflexivity condition it follows that the sovereign itself cannot have the power to interpret these norms; from (6) and from the asymmetry condition it follows that the interpreter cannot be any of subjects. Thus there cannot be such norms.

But those Lawes which the Soveraign himselfe, that is, which the Common–wealth maketh, he is not subject. For to be subject to Lawes, is to be subject to the Common–wealth, that is to the Sovereign Representative, that is to himselfe; which is not subjection, but freedome from Lawes. Which errour, because it setteth the Lawes above the Soveraign, setteth also a Judge above him, and a power to punish him; which is to make a new Soveraign; and again

> for the same reason a third, to punish the second; and so continually without end, to the Confusion, and Dissolution of the Common–wealth. (Hobbes 1973, ch. xxix, 173)

For these reasons there cannot be constitutional norms constraining the power of a sovereign. Neither can there be any International Law in the proper sense.

A legal system is, for Hobbes, a set of persons united by relations of authority; in modern terms it is a partly ordered set with a maximal element, a sovereign. However, I have not proved yet that there must be a single maximal element. This would mean that sovereignty is *indivisible*. In order to prove it, we need an additional postulate.

For Hobbes it is essential that "ought" implies "can". This follows directly from his attempt to merge the requirements of the law of nature with individual rationality. In the Leviathan, ch. xxvii, Hobbes discusses contradictory laws and concludes that a contradiction in law is always an excuse for a transgression. Therefore, it is clear that the following condition holds:

(7) The set of norms valid for x is consistent.

Suppose that sovereignty is divided so that both y and z are the sovereign of x. Then either y and z can give mutually inconsistent commands to x or they cannot. If they can, condition (7) is not satisfied. Therefore their power to give commands must be limited. But, by (L), the limitation is possible only through valid norms. If these norms are issued by one or the other of the two sovereigns, then either this sovereign is limiting its own power, which is impossible, or it is limiting the power of the other sovereign, in which case that other cannot be a sovereign. On the other hand, if the limiting norms were issued by some third party, neither y nor z could be a sovereign. Hence, sovereignty is indivisible.

Hobbes believed that the traditional English doctrine of the mixed constitution, accepted by both the Parliament and Charles II in their public declarations, was one cause of the Civil War. Indeed, any attempt to divide sovereignty would sooner or later push the commonwealth back to the state of nature:

> For that were to erect two Soveraigns; and every man to have his person represented by two Actors, that by opposing one another, must needs divide that Power, which (if men will live in Peace) is indivisible; and thereby reduce the Multitude into the condition of Warre, contrary to the end for which all Soveraignty is instituted. (Hobbes 1973, 97, [xix]; cf. 95, [xviii]; 173, [xxvi]; Hobbes 1983, 149–50, [xii.v])

The fact is that there was no clear theory of how disputes between ruling authorities should be solved in a divided system. Grotius, for example, admits that sovereignty can be divided (1853 p. 46, [I.III.xvii]). But because this division can only be based on an express law, and because the possibility of enforcement of rules was for Grotius as important as it was for Hobbes, the only possibility was that the parties should enforce their rights themselves:

> if the king have a part only of the Sovereignty, another part being in the Senate or the people, and if the king invade the part which is not his, he may justly be opposed by force, because in that part he has no authority. (...) And since each party has its portion of the Sovereignty, it must also have the right of defending that part. When this is the case, the king may lose his portion of the Sovereignty by the right of war. (Grotius 1853, 58, [I.IV.xii])

This is in accordance with Grotius' theory that the laws of nature were laws in the proper sense, and enforceable by sanctions. External war between sovereigns was a legal measure. Sanctions were not necessarily applied by superiors against subjects. Thus, two political bodies sharing the sovereignty inside a state could legitimately compel each other. It is no wonder that Hobbes was not satisfied with this theory (called by Julian Franklin the "winner takes all –doctrine"). We may admit that constitutional disputes are sometimes actually solved only by violent means. But we are not happy with a constitution which *prescribes* a civil war as a solution to certain disputes.

In the *Leviathan*, the consistency argument is directed against the temporal jurisdiction of the churches:

> For seeing the *Ghostly* power challengeth the Right to declare what is sinne it challengeth by consequence to declare what is law... and again, the *Civil* Power challenging to declare what is law, every subject must obey two Masters, who both will have their Commands be observed as Law, what is impossible. Or if it be but one Kingdome, either the *Civill* which is the Power of the Common–wealth, must subordinate to the *Ghostly,* and then there is no

> sovereignty but the *Ghostly*, or the *Ghostly* must be subordinate to the *Temporall*, and the there is no Supremacy but the *Temporall*. (Hobbes 1973, ch xxix, 175)

Contrary to what is sometimes asserted, the indivisibility of sovereignty is a necessary consequence of the Hobbesian theory of law.

There is no fault in Hobbes' logic. His only mistake was to believe that it was empirically necessary that a system in which there was no single superior would sooner or later dissolve itself. As Leibniz said, commenting on Hobbes' doctrine of indivisiblity: "Hobbes' fallacy lies in this, that he thinks things which can entail inconvenience should not be borne at all". According to Leibniz, a division of supreme power may rise dissensions and even wars, if everyone holds stubbornly to his opinion. "But experience has shown that men usually hold to some middle road, so as not to commit everything to hazard by their obstinacy." (Leibniz 1988, 119) The fact that a legal–political system could create contradictions does not imply that it is bound to create them. Most notably, many political structures inherited from the Medieval world did not obey the Hobbesian logic. Thus, the German Empire was recognized as an anomaly by those (e.g. by Pufendorf) who adopted their notion of sovereignty from Hobbes.

As we have noticed, it is a theorem of the theory that if there are valid norms, a legal sovereign must exist. Therefore there is necessarily *a rule of succession* in every enduring legal system, i.e. a rule of the following form:

(C) If x ceases to be the sovereign, y becomes the sovereign.

If there were no rule of succession, it would be impossible to identify the successor of a sovereign, and after the death of x, the system would disappear. The rule of succession is a valid norm and must be based on the existing sovereign's express or tacit command:

> For the death of him that hath the Soveraign power in propriety, leaves the Multitude without any Soveraign at all; that is, without any Representative in whom they should be united, and be capable of doing any action at all: And therefore they are incapable of Election of any new Monarch, every man having equall right to submit himselfe to such as he thinks best able to protect him... Therefore, it is manifest, that by the Institution of Monarchy, the disposing of

> the Successor, is alwaies left to the Judgement and Will of the present Possessor. (Hobbes 1973, ch. xix, 102)

Indivisibility, illimitability and continuity are the essential properties of a Hobbesian sovereign. The conceptual role of a legal sovereign is very similar to that of the omnipotent God in theology. As it has on occasion been pointed out, the concept of omnipotence is ambiguous in both cases. (See e.g. Hart 1961, 144–50) Can a necessarily omnipotent being voluntarily give away some part of its omnipotence? Both affirmative and negative answers seem to be inconsistent with the idea of *necessary* omnipotence.In imperative theories of law, this problem (which is analogous to the Stone Paradox in theology) can be formulated as follows. Suppose that a Hobbesian sovereign gives an order to his subjects:

(O) x ought not to obey any commands of the sovereign concerning the matter M.

Has the sovereign succeeded in limiting his own power over his subjects? If (O) establishes a valid norm for x, then the commands of the sovereign concerning the matter M are not valid norms for x. On the other hand, if (O) does not establish a valid norm, then there is at least one command of the sovereign which is not valid. Both conclusions seem to be against the theorem that the sovereign is necessarily omnipotent.

Hobbes' solution to this problem is that in spite of its form (O) does not constitute a real command. By expressing (O) , the sovereign has not performed a meaningful speech act:

> If the monarch promise aught to any one, or many subjects together, by consequence whereof the exercise of his power may suffer prejudice, that promise or compact ...is null. ...he who sufficiently signifies his will of retaining the end, doth also sufficiently declare that he quits not his right to the means necessary to that end. Now he who hath promised to part with somewhat necessary to the supreme power itself, gives sufficient tokens, that he no otherwise promised it than sofar forth as the power might be retained without it. Whensoever therefore it shall appear that what is promised cannot be performed without prejudice to that power, the promise must be valued as not made, that is, of no effect. (Hobbes 1972, ch. vii, 98)

Hobbes seems to have thought that when a sovereign tries to give a command like (O), he actually intends to use his power concerning the matter M, and the validity of the command is dependent on that power. The command produces a paradox of self-referentiality: it is valid only if it is not valid. A sovereign can give his power away only by resigning. This interpretation of illimitability is fatal for all attempts to base International Law on valid norms. The sovereign is equally unable to make contracts with other sovereigns, for that would limit his powers, too. Agreements between sovereigns cannot be but mutual declarations of intentions, without any normative impact.

6.2. Hobbes' logic and Natural Law theories

The Hobbesian conception of sovereignty became the starting- point of almost all theoretical discussion on law and politics in the seventeenth and eighteenth century. It is interesting how authors writing from completely opposite viewpoints accepted the same basic set of presuppositions. There had to be an ultimate, unlimited authority inside every politico-legal system; it had to be there for the logical reasons formulated by Hobbes. And even those who rejected his presuppositions had to struggle with them. Thus, those who tried to show that sovereignty could be limited in a legal way had to counter the problems associated with reflexivity; those who defended divided sovereignty had to face the problem of inconsistency, and for the defenders of popular sovereignty Hobbes' critique of symmetry constituted an important obstacle. For the constitutionalism of the eighteenth century the problem was to find a system in which every authority were subject to some other authority – the problem of checks and balances. Thus, the most important disputes on the foundations of law during the era of the Englightenment can be seen as a continual wrestling with a theory which is basically a Hobbesian one.

The supposed symmetry of authority –relations is a real problem. Although relations of authority can well be symmetrical in the sense that x and y have authority over each other in some issues, this symmetry is still restricted in the sense that they cannot have complete authority over each others' *exercise of that authority*. If the people, for example, have an effective right to throw out their otherwise omnipotent rulers, the rulers cannot have a right to control the people's exercise of that right. The German sociologist Niklas Luhmann has formulated the problem in quite similar terms to those used here by me. In his rather difficult article (Luhmann 1980), Luhmann describes the development of modern political doctrines as a progress from an a–symmetrical two–place relation (sovereign -> subject) to a symmetrical three–place relation (people -> politics -> administration -> people). The necessity of the third mediating position comes from the fact that a fully symmetrical authority system would be indeterminate (Luhmann 1980, 70–1). This implies that the relations between authorities must be intransitive: from the fact that the electorate exercises control over politicians, and the politicians, in their turn, over the administration, it does not follow that the people can control the administration. (A related point on nontransitive authority patterns is made by Karl W. Deutsch (1963), 54–5.)

While almost all theorists rejected Hobbes' proto–positivist legal theory and adopted some version of Natural Law, they invariably presupposed his basic postulates. Thus, the conclusion that there has to be a single, unlimited authority in every legal–political system was seen as a conceptual necessity. Henry Parker, one of the ablest English spokesmen of the parliamentary cause during the crises in the 1640's, declared that

> That there is an Arbitrary power in every State somewhere, tis true, 'tis necessary, and no inconvenience follows upon it; every man has an absolute power over himself; but because no man can hate himself, this power is not dangerous, nor need to be restrayned: So every State has an Arbitrary power over it self, and there is no danger for the same reason. (p. 200, [34])

This could be compared with the view expressed by Sir Robert Filmer, the most extreme representative of royal absolutism:

> We do but flatter ourselves, if we hope ever to be governed without an arbitrary power. No: we mistake; the question is not, whether there shall be an arbitrary power; but the only point is, who shall have that arbitrary power, whether one man or many? There never was, nor can ever be any people governed without a power of making laws, and every power of making laws must be arbitrary: for to make a law according to a law, is *contradictio in adjecto*. (Filmer 1949, p. 277)

Filmer relies on the irreflexivity postulate. Parker, while nominally accepting the traditional English doctrine of the mixed constitution, utilizes the consistency requirement to show that the supreme authority cannot be divided. Then, he uses the regress argument in order to prove the necessity of arbitrary power:

> To what kinde of tryall the judgement of a Parliament shall be submitted: If we call another Parliament to judge of this, so we may appeal in *infinitum*; and why another should clearer than this, we cannot imagine: If we could constitute a higher Court for this appeal, so we might do in *infinitum* also, but we know no higher can be imagined: and if we appeal to a lower, that were to invert the course of nature: and to confound all Parliaments for ever; if we call all the Kingdom to judge of this, we do the same thing as to proclaim Civill Warre, and to blow the Trumpet of generall confusion: And if we allow the King to be the sole supream competent to Judge in this case, we resigne all into his hands, we give lifes, liberties, Laws, Parliaments, all to be held at meer discretion? For there is in the interpretation of Law upon the last appeal, the same supremacy of power requisite, as it is in making it; And therefore grant the King supream interpreter, and 'tis all one, as if we granted him to be supream maker of Law; and grant him this, and we grant him to be above all limits, all conditions, all humane bonds whatsoever. (Parker 1965, 210, [44]).

This argument presupposes all the postulates of the Hobbesian theory, and the conclusion is the same. The dispute between Parliament and King could be reduced to the question: who holds supremacy inside the Constitution. "Either the one or the other must be predominant, or else by a mutuall opposition all must perish"(p. 188, [22]). Here the rejection of inconsistency leads into an inescapable conclusion: there must be somewhere a final judge in constitutional issues, a judge who has the ultimate power to interpret the law and who necessarily holds unlimited power:

> In matters of Law and State both, where ambiguity is, some determination must be supream, and therein, either the Kings power and trust must be guided by the discretion of the Parliament; or else the Parliament, and all other Courts must be overruled by the Kings meer discretion.(Parker 1965, 202 [36])

Parker, his assertions to the contrary notwithstanding, actually was forced to reject the theory of divided sovereignty and to put Parliament at the place which was reserved for King in absolutist theories.

The victorious new ideology of the eighteenth century, the doctrine of the sovereignty of the people, adapted the predominant Hobbesian conception of the sovereignty. The people as *pouvoir constituant* would take the place of King or Parliament as the ultimate source of all positive law. This new power–holder was supposed to possess all the authority characteristic of a Hobbesian sovereign. The problem, then, would arise from the postulate of asymmetry. How could the people be simultaneously the supreme lawgiver who might give commands for the lesser authorities, and the subject of authoritative commands of those authorities? This is the problem Rousseau sets for himself: "The problem is to find a form of association... in which each, while uniting himself with all, may still obey himself alone..."

In *Du Contrat Social* Rousseau uses both the irreflexivity postulate and the asymmetry postulate. His use of them shows how the Hobbesian basic logic of sovereignty is preserved even when the people takes the place reserved for the absolute monarch:

> It is, consequently against the nature of the body politic for the Sovereign to impose on itself a law which it cannot infringe. Being able to regard itself only in one capacity, it is in the position of an individual who makes the contract with himself; and this makes clear that there neither is nor can be any kind of fundamental law binding on the body of the people...
> (Rousseau 1975, 176; I.vii)

> The supreme authority can no more be modified than it can be alienated; to limit it is to destroy it. It is absurd and contradictory for the Sovereign to set a superior over itself; to bind itself to obey a master would be a return to absolute liberty. (ibid. 243; III.xvi)

Rousseau's solution to the logical problem was to distinguish between two types of legal commands: general laws made exclusively by the sovereign and particular decisions made by other authorities. Every citizen had two corresponding legal capacities: as a member of the legislating Sovereign he could participate in the act of giving general commands, as a private citizen he had to obey those commands as applied by authorities authorized by the sovereign. Rousseau stressed that the people could not make particular decisions; this was as essential for his construction as the conviction that the people should make all legislative decisions. This can be seen as an attempt to relax the *transitivity* postulate. For conceptual reasons, the sovereign could only give commands of type A (general laws), while other authorities could only give commands of type B (particular decisions based on the commands of the sovereign). Thus, the sovereign governed only through other authorities. These distinctions were not contingent, i.e. not themselves dependent on positive law. If they were not respected, the sovereign's commands would no longer be valid, binding reasons for action:

> If the sovereign wishes to govern, of if the prince wishes to give laws, or if the subjects refuse to obey, disorder takes the place of regularity and the State is dissolved and falls into despotism or anarchy. (p. 306)

The democratic versions of the sovereignty doctrine were dependent on the idea of the Natural Law in a double sense. For Hobbes and Bodin, Natural Law was also the basis of the authority of the sovereign. But because they defended the status quo, they did not need to rely on normative concepts in the *identification* of the sovereign and its will. The identification criteria were provided by empirical facts: the sovereign was he or those who were actually in charge – the legitimate king, a successful usurper, an aristocratic or democratic assembly. The radical proponents of popular sovereignty, however, had to rely on the Natural Law in this issue, too. The question, sharply posed by Hobbes himself, was: If the people was the sovereign, how is it constituted and how do we recognize its will? The people is a collective entity. A will can ascribed to a collective only by referring to some normative procedure of decision–making. Without some pre–existing rules "the people" was just a collection of separate individuals. Both Burke and Hegel utilized this kind of argument against the French revolutionaries. In order to legislate, the people had to make decisions according to some established norms. But these norms could themselves be but positive norms. The majority principle, for example, was, according to Burke, no more sanctioned by the Natural Law than other normative principles. The only possible answer to this argument was that it was not only the existence of an ultimate authority but also its locus and the mode of its exercise that could be derived from non–positive norms.

In his *Rechtslehre*, Kant relies on a normativistic version of the theory. For Kant, the ultimate foundation of a legal system is the rational law of nature. This prescribes that the people are the source of all positive law and simultaneously necessitates the separation of the legislative, executive and judicial functions. The basic division of authority in the State is derivable from the law of nature. In effect, Kant's theory is an attempt to put a norm in place of the sovereign authority. At least in this respect, Kelsen could rightfully call his theory a "Kantian" one. Sometimes it is claimed that Kelsen's Kantianism is purely methodological, that it takes its inspiration from Kant's epistemological writings but not from his *Rechtslehre*, for Kant's legal theory was a version of Natural Law. If, however, we recognize that both Kant and Kelsen tried to provide a normativistic solution to the problem of the ultimate foundations of law, this claim is not strictly correct. In their theories the Hobbesian postulates take on a new interpretation. Instead of speaking about the logic of command–obedience relationships, they speak about the logical properties of norms belonging to legal systems.

Kant's version of the Hobbesian regress appears, in its most explicit form, in his essay on 'Theory and Practice':

> But all who are subject to laws are the subjects of a state, and are thus subject to the right of coercion along with all other members of the commonwealth; the only exception is a single person (in either the physical or the moral sense of the word), the head of the state, through whom alone the rightful coercion of all others can be exercised. For if he too could be coerced, he would not be the head of the state, and the hierarchy of subordination would ascend infinitely. But if there were two persons exempt from coercion, neither would be subject to coercive laws, and neither could do the other anything contrary to right, which is impossible. (Kant 1970, 75)

Kant formulates the problem in terms of the consistency of a public constitution. For him, the sovereignty of the people could not mean that the people possessed a right to resist legally constituted authorities – that would either create a symmetric authority relation or lead to regress. This argument is repeated in 'Theory and Practice', in *Perpetual Peace*, and in the *Rechtslehre*. In *Perpetual Peace*, the formulation is the following:

> It is easily seen that if one were to make it a condition of founding a political constitution that force might in certain eventualities be used against the head of the state, the people would have to claim rightful authority over its ruler. But if this were so, the ruler would not be the head of the state, or if both parties were given the authority as a prior condition of establishing the state, the existence of the state itself, which it was the people's intention to establish, would become impossible. (Kant 1970, 126–7)

Kant, the great advocate of the *Rechtsstaat* and republicanism, ultimately accepted a theory which had very Hobbesian conclusions: there is no right to resistance, the head of the State is above positive law, the validity of the constitution should not even be questioned publicly; nevertheless, after a successful revolution, the new rulers necessarily acquire the right to be obeyed. We can see how convincing Hobbes' logic of sovereignty was. Those who opposed his political theory from different viewpoints were, nevertheless, forced to accept his view on the foundations of legal systems.

6.3. The positivistic theories

In his own theory, John Austin, the great English positivist, adopts the main points of Hobbes' theory of law. For Austin, as for Hobbes, laws are commands addressed by a political superior to a subject. At the top of the legal system there is a supreme authority, the sovereign, who is habitually obeyed by the rest of the population of a political society, but who himself does not obey anyone. The sovereign's power is illimitable. Hobbes' infinite regress –argument reappears in Austin's works:

> The power of the superior immediately imposing the restraints [for a sovereign, EL], or the power or some other sovereign superior to that superior, would still be absolutely free from the fetters of positive law. For unless the imagined restraints were ultimately imposed by a sovereign not in state of subjection to a higher sovereign, a series of sovereigns ascending from infinity would govern the imagined community. Which is impossible and absurd. (Austin 1954, 254)

This proof is valid only if Hobbes' conditions of irreflexivity and asymmetry are accepted. Otherwise authority x would be able to limit the power of another authority y and *vice versa*, or x could limit its own power.

The conditions (2)–(4), however, seem to be incompatible with Austin's attempt to reduce legal–authority relations to facts about habitual obedience. As Austin himself recognizes, empirically observable habits of obedience are not necessarily asymmetric (Austin 1954, 25). For example, a legislature may habitually obey the prescriptions of a supreme court in certain matters, while the court may accept the superiority of the court in other matters. It is possible that a system in which the supreme authority is divided between several agencies controlling each other may generate inconsistencies in some situations. If such an inconsistency emerges, so that the decisions of the legislature and the court conflict, it may be only the contingencies of the political situation which determine who has the last say. It is not necessary for the solution to be somehow predictable from the present habits of obedience existing between the legal organs.

There are other problems in the theory. For Austin, all constitutional as well as international law is merely "positive morality". This is problematic, because the source of this morality is often the same as the source of laws, namely the supreme legal authorities. And even if constitutional norms are only a part of morality, it must be admitted that it often effectively constrains the activities of legal authorities. Contrary to Austin and Hobbes, sovereigns seem to be able to limit their own power. Here, it is the irreflexivity condition which creates problems.(cf. Morawetz 1980, 20–21)

Austin tried to accommodate the idea of popular sovereignty by suggesting that in democracies, the electorate is the sovereign. But Austin agrees with Hobbes that no one can command himself. (Austin 1954, 284). Austin's solution is that the sovereign body can impose obligations on its individual members. The members of a sovereign body can collectively and in their official capacities command all the members distributively and in their personal capacities.(This looks quite like Rousseau's solution to the same problem). But there is still a problem, noticed (among many others) by David Lyons (1984, 50): "we cannot identify the members of the electorate without having recourse to those legal rules that establish voting privileges". One of the problems appearing in Austin's theory is the difficulty of identifying the legal authority which is supposed to be the source of all laws without referring back to these laws. Again, this problem is by no means unique to Austin. A similar problem arises from the Realist doctrine that all law is created by courts.

The form of legal positivism adopted in Germany during the nineteenth century answered the identification problem in the following way: Law is the will of the State, and the State is identifiable as a social fact, without recourse to legal norms. (The latter view was shared by Austin, whose starting point was the existence of "independent political societies".) The problem raised by constitutional and international law was solved by supposing that the State was capable of self-limitation (Selbstverpflictung) (see Jellinek 1921, 367–79). This is the other possible answer to the omnipotence dilemma created by commands like (O).

In the beginnings of the twentieth century, the Dutch legal theorist Hans Krabbe gave a theoretical formulation for to an alternative idea of central import in for more liberal versions of constitutionalist legal theory. According to Krabbe, the traditional notion of sovereignty was adequate in the early modern State in which the ruler – the King or a representative assembly – was actually above the law, giving commands but not obeying any. But in a constitutional state, there was no such entity. Thus, the existence of a Hobbesian sovereign was a contingent property of a system. The idea of the German positivists that the State could replace the sovereign was nonsense. For the State itself was a legal entity, not a social fact. "A people is a state because of legal relations existing within it" (Krabbe 1930, 209). Therefore, the State could not be the fundamental source of laws. Rather, the law itself had taken the place of the sovereign.

In a way, what Kelsen tried to do was to restore the logical structure originally created by Hobbes. There are hardly any references to Hobbes in Kelsen's main works. Nevertheless, the basic logic of their theories is similar, and they both shared the 'geometrical' conception of method (Kelsen 1911, 92–5. The comparison between Kelsen and Hobbes is made by Gentile in Moulakis 1986, 44–59. Gentile, however, emphasizes other aspects in their works than those stressed here).

Kelsen rejects the idea of the State's self-limitation (Kelsen 1970, 312–13). He also rejects Austin's and the German Positivist's attempt to find a non-normative foundation for law. For Kelsen, sovereignty and the State were normative concepts and the latter is, for juristic purposes, defined in terms of the former. Here he explicitly follows Krabbe. But for Kelsen, the primacy of the normative was a conceptual, not an empirical matter. It did not hold only in the constitutional State. Legal norms simply could not emerge from non-normative facts, nor could they be founded on pre-existing morality. His way of formulating the question about the ultimate foundations of legal systems is epistemological: How is it possible to conceive something as a normative order?

Kelsen's theory is normative and "pure" in two senses. It is supposed to be purified from all factual considerations. It is also normative in the sense that relations within the legal system are relations between norms, not between persons in different positions. At the same time, Kelsen shares the positivistic intentions of Austin: the ultimate foundations of legal systems cannot be found in the pre-existing norms of Natural Law or critical morality.

For Kelsen, the predicates "higher" and "lower" or "superior" and "inferior" refer to the properties of norms. Lower norms are derivable from the higher norms in the sense that higher norms *authorize* the creation of lower norms. The following passage is typical of Kelsen:

> The reason for the validity of a norm is always a norm, not a fact. The quest for the reason of validity of a norm leads back, not to reality, but to another norm from which the first norm is derivable... (Kelsen 1949, 111)

Thus we can formulate the following:

(1') N is a valid positive norm -> there is a norm N' such that it authorizes the creation of N, and N is created according to N'.

It is this relation which compels a legal system into a hierarchical structure:

> To the question why a certain act of coercion – e.g. the fact that one individual deprives another individual of his freedom by putting him in jail – is a legal act, the answer is: because it has been prescribed by an individual norm, a judicial decision. To the question why this individual norm is valid as part of a definite legal order, the answer is: because it has been created in conformity with a criminal statute. This statute, finally, receives its validity from the constitution, since it has been established by the competent organ in the way the constitution prescribes. (Kelsen 1949, 115)

The quoted passage reveals the two ways a lower norm can be derived from a higher one. Either the content of the lower norm can be inferred from the content of the higher one (material authorization) or then the higher norm confers power on some legally defined organ to create the lower norm (formal authorization).

Ultimately norms belong to one and the same legal system because their validity can be traced back to the first constitution which established the legal order in question (Kelsen 1949, 115). In order to create this kind of unified hierarchy between various norms, Kelsen must accept the normative counterparts of the Hobbesian conditions (2)–(4):

(2') Norm N authorizes norm N' -> it is not true that N' authorizes N.

(3') No norm authorizes itself.

(4') N' authorizes N and N" authorizes N' -> N" authorizes N.

These principles are not sufficient to guarantee the *unity* of legal systems supposed by Kelsen. They do not imply that all the chains of authorization have a common starting point: the fact that every lower norm is derivable from some higher norm does not imply that there is a higher norm from which all lower norms are derivable. This is a point made by Munzer (1972, 48; cf. a similar point against sovereignty made by Lucas 1966, 30). However, the unity requirement follows from the idea of Kelsen that a legal system is necessarily a consistent system of norms. Kelsen supposes that a legal system itself must provide means to solve conflicts between alleged norms: when two legal requirements seem to be mutually inconsistent, there must either be a third norm saying which of the two norms is valid, or an organ authorized to solve the dispute. This organ must base its competence on some norm belonging to the same system. Thus Kelsen has a principle of indivisibility of normative systems comparable to Hobbes' principle of indivisibility of sovereignty. In order to avoid contradictions, only one normative system can be considered as the binding one:

> If one assumes that two systems of norms are considered as valid from the same point of view, one must also assume a normative relation between them; one must assume the existence of a norm or order that regulates their mutual relations. Otherwise insoluble contradictions between the norms of each system are unavoidable and the logical principle that excludes contradictions holds for the cognition of norms as much as for the cognition of natural reality. (Kelsen 1949, 115)

The principle of consistency leads into the principle of unity:

(5') N and N' are valid positive norms -> there is a norm N" such that it authorizes both N and N".

The principles (1')–(5') and the exclusion of infinite regress imply the conclusion that for every system of valid positive norms there is a unique maximal element which is not authorized by any positive norm but which itself authorizes all other norms of the system. This is Kelsen's famous Grundnorm or the basic norm. The proof is exactly the same as Hobbes' and Austin's proof of the existence of a sovereign:

> The norm which represents the reason for validity of another norm is called, as we have said, the 'higher' norm . But the search for the reason of a norm's validity cannot go on indefinitely like the search for the cause of an effect. It must end with a norm which, as the last and the highest, is presupposed. It must be *presupposed*, because it cannot be 'posited', that is to say: created, by an authority whose competence would have to rest on a still higher norm. This final norm's validity cannot be derived from a higher norm, the reason of its validity cannot have been questioned. Such a presupposed higher norm is referred to in this book as a basic norm. (Kelsen 1970, 195)

We notice the parallelism between the arguments of Hobbes and Kelsen. And similar *regressus ad infinitum* arguments appear in other philosophical contexts. Every chain of justification must ultimately either go on *ad infinitum*, or refer back to itself, or stop at some point. A common solution in philosophy is to stop the regress on a justificatory ground which is supposed to be qualitatively different from the earlier steps of the argument (The Immovable Mover, statements which are beyond doubt, and so on). Kelsen's basic norm has a comparable function.

Several of the criticisms directed against Kelsen's theory are attacks against postulates (1')–(5'). For example, Castberg, Lloyd and Raz have considered the possibility that there might be several basic norms in a system: this implies a denial of (5'). Eckhoff and Sundby (1975, 140) "hold it to be quite a common phenomenon in legal reasoning that norm A serves as part of the reasons behind norm B, while norm B in its turn helps to back up A" – i.e. they deny postulate (2'). Hart has argued that norms can refer to themselves, which can be a reason for denying (3').

As compared with the Hobbesian notion of the sovereign, the basic norm has certain advantages. It avoids the problem of self–limitation, and makes it possible to base the highest authority on law, not only on the pre–legal fact of sovereignty. There are, however, several problems in Kelsen's solution. One problem is the ontological status of basic norms. In chapter 7., I shall consider Hart's attempt to improve Kelsen's construction. I try to show how the notion of conventional fact might be used to explain the ontological status of the ultimate foundations of legal order. However, it can be done only by abandoning both the hierarchical logic inherited from Hobbes, and the aspirations to "pure theory".

The "impure" social facts creep into Kelsen's pure system by two routes. Firstly, Kelsen cannot ignore the fact that legal organs often seem to break the rules regulating their conduct: legislatures can enact norms which are apparently inconsistent with the limitations prescribed by the constitutions, courts can refuse to apply ostensibly valid norms, and so on. Such unauthorized actions can have their intended effects. If this is the case, we have to suppose, according to Kelsen, that the higher norms have actually authorized these acts. So, if there is no constitutional review, it has to be assumed that there is a constitutional norm which authorizes the legislature to enact norms which are "unconstitutional". Such a legislature is in the position of the Hobbesian sovereign. And this idea goes all the way down. Coups, conquests and revolutions often change the national legal systems in an irreversible way, and the international community just recognizes these changes. Thus, ultimately International Law recognizes that such uses of force which are illegal from the national point of view can create new legal facts. Indeed, this is the origin of any legal system. For the history of any system can be traced back to the first constitution, and that constitution was necessarily produced by extra–legal means. It became valid because it was effective, i.e. norms authorized by it were applied by officials authorized by the very same constitution, and obeyed by the people made its subjects by the constitution itself.

There is another, related "impure" aspect in Kelsen's system. Effectiveness is a necessary condition for the existence of a legal system:

> The principle of effectiveness is the general basic norm that juristic thinking assumes whenever it acknowledges a set of norms as the valid constitution of

> a particular state. This norm may be formulated as follows: men ought to behave in conformity with a legal order only if this legal order as a whole is effective. (Kelsen 1957, 224)

This norm is the norm judged by Hobbes to be superfluous: the obligation to fulfil our obligations. Here Austin is more plausible than Kelsen. Effectiveness, or "the habit of obedience" is a social precondition for the existence of a system, not something prescribed by the system itself. It is useless for the law to proclaim its own bindingness, for such proclamations are no more binding than the rest of the law.

In *The Pure Theory* Kelsen makes effectiveness a necessary condition for the validity of any law, not only of the system as a whole. If a law is systematically disregarded, it is no longer a law. Every legal system tacitly recognizes the force of the "negative custom" of disregarding certain laws. Thus, "impure" social facts finally infect the entire system. These problems show that a legal theory might be made independent either of moral considerations or of social facts, *but not of both*.

6.4. Ross and the problem of self–referring norms

In his important work *On Law and Justice*, the Danish legal theorist Alf Ross tried to moderate the extreme decisionism of the Realists by combining it with certain normativist aspects. Ross' treatment of the problem of validity of individual laws is in accordance with the general Realist programme. In his view, "assertions concerning valid law are according to their real content a prediction of future social happenings" (p. 49). Such a prediction says that courts and other officials are likely to behave in a certain way *because* they feel that the law in question requires such a behaviour and they think that the requirement is binding. Assertions concerning valid law speak, then, not just on regularities governing the behaviour of officials, but on regularities of certain type. From this it follows that validity is not a systemic property. An individual law can be invalid, even while it in some sense follows from the other parts of a system, if it is not considered as binding by the relevant officials.

Obviously, when the validity of laws is discussed in courts, the judges are not making predictions on their own future behaviour (cf. ch. 2.1.). Ross may answer, however, that judges' officially performed speech acts are not simply assertions concerning validity; judges declare laws as valid, or recommend or prescribe that others should take them as valid. At the descriptive meta-level, assertions concerning validity are predictions of official behaviour. One aspect of this behaviour is linguistic behaviour: which laws are declared as valid, appealed to, used as justifications etc.

However, when Ross discusses about the sources of law, he creates a system similar to that of Kelsen. The real novelty in his treatment is at the level of the supreme norm.

> Let us call the authority we are considering A_1, then A_1 is constituted in a set of (formal and material) rules of competence. If we call these rules C_1, then C_1 itself must either be authoritatively enacted by a superior authority A_2 or not. If they are enacted by A_2, then A_2 must be constituted by C_2 which must be authoritatively enacted by A_3, or not. Since the series of authorities cannot be infinite, the inevitable conclusion follows that in final instance the highest norms of competence cannot be enacted – they must be presupposed. (Ross 1958, p. 80)

This is the normativist version of the Hobbesian regress – the decisionist solution would be that A_3 does not derive its authority from any rule. But, according to Ross, C_3 is not a transcendental entity like Kelsen's Grundnorm or its counterparts in theories on Natural Law. For the norms which constitute an authority and its competence are at the same time norms for determining how a law created by that authority can be amended. Thus the master rule in a system is the rule concerning the amendment of the rules which constitute those authorities which can enact other rules. It is a part of the system, not something standing behind it.

This idea is a continuation of the main theme of my discussion. The separation between ordinary norms and the norms of constitution produces a modification into the Hobbesian–Austinian basic definition. The *terminus ultimus* of the Commonwealth is not the authority who has the power to make laws, but the authority which has the power to make those laws according which the other laws are made. Or, in the words of Herman Finer: "Who has the power to alter the Constitution is the master of the state, and the amending clause gives that power". (Finer 1932, 204; cf. Freund 1965, 348) This authority is based on the positive norms which define the methods of amending the constitution. But behind those positive norms there cannot exist any further norms; they rest on the social fact that the legal system is taken as binding. In the words of Ross:

> In the United States, the highest authority is the constituent power constituted by the rules in art. v of the Constitution. These rules embody the highest ideological presupposition of the American law system but they cannot be regarded as enacted by any authority and they cannot be amended by any authority. Any amendment of art. v of the constitution which in fact is carried out is an alegal fact, and not a creation of law by way of a procedure that has been instituted. (p. 81)

Here the irrefelexivity postulate is made explicit:

> It could be maintained that a certain authority, for example, A_3 can be established in norms enacted by itself, which amounts to saying that it is possible for a norm to determine the conditions for its own establishment, including the way in which it can itself be changed. A "reflexivity" of this kind, however, is a logical impossibility, and is generally recognized as such by logicians. A proposition cannot refer to itself. (p. 81)

There is a problem in a theory which denies the possibility of self-referential statements. For any such a theory is itself a victim of the very same paradox it tries to solve. Consider the statement made by Ross:

> ...genuine self-reference, whether direct or indirect, whether total or partial, deprives the sentence of meaning as far as self-reference is involved. (Ross 1969, 17)

Now this sentence refers to the (infinite) *set of all sentences*. It says that for any sentence it is true that if a sentence is self-referential, it is meaningless. By referring to the set of all sentences, the sentence quoted above refers indirectly to itself. In this sense it is like a law which says something about all laws. Therefore, if the quoted sentence is true it is meaningless. Any theory which tries to banish even indirectly self-referential sentences from a language has to contain some indirectly self-referential sentences. Thus, the theory cannot be formulated in the same language.

Is the situation different if the theory is limited to norms only?

Functionally, Ross' postulate plays exactly the same role as Hobbes' denial of self–obligation (3). Like the Hobbesian sovereign, the amendment rule cannot alter its own power in a legal way. But Ross' justification for the irreflexivity postulate cannot be the same as Hobbes' was. It is plausible to say that no one can command him– or herself except in a metaphorical sense, and if all laws are commands, self–legislation is excluded. This follows from the pragmatics of commanding. Ross, however, conceive laws as "propositions", not as commands, so the irreflexivity postulate has to be justified on other grounds. As a general principle of the logic of normative propositions, it is unsound. An everyday counterexample can be found from the initial pages of almost every book printed in English: "Conditions of Sale: This book is sold subject to the condition that it shall not... be lent, re–sold, hired or otherwise circulated... without a similar condition *including this condition* being imposed on the subsequent purchaser". The italized expression makes this commonplace norm (or prescription) self–referential without making it paradoxical in any obvious sense.

It can still be true that in the case of constitutional self–amendment a paradox is still involved. The basic argument is the following: Suppose that at time t_1 there exists in some constitution an amendment rule:

C_1: An amendment of the Constitution will be valid law iff K_1.

An amended constitution existing at some later time t_2 will contain the following rule:

C_2: An amendment of the Constitution will be valid law iff K_2,

so that the condition K_1 is not identical with K_2. Now C_2 is supposed to derive its validity from C_1. It is produced by applying C_1 under the condition K_1. This can be written in the form of a logical inference:

$$C_1$$
$$C_1 \rightarrow (K_1 \rightarrow C_2)$$
$$K_1$$

therefore: C_2.

But C_1 and C_2 are practically incompatible; hence the propositions which say that both rules are valid are mutually inconsistent.

It is possible to present an internal criticism of Ross' position. On p. 81 in *On Law and Justice* Ross admits that actually legislators would agree that there is a legal way to change a rule of constitutional amendment, e.g. art v of the U.S. Constitution, namely by applying it on itself. He accepts this as "a social-psychological fact which will exert a great influence on the actual course of political life". But his own earlier analysis of validity statements says that ultimately they all are statements about such facts. If the relevant officials believe that an amendment of the amendment rule of a constitution is binding, and that it is binding because it is made in accordance with the old rule, would it not be valid according to Ross' own analysis of validity? We noticed that a statement which says that a rule is valid is, for Ross, a predictive statement. The statement which says that the old amendment rule C_1 was valid until it was amended at the moment t by a new valid rule C_2 has, then the following content. "Before time t, the officials treated the rule C_1 as binding and acted accordingly; after t, the officials shall treat the rule C_2 as binding and act accordingly."

Ross' predictive analysis would handle any replacement of an old law by new one in the same way. The difference between an ordinary amendment and self-amendment is visible only in the light of the theory of Ross, not in the consciousness of judges and Members of Parliament. It seems that in this fundamental question Ross rejects his Realist programme that "the study of law must in final analysis be a study of social phenomena... and jurisprudence must have as its task the interpretation of the 'validity' in terms of social effectivity" (p. 68). In respect of the ultimate norms, however, social phenomena have to give the way to the logic of norms in Ross' analysis. As Suber (1990) remarks in his magisterial treatment of self-reference in law, Ross relies on a model which envisions legal change as a series of deductive inferences.

Here, Kelsen's notion of authorization is useful. According to Kelsen, two norms N_1 and N_2 can be interrelated in two different ways. N_2 can be inferred from N_1 with the help of relevant facts (and, perhaps, of additional norms and legal definitions). Or then, N_1 can authorize the creation of N_2 by conferring to some legal organ the power to create it. This latter operation is not a deductive inference. There is no logical reason why a norm could not confer the power to change itself. From my less "pure" point of view the essential thing is whether the authority of the organ to make such a change would actually be accepted in the relevant community. If Ross were loyal to his Realist methodology, that should be the central question for him, too.

In his later article in *Mind* (Ross 1969) Ross explicitely adopts a Kelsenian solution to the puzzle of ultimate norms. Because self–amendment is impossible for logical reasons, and because officials would nevertheless treat a self–amended rule as valid, Ross postulates a basic norm which stands behind the amendment rule in every system. It has to be of the form: "Obey the authority instituted by the amendment rule C_1 until this authority points itself points out a successor (by establishing a rule C_2); then obey this authority, until it itself points out a successor; and so on indefinitely." This is just like Kelsen's formulation of the Grundnorm for legal systems considered from the dynamic point of view; the ultimate reason for validity of rules is a norm standing behind the first constitution. The meta–systemic status of Ross' basic norm become obvious when we notice that *it* cannot be changed by means of C_1. If it could be changed, the paradox would return.

An alternative to the Rossian view would be the rejection of the inference model of validity. We should admit that the asymmetry postulate shared by all thinkers discussed here, from Hobbes to Ross, is not a conceptual truth. Law can refer to itself. This forces us to modify the hierarchical idea which, as we have seen, has characterized not only the positivist tradition but also its main competitors in the field of legal theory.

CHAPTER 7

CONVENTIONALISM AND LAW

The defining property of those theories which are usually collected under the label "legal positivism" is the thesis that certain social facts form a sufficient condition for the existence of law and legal systems. The acceptance or rejection of this thesis has important consequences, but there are other issues in legal theory which are of equal importance. Thus, the positivism–antipositivism issue is only one possible way of classifying different theories.

The modern theory of legal positivism, formulated by H.L.A. Hart and brilliantly developed by such theorists as Joseph Raz, has several other characteristics, some of them shared by many non–positivist theories. According to this theory, law has an irreducible normative character. Law is institutionalized in the sense that it is created and maintained by institutions and largely addressed to them. Law is systemic and reflexive: different laws are interconnected and regulate their own creation.

This form of positivism enjoys a wide support in the Anglo–Saxon countries; so wide that in a recent critical book it has even dubbed "the Jurisprudence of Orthodoxy". I must add that it does not enjoy a similar status in the Nordic countries, for example.

What follows is essentially an attempt to reconstruct a part of the theory of law presented in H.L.A.Hart's "The Concept of Law" (CL, for short) in terms of conventionalism. My starting point is to show how Hart's notion of The Minimum Content of Natural Law is consistent with the supposed coordinative role of legal norms.

7.1. Hart's theory of human nature

Some of Hart's critics have remarked that in spite of the name the theory of the Minimum Content (CL, ch. 7) has nothing to do with Natural Law in the classical sense. Be that as it may, what Hart certainly provides us with is a theory of human nature. It seems that a theory of human nature is an essential part of any comprehensive social theory. Several theorists, including many existentialists, Marxists and behaviourist psychologists have claimed that human beings have no nature. This claim is, strictly speaking, unintelligible. Even if human beings were completely plastic and malleable in their behaviour, that infinite plasticity would be one of their essential properties. It would be a property distinguishing them from the rest of the living nature, and it should be explained, at least in part, in terms of their inherited biological constitution.

However, the claim that human beings are not constrained in any way by their inherited constitution is implausible. But we may accept that human beings have a nature without supposing that we need a biological theory to inform us what that nature is. It seems that biological accounts of human nature, such as sociobiology, have not been able to tell us much new about the subject. We can perhaps learn more about human nature by studying the problems and solutions of mankind as revealed in history, philosophy or novels than by studying biology.

In his theory, Hart focuses on those properties of human nature which he sees as important from a legal theorist's point of view. His list of the properties is not new. It is almost the same as Hume's list of The Conditions of Justice. After Hart, similar lists have been produced, with slight modifications, by Lucas (1966), Rawls (1971), Downie (1971), MacPherson (1970), Mayo (1986) and Flodin (1986). Hart's list includes the following properties (CL, 190–95):

(i) *Human vulnerability*. The constitution of human beings is such that it is easy for them to harm each other, physically or mentally. Therefore arises the obvious and general need to constrain their interactions.

(ii) *Approximate equality*. In spite of their differences, human beings are relatively similar in their strength and skill, compared with, say nations of different size. At least with respect to certain types of actions (acts of violence, for example), it is likely that all individual humans would benefit from adopting a common set of constraints.

(iii) *Limited altruism*. As Hart says, men are neither "devils dominated by a wish to exterminate each other", nor "angels, never tempted to harm others". Human altruism is limited in its intensity and its scope. It is not sufficiently strong to prevent conflicts, still it is usually present, and it can have either an intensifying or a tempering effect on conflicts.

(iv) *Limited resources*. Scarcity is the fundamental supposition behind economic accounts of human nature. Scarcity is a function of both the amount of external resources and of the amount of human needs. Therefore, it is possible to claim that scarcity is a part of the modern condition only, and that in the Stone Age, for example, there was no material scarcity (see Sahlins 1974). Nevertheless, scarcity is an important factor in the present world, and that fact may be irreversible. This creates the need for the rules of distribution of material resources.

(v) *Limited understanding and strength of will*. Under this title several properties can be collected:
(a) Limited capacity of information gathering.
(b) Limited capacity of information processing.
(c) The possibility of individual or collective short–sightedness.

These properties of human nature are sources of the interaction–problems discussed in ch. 2. and exemplified in formal games. The combination of scarcity and limited altruism produces PD–situations, which, because of vulnerability, can be dangerous for all parties involved. Short–sightedness can prevent cooperation in recurrent games. Our limited capacity to gather and process information can create uncertainty which prevents coordination in coordination games. Game theory has been used to illustrate the problems perceived by Hobbes and Hume in their treatments of human nature; it can do the same service here.

It should be noted that Hart does not suppose human beings to be destructive or uncooperative by their nature. That supposition would constitute an essential change in his theory of law. The destructive nature of conflicts is an avoidable consequence of the inherent limitations of human nature. Human beings can behave in a destructive way, not because they are so evil, but because they are not perfect. Because of their limited intellectual and emotional capacities, their cooperativeness, altruism, and sense of justice can be utilized for destructive purposes.

Hart stresses the role of material scarcity; here he joins the great liberal thinkers. Indeed, it may be claimed that, through economics, scarcity has become *the* liberal justification of law and government.

My present account is a departure from the liberal–economic main road. The most important property of human nature is, from the conventionalist point of view, (v). Scarcity of information is an even more universal and general property of the human condition than material scarcity. Even in a superabundant society (in Marx's communism, for example) human beings have to act on the basis of limited information, and that is still likely to create difficulties in their interactions. Even a complete knowledge of the external nature cannot make human agents completely transparent and predictable to each other. Because of this, the ultimate limits on the perfection of society and individual are set. That is why we need institutions, including the legal institutions studied by Hart. This has also be noted by some economists:

> It is only because human beings are limited in knowledge, foresight, skill, and time that organizations are useful instruments for the achievement of human purpose.(Simon 1957, 199)

Hart's notion of "limited altruism" should not be equated with the individual–egoism postulate typical of Hobbesian theories of human nature. Human beings are limited in their altruism in the sense that they are generally acting according to particularistic commitments. Their concrete concern is the welfare and moral good of those individuals and groups with which they have special ties, not the abstract good of mankind. Their conceptions of good and justice are necessarily partial and conflicting. Both moral and factual components of their belief systems are necessarily restricted by the fact that they are not omniscient beings.

In his dissertation, Mats Flodin (1986, 126–30) wants to make two amendments to Hart's description of human nature. He supposes that human beings have only a "limited tolerance of social inequality" (130) and a universal "dislike of disorder... It is unknown that a society can exist without some form of social arrangements" (131). For me, these additions seem to be unnecessary. As far as Flodin's first postulate is concerned, it may be too good to be true. Historically, societies with extreme inequalities have survived long periods. We may say that a sense of justice is perhaps a universal feeling, and that claims of justice, for conceptual reasons, must be expressed as demands for equal treatment. But they may be compatible, or even imply, extreme inequalities in respect of some properties. The second postulate seems to express tautology: what we mean by a society is a system of social arrangements. The reason why people end by establishing social arrangements is that these can help them to solve the interaction problems resulting from the other properties of human nature.

In his excellent exposition of Hart's theory, Michael Martin (1987, ch. 1) asks whether Hart's postulates (i)–(v), when strengthened with some additional postulates (humans want to survive, they are rational, they know that (i)–(v) hold, they are not prevented from carrying out their plans) logically entail that there has to be a legal system with a specific content. His answer is in the negative.

There is no need to go into the details of Martin's critique. Hart's theory of the Minimum Content of Natural Law is basically an attempt to explain in functional terms why human societies have developed legal systems. The core of Martin's criticism is common to all critiques of functional explanations in social theory. Firstly: functional explanations do not usually provide *sufficient* conditions for the existence of the institutions they purport to explain. For even if it were rational for human beings living under certain circumstances to develop institutions performing collectively useful functions, it would not guarantee that these institutions emerged. Human beings are not always individually rational, and even when they are, they are not always able to perform the collective actions required for the creation and maintenance of institutions. For example, it might be very useful to have an effective world government; alas, people have not created one. Thus, it is not true that the functional usefulness of an institution is a sufficient condition for its existence.

Secondly, functional explanations do not provide *necessary* conditions for the existence of institutions. We can always imagine alternatives which would perform the same tasks equally well. Martin imagines a society in which there are no laws forbidding violence, but where

> everyone is trained in self–defense from childhood; people are always armed. Housing and clothing are designed with self–defense in mind. (...) Second, people in such a society are psychologically prepared for violent attack and are determined to defend themselves. Thirdly, people in this society have a sophisticated defense technology. (Martin 1987, 187)

Martin believes that in his imaginary society "the chance of survival is close to ours". His point is that in regard to the purpose of human survival, there can be functional alternatives.

We might answer that even if survival is the most important motivational factor, it is not the only one. Human beings have other aims, too, and these other aims are better realized in a society with a legal system than Martin's state of nature. But then, it might be answered, these other aims should be added to Hart's theory. The resulting theory would not be "minimal" anymore; it would become more like a traditional (e.g. Aristotelian – Thomistic) theory of Natural Law.

It is undeniably true that human beings have other purposes than their own survival. Unlike the Aristotelians and Thomists, I do not think that attempts to list these purposes are very useful. The purposes and values vary radically in different cultures and societies. What is important is that people universally have values and purposes, that they are shared between the members of societies and social groups, and that their realization invariably requires cooperation and coordination among the members. The list provided by Hart need to be completed with the following postulate:

(vi) *Partial sociableness*. Human beings have values and purposes which can be realized only through common action.

What is presupposed here is not the classical idea of common good. Postulate (iv) just states that in every society there are *group goods*, i.e. purposes and values which are shared by the members of various sub–groups of political communities, and which cannot for conceptual and/or practical reasons be realized without common action. However, it is not self–evident that people are able to perform mutually beneficial common actions. In this work, I have tried to show that problems of common action are often coordination–problems, and that in coordination problems the observance of conventions is a generally rational strategy.

I think that the standard criticism against functional explanations is correct in the sense that the functional explanations provided in the literature are usually imperfect. Because Hart's theory, as I see it, is an attempt to explain institutions in a functional way, it is subject to criticism. This does not make the theory worthless. Hart's theory of human nature provides certain background reasons for the existence of legal institutions. A necessary and sufficient explanation for their existence (a rare thing in the social sciences) could be constructed only by telling the full story. That story would explain in causal and rational terms why people have picked up those particular functional solutions which characterize our legal systems.

It should be noted that in any comprehensive story intended to explain the emergence of modern legal institutions, conscious action should play an important role. The functionality of law, unlike that of, say, language, is not guided only by an invisible hand. One important reason why legal institutions are able to solve the problems arising in human interaction is that they are designed to do that. Usually we cannot find any designing act or actor (the Original Contract or the Great Legislator) in the history of legal institutions. Even if we can, the actual institutional practices are necessarily changed and modified by innumerable actors (legislators, courts, officials and citizens) striving for different and sometimes incompatible aims. It may nevertheless be true that one aim shared by most actors involved in the development of modern institutions is that of solving the problems described by Hart. This aim may be important not because it is felt to be important but because it is – unlike other aims such as justice, religious belief or the glory of the nation – generally shared through time.

The Hartian form of functional explanation does not make the claim that legal systems in their present form are globally optimal solutions for the problems generated by human nature. For example, one thing left out of the Hartian theory of human nature is that human beings are dependent on their ecological environment and that the environment sets constraints on our actions. If the mutual arrangements adopted by us do not reflect that fact, it may be detrimental for our survival. It may be argued that the existing legal–political systems are not functional in this respect, and in the long run, we have either to change them radically or to perish. Thus, a functionalist theory of law need not imply universal optimism or conservatism.

7.2. The nature of obligation

In the discussion about the nature of rules we again find a terminological confusion, which cannot be solved by our linguistic intuitions. Here I use 'rule' as the most general classificatory term. 'Norm' refers to a sub–species of rules, and 'obligation' or 'duty' to a sub–species of norms. Several authors (especially sociologists) equate norms with what I call obligations.

'Social obligations' or 'social rules of obligation' refer to a class of norms which are in force in societies at certain times.Their existence is a social fact. I accept the view that at least many legal obligations, as well as obligations of positive morality, belong to that class. What are the conditions for the existence of such obligations? Both sociologists and legal theorists have tried to answer this question.

Sometimes, norms or obligations are simply equated with social regularities or frequencies. A norm proposition "In the situations of type C, doing A is obligatory in S" is true if and only if the members of S generally do A, when C. This seems to be the thinking behind some Realist theories of law. However, there are social regularities which do not have any obligatory character. To use the example given by Weber, the regularity with which people usually open their umbrellas when it rains is not based on any obligation to do so. Similarly, we may predict that elderly judges are likely to give longer sentences for crimes of a certain kind, but this prediction is not based on the existence of a legal obligation to do so. Neither is the fact that failing to do A when C is regularly punished a sufficient ground for the existence of an obligation. Punishments or critical reactions may be necessary elements of obligations. But if a protection racket punishes shopkeepers for not paying protection money, we cannot say that there is an obligation on the shopkeepers to pay. For the shopkeepers do not accept the legitimacy of the demand, nor the legitimacy of the punishment. Neither do the protection racketeers claim any legitimacy for their actions (see the related discussion on authority and coercion in ch. 4.2.).

Several other authors equate the existence of obligations with expectations concerning actions. For example, Bierstedt (1963, 222) says that a norm "is a societal expectation. It is a standard to which we are expected to conform whether we actually do so or not". Of course, not all societal expectations are norms. Hart's example of people going regularly into taverns makes the point. People may go into taverns partly because they expect to meet other people there: the expectations are interrelated. But there is no obligation that they should go into taverns. In the case of an obligation, the expectations in question are themselves normative. Homans (1950, 124) claims that norms "are not behavior itself, but what people think behavior ought to be". This kind of definition is interesting because it is "circular". The relevant expectations cannot be described without mentioning normative concepts. However, obligations cannot be shared normative *beliefs* only. They must also be linked to actual behaviour.

The theory of obligations presented in Hart's CL (54–6) incorporates the elements discussed here. Hacker (1977) provides an explication of Hart. (Hacker uses the term "social duty–imposing rule". My corresponding term is "social rule of obligation", or "SO" for short.)

(SO1) A social rule of obligation exists (in S) iff

(1) the subjects are required to do or abstain from a given act upon specific occasions;
(2) the rule is thought by most members of S to be important because it is believed to be necessary for the maintenance of social life or some valued feature of it;
(3) the conduct required by the rule may conflict with the wishes of the norm–subjects;
(4) the compliance with the rule must be general;
(5) in the event of deviation from the rule, serious critical reactions characteristic of rule– acceptance usually ensue;
(6) deviation is usually regarded as a good reason for critical reactions;
(7) critical reactions are usually regarded as legitimate, there is no general counter–criticism;
(8) normative language is extensively used in the expression of critical reactions.

This description, taken from Hacker, catches the essence of the Hartian notion of obligation. My task is now to try to answer to the following questions: (1) How is Hart's description related to the general conventionalist approach adopted here? (2) How is it related to Hart's theory of human nature? (3) What are the conditions for existence of normative (especially legal) systems? (4) What could be answered to the criticisms of this Hartian definition of obligation?

The answer to the second question is rather obvious. Given the fact that cooperation is a necessary condition for maintaining social life and realizing social values, and given the description of human nature, SO:s are necessary. Individuals in a society need rules protecting their life and limb, rules which determine their rights over material resources, rules which regulate their daily interactions, and rules concerning the maintenance of their offspring. (In modern conditions, we must add the rules protecting the human environment.) Critical reactions are needed to enforce these rules in the cases when individual wishes conflict with the requirements of the rule, or when individuals are ignorant of the consequences of their actions. Imperfectly rational individuals cannot do without rules, but they are likely to develop rules.

As Hacker has noticed (see Hacker 1973), the Hartian theory of obligation is a "sanction" theory of duty – a variation of the theme discussed in ch. 7. However, the notion of "critical reaction" covers much more than institutionalized sanctions typical of legal systems, although legally determined punishments (as well as damages, nullities and impeachments) are one form of critical reactions. A critical reaction can involve verbal criticism ("That is wrong", but also, "That is stupid", "That is imprudent", etc.), social ostracism, religious or magical condemnation, public ridicule, private revenge etc. There can be, but need not be, further rules regulating critical reactions. These informal sanctions are equally essential for the existence of legal systems. What is important is that if an SO exists, it always gives reasons for some critical reactions.

The notion of mutual belief, essential for conventionalism, may be said to be implicit in Hart's theory: he speaks, for example, about rules as "shared standards". However, he seems to emphasize the idea expressed in (3) that there is a potential conflict between individual will and rules which are necessary for social life (2); therefore the need for enforcement (5). Behind this are the competition for scarce resources and a limited human altruism. As Ullmann–Margalit notices, SO can be conceived as a norm compelling individuals to cooperate in a Prisoners' Dilemma (Ullmann–Margalit 1977, 13). But the fact that obligations can conflict with personal wishes is not the only reason why people fail to conform to them. Another reason is that they are not convinced that *others* will follow their example. They are afraid that their attempts will either be useless or will be exploited by others. These problems are related to the necessary limitations of human knowledge. People may expect others to deviate from the rules because of selfish interests, or because of irrationality or ignorance, or because of uncertainty at a higher level. Here the notion of mutual belief is crucial. In these cases, the underlying interaction situation does not have the character of a PD.

It is important to notice that the deliberate immorality of an action is not the only reason for critical reactions. We frequently criticize people (including ourselves) because we find their actions to be irrational, imprudent, arbitrary, ambiguous or capricious. Critical reactions do appear even in situations in which the aims and interests of actors are normally compatible and the regulative rules are, in principle, self–enforcing. A typical example is a communication situation in which participants are criticized for violating the postulates of conversation. Thus, the role of "sanctions" in the wide sense is not just to change an underlying PD–situation. Their role is not only to work as a deterrent against those who deliberately want to break rules. They have other roles, too. Firstly, critical reactions have an expressive function: they inform people about the limits of acceptable conduct. Secondly, they maintain trust in the community. The latter theme is discussed in chapter 9. of this book.

The following amended definition makes the connection with my theory explicit:

(SO2) A social rule of obligation R (with the content "Every member of S ought to do A when C") exists in S iff

(1) the members of S, when the situation is believed to be C, generally do A;
(2) the members of S believe that R is a rule in S;
(3) the members of S believe that (1) is instrumental for the realization of ends considered as valuable in S;
(4) individuals for not doing A when C are generally subjected to critical reactions;
(5) propositions (1) – (4) are mutually believed in S;

(6) (3) is at least partly a reason for (4);
(7) (5) is at least partly a reason for (1).

According to this definition, the existence of a social rule of obligation is a conventional fact. This set of existence conditions of SO has a lot in common with "the existence conditions of a social norm" listed by Rolf Sartorius (1987, 49–51). Sartorius, however, does not utilize the notion of mutual belief. Instead, he iterates higher–order beliefs and preferences, finding ultimately 153 (!) conditions for the existence of a social norm. This is un–economical and arbitrary. As in the case of Bach's definition (see cf. 1.2.) any attempt to fix the number of iterated beliefs at some definite level of complexity is ad hoc. Depending on the circumstances, people can be more or less reflective in their shared beliefs.

Sartorius knows this, for he comments that "few of the conditions... can be claimed to be logically necessary to the existence of a social rule and... those (if any) which are so are not jointly sufficient" (Sartorius 1987, 51). There is then no reason to suppose that the 153 conditions listed by him are ever satisfied, except occasionally. More controversially, he extends this to my condition (1) ((4) in SO1) that the behaviour required by the rule must be general. Here he claims to be arguing against "a virtually universal assumption among philosophers" (p. 51). He offers the following example of a rule which is not generally followed:

> For instance, I take it that contemporary American sexual morality contains a prohibition of adultery. I also think that it might be true that the majority of married individuals commit adultery at least once in their lifetimes. (Sartorius 1987, 51)

Perhaps so. But this can hardly be seen an example of a rule "without the external aspect", a rule which is preached but not followed. "Once in a lifetime" is not, after all, very often.

There are better examples to illustrate his point. For example, very few persons possessing a personal computer pay any respect to the legal rules against unauthorized copying of programmes. Another example: in Finland, a law prohibiting professional fortune–telling is still on the statute–book, but it has not been applied by the courts since the war. The statute against blasphemy has a more unclear status:

the last case of application is from the early seventies. It seems to be plausible to say that all these rules, although not generally followed, do exist in Finnish society. But they exist for a special reason. They belong to systems of rules. The existence conditions of such systems are more complex than the existence conditions of individual rules, for systems can themselves provide criteria for the existence of individual rules. Systems can guarantee the existence of member rules even when these rules do not satisfy the existence conditions listed in (SO2). What is required is that violating the rules of a system is by and large considered a justification for formal or informal critical reactions, and that at least the most important rules (from a social point of view) are actually enforced by such reactions. Among the latter have to be those duty–imposing rules which are essential for the existence of the other rules, e.g. rules regulating the conduct of the courts.

Here the rules of etiquette, fashion, positive morality, etc. are different. They are not parts of systems in the same sense. Consequently, if Americans were sufficiently promiscuous, the rule of positive morality against adultery would not exist in American society. Of course, we cannot say exactly how much rule conformity is needed for a rule's existence.

7.3. A note on "obligation"

Hart's theory of obligation has been criticized by several authors. The theory seems to be intended to give a general analysis of obligations, both moral and legal ones. It is supposed to catch the general meaning of our everyday notion of 'obligation'. But are moral obligations really social rules in this sense?

Let us consider an example presented by Dworkin. A convinced vegetarian living in our society claims that he is under an obligation not to eat meat. By making this claim, he is not asserting that it is a general practice in society to abstain from meat eating, or that in the cases of meat eating a serious criticism will usually be forthcoming, or that the duty not to eat meat is generally considered important for social life. Nevertheless, the vegetarian insists that *there is* an obligation or duty, not only that it is a good thing if people followed his ideals.

Thus it seems that the Hartian description (SO1) or my revised description (SO2) does not give us the meaning of the term 'moral obligation', nor even a part of that meaning. But does it nevertheless catch the meaning of 'legal obligation'? Some legal obligations are generally considered trivial (and not important for social life). Some of them are left unenforced, and acts of deviation do not usually arouse serious critical reactions (cf. the examples given above). Some of them are not generally followed at all. (SO1) does not give the meaning of 'legal obligation' either.

These criticisms take it for granted that Hart's intention is to give an analysis of the meaning of the ordinary language notion 'obligation'. And certainly Hart himself, for example in the Preface of CL, gives the impression that he is doing "linguistic philosophy" and that his study is mainly "about words". My proposal is, however, that we should not take (SO1) as an exercise in linguistic analysis. Instead, it is a theoretical description of a social phenomenon, related to a constructive theory of law and society.

Nevertheless, there is a linguistic dimension in Hart's work, but it is not about the meaning of certain English expressions. It is about the use of language. Probably all languages have a normative vocabulary – in English, such expressions as 'obligation', 'right', 'ought', and so on, belong to it. These normative expressions can be used for two different purposes (perhaps there are other purposes too). They can be used either to *describe* (1a) moral or (1b) legal practices existing at a certain time in a certain society, or to *criticize* and *evaluate* actions and practices from (2a) the moral or (2b) the legal point of view.

The difference between the uses (1a) and (2a) is not between two kinds of morality ("positive" and "critical"), but between two kinds of judgements or points of view. When the vegetarian says that there is an obligation to abstain from meat eating, he is making a critical moral judgement (of type (2a)), not describing an existing practice. There are, however, connections between the different judgements. The vegetarian, when making his critical claim, is committed to the further claim that it would be preferable if the practice of not eating meat existed in his society, and the corresponding descriptive claim (1a) were true. If he really thinks that there is an obligation or a duty not to eat meat (at least for a person like himself), he is a "moral legislator". Similarly, a judgement about an existing moral practice implies that in society people generally make the corresponding critical judgements (2a). If the described practice really is a moral practice, it is a part of the critical morality of at least some people. "Positive morality" is not a special kind of morality. It consists of the moral opinions which are common and shared in some community – looked at from the point of view of descriptive social theory. Because the rules of positive morality are SO:s in relevant communities, they are, unlike the morality of a vegetarian in our society, backed by critical reactions. They are often followed for hypocritical reasons. In a limiting case, they are followed just for hypocritical reasons.

Critical (or action–guiding) legal judgements (2b) have a special property: Their acceptability (unlike the acceptability of critical moral judgements) is dependent on the truth of the corresponding descriptive judgements (1b). "That is against the law" is appropriate as a critical comment only if it is true that the action referred to is prohibited by some valid law. The same is not true of critical moral judgements. The appropriate use of legal, but not moral, critical expressions is dependent on the existence of corresponding practices. In a sense, the legal "ought" implies "is".

MacCormick remarks that there is a difference between descriptive or "detached" moral and legal judgements:

> detached moral statements are statements of somebody's views of morality, not statements of what is moral; whereas detached statements of law are not statements of somebody's view of legality, but statements of what is legal – in some jurisdiction at some time. (MacCormick 1987, 110)

But the issue is more complicated. If, as I have supposed, law is based on conventional practices, the statement of what is legal in some jurisdiction at a certain time is a statement of what the relevant officials believe to be legal there at that time. Thus both moral and legal descriptive judgements have the same explicit form: "According to X, there exists a requirement R". But in the legal case the judgement is self–grounding when X is identical with a relevant group of officials. In a sense, it is a statement of the officials' shared view on legality. This is not so in the moral case – unless we accept some form of moral conventionalism. Descriptive and critical legal judgements presuppose each other.

For Hartian positivism, the distinction between different judgements is fundamental. When we recognize it, another alleged distinction becomes unnecessary. It is often claimed that for positivism, the fundamental claim is that there is a *semantical* difference between 'legal obligation' and 'moral obligation'. The institutional separation of moral and legal practices is, however, socially contingent. In some, "primitive" societies it is impossible to draw the line. And all legal systems certainly embody at least some elements from the shared morality of society (on this issue, see chapter 8.). "Law as it is" necessarily reflects at least somebody's opinion on "law as it should be". A Hartian positivist can consistently say that existing legal and moral practices are necessarily interconnected, indeed, that law is only a highly institutionalized form of morality, but that law (and existing morality) as it is and as it should be are different things.

The fundamental difference is that the rules of positive morality are always SO:s. They exist only as human practices. Some legal obligations can exist without being SO:s because they belong to systems which ultimately exist by virtue of SO:s.

The claim that there is no deep difference between descriptive judgements on law and descriptive judgements on positive morality is not inconsistent with a general positivistic view of law. For we can equally have a 'positivistic' description of the morality of some society. What is essential for this outlook is the separation of the descriptive and critical–evaluative uses of normative expressions. We can describe an accepted system of 'oughts' as a moral or a legal system without accepting it.

The systematic use of such descriptive judgements is actually one of the most important "inventions" of modern social theory. The pioneers of positive social theory, Durkheim and Westermarck, for example, extended our view of the world by showing how we can (i) see the practices of other cultures internally, how they play a similar role in the lives of the other people as our practices play in our lives (the dimension of understanding); and how we can (ii) see our own practices externally, as social facts existing contingently in certain historically and geographically limited societies (the dimension of explanation). Our ability to switch between descriptive and evaluative viewpoints is an important aspect of our ability to understand the social world which includes such "sacred" practices as religion, morality, and law.

The minimum presupposition of evaluative–descriptive understanding is that the practices which we try to understand are of the relevant kind. We can understand a system of prescriptions as a legal system only if it satisfies certain minimal requirements. It has, by and large, to be effective, and it has to satisfy certain functional requirements. These issues are discussed in chapter 8.

Legal statements such as "A has a legal right to x", "y is legally prohibited", "According to the law B ought to be punished", etc. are not only used to make descriptive or critical legal *judgements*. They have a different, constitutive use. They can be used by a judge when formulating a verdict or by a legislator when enacting a new rule. Because moral rules are not institutionalized, moral statements have no comparable use. Several theorists have remarked that law "presents claims". Law is said to claim authority and moral correctness. What do these antropomorphic expressions mean? An empirical study of existing constitutions shows that they almost always contain references to such basic social values as the dignity of man (56 cases), justice (71 cases), the common good (96 cases), or democracy (107 cases) (van Maarseveen and van der Tung, 1976). Quite often, these words have very little to do with political realities. But they show that law is always presented as an embodiment of certain parts of accepted social morality. That claim is not dependent on such ideological pronouncements; they just make the claim of law explicit.

Law's relation to authority and moral acceptability can be compared to the relation a scientific theory has to truth. From the history of science we learn that innumerable false theories have been claimed to be true. It is quite likely that none of the theories accepted by us as scientific truths are actually true. Correctness is not an essential property of a scientific theory. It is, however, an essential property of a scientific theory that it claims to be true. Similarly, it may be that most or all legal systems are actually unjust. But law claims to be correct, it claims that its requirements should be accepted because they are at least permitted by independent morality, and because law has a moral right to be recognized as authoritative.

7.4. Primary and secondary rules

A society living under the regime of SO:s or primary rules is able to overcome some of the difficulties arising from human nature. Such a society is a kind of Lockean state of nature (cf. Bobbio 1971, 115–6).

There are mutually recognized standards of conduct, so that individuals can assume in their expectations that the others will follow a general pattern in their actions. But the problems created by human nature are still there. Therefore, the interactions in a community having only SO:s tend to remain in a sub–optimal state in regard to the realization of the values protected by the rules. Firstly, the critical reactions related to a rule can have an effect only if the reactions are appropriately coordinated, i.e. they arise if and only if a member of S has not performed his role in a normatively regulated situation. In a decentralized system of rule enforcement, there may be too many underreactions (violators are not punished) or overreactions (they are punished several times) or wrong reactions which can create counterreactions. The enforcement itself poses a coordination problem for the members: who should enforce the rules, when and how should it be done? The members of S need further rules to govern the critical reactions: all this seems to lead into an infinite regress.

Secondly, a regime of primary rules tends to be too static. When external circumstances change, social values could perhaps be realized in a better way by adopting new rules. But somebody should initiate the needed change, and the fact that the rules are going to change should be communicated to the members of society in such a way that a new mutual belief will arise. The difficulties are obvious: in a system of SO:s there is no centre of normative authority to perform the task.

Uncertainty in interpretation, inefficiency in enforcement and the static nature of rules are the main problems in a system where people have only SO:s regulating their conduct. It is worth noticing that Hart's description of such a system is not intended to be an anthropological description of early societies. Most, perhaps all, "primitive" societies studied by historians and anthropologists have institutional properties which go beyond Hart's ideal type. It is, like the state of nature of the early contract theorists, a theoretical abstraction. Like the contractarians, we can still try to find illustrative examples of this state. For example, International Law seems to be closer to this state. So are we all in many of our daily interactions in which shared morality and custom play a much more important role than law.

A further example of a relatively "primitive" normative system would be the Finnish Council of Public Speech – a voluntary organization established by Finnish journalists and publishers. Its task is to act as a guardian of "good journalistic manners", e.g. to ensure that a person publicly accused has an opportunity to respond. It applies a code which contains a set of simple obligations ("a journalist has a duty to protect his or her source", etc.) and exercises only moral censure: newspapers which ignore its decisions have only to suffer from bad publicity. It interprets and applies pre–existing rules; it can neither enforce nor change them. Thus, it is an example of partially institutionalized positive morality. The example shows that for many purposes, "primitive" systems are more useful than developed ones. Obviously, an institution vested with full powers to enforce and change the rules would constitute a danger to the freedom of expression.

The defects of a regime of primary rules are not equally present everywhere. The factors which tend to make the coordination of human activities more difficult have already been discussed (in ch. 5.3.). Such factors are the number of members in a community, a changing or heterogeneous population, the complexity of tasks which have to be performed, and sudden changes in the external (including social) conditions which made the need for changes in rules more urgent. All these things make it more difficult to create, maintain, and change the mutual beliefs necessary for cooperation. Hart himself comments:

> Disputes as to whether an admitted rule has or has not been violated will always occur and will, in any but the smallest societies, continue interminably, if there is no agency specially empowered to ascertain finally and authoritatively the fact of violation. (CL 91)

For Hart, uncertainty, inefficiency and the static nature of the regime of primary rules are reasons for a community adopting *secondary rules*, "rules about rules" (CL, ch v). Secondary rules "provide for operations which lead not merely to physical movement or change, but to creation or variation of duties or obligations" (CL, 79). These secondary rules govern the interpretation, enforcement and change of the primary rules.

Here is an unnecessary ambiguity in Hart's account. Probably all societies have rules which correspond to Hart's description of secondary rules in the sense that they make it possible to "create or change" obligations: e.g. rules for promising, contracting or marriage.

Only those secondary rules which have an effect on the general rules of the whole society are relevant here. Moreover, not all rules which are relevant are secondary in the described sense – the famous rule of recognition, for example, is a duty–imposing rule, although it is a "rule about rules". Thus, I use the term *metarule* to refer to those rules which are related to the interpretation, enforcement and change of all other rules of the system.

Here, however, my presentation differs from that of Hart. The most fundamental change needed is not the introduction of rules of a new kind, but the creation of *authoritative positions*. The reasons for authority have already been discussed in ch. 5. Under a system of primary rules, the rules are considered authoritative, but there is no special group of authorities, no "agency" (Hart above). There are three important things which are present in modern legal systems, but not in a system governed merely by SO:s:

(1) *Political division of labour*. There is a special sub–class S' of the population S, which claims and is generally recognized as having legal–political authority in S.

(2) *Secondary or meta–rules*. There are rules which determine the membership of the authoritative group S' and regulate its conduct in its authoritative capacity. The meta–rules discussed by Hart are those which regulate the identification, interpretation, change and enforcement of other rules. The obligation–rules belonging to this class are SO:s in S'.

(3) *The change in the status of primary rules*. In this more complex society not all obligation rules regulating the conduct of the members of S are SO:s. Because the authoritative group has a power to accept new rules for the whole society, as well as to enforce them, there may be obligations which do not satisfy the conditions for existence SO. They are perhaps not generally followed, or not regarded as important, and so on. Nevertheless, they exist as members of a more complex structure.

These properties are essential for the existence of a normative *system*, as distinguished from a mere set of rules existing in some community. But this picture is still a simplified one. In modern legal systems, the political division of labour is more complex. What is important in modern legal–political systems is that there are authoritative institutions with their own internal rules. There are legislative institutions which are defined and regulated by the rules of change, interpretative institutions defined by the rules of adjudication and regulated by the rules or recognition, and enforcement institutions regulated by the rules of enforcement.

When describing the modern State–centred legal system as functional, Hart seems to provide an apology for the existing order. Behind the description there seems to be a basically Hobbesian argument that without modern legal institutions we are doomed to be, if not in a state of war, at least in a state of chaos or stagnation. Is the theory ultimately an ideological one in the pejorative sense of the term?

My answer is, firstly, that even if anarchy were a viable alternative, no sincere anarchist could claim that there is no moral trade–off between the State and anarchy. Some people may value liberty so highly that they are willing to reject the security and predictability provided by the *Rechtsstaat*. But it is implausible to say that the goods provided by the State have no value whatsoever. It is possible to accept the functionalist description of law and nevertheless conclude that some form of anarchy would be a better form of human organization, even if it could not fulfil all the functions performed by the modern State.

Secondly, the Hartian theory does not imply that the existing legal institutions are the best we can have. It does not, for example, imply that the modern penal system is the most rational way to institutionalize the critical reactions to lawbreaking, or that the nation–state is the natural centre of law–creating authority, or that the existing division of labour between the legislative, executive and judicial organs of the State is the best one.

7.5. Meta–rules

How do the meta–rules work under the system of a political division of labour? Suppose that in a community S there is a group with authority, S'. Its function is to apply the rules which exist in S. What the judicial institution S' needs is a rule which says which rules should be applied. It is a rule of the following form:

(RR) A rule R is valid and ought to be applied by S' iff there is a source for R which belongs to the set L.

Sources belonging to L can be decisions of legislative institutions, precedents, customs and so on. But there must be one exception to RR. S':s obedience to the rule RR itself cannot be based on the fact that RR has a source in L. It can, of course, have one. Finnish law, for example, says that all officials have to follow Finnish Law. But that cannot be the basis of judicial obedience, for there could be a competing rule RR', designating a different set of sources, L', and these sources can include a source for RR' itself.

Hart calls rules like RR "rules of recognition". He describes them in the following terms:

> The rule of recognition providing the criteria by which the validity of other rules of the system is assessed is in an important sense, which we shall try to clarify, an *ultimate* rule: and where, as is usual, there are several criteria ranked in order of relative subordination and primacy one of them is *supreme*. (CL, 102)

> We only need the word 'validity' and commonly only use it, to answer questions which arise *within* a system of rules where the status of a rule as a member of the system depends on its satisfying certain criteria provided by the rule of recognition. No such question can arise as to the validity of the very rule of recognition which provides the criteria; it can neither be valid nor invalid but is simply accepted as appropriate for use in this way. (CL, 105–6)

> The assertion that it [the rule of recognition] exists can only be an external statement of fact. For whereas a subordinate rule of a system may be valid and in that sense 'exist' even if it is generally disregarded, the rule of recognition exists only as a complex, but normally concordant, practice of the courts, officials, and private persons in identifying the law by reference to certain criteria. Its existence is a matter of fact. (CL, 107)

There are several important points in this description. Firstly, we can see why the notion of SO is important even for the understanding of modern, complex legal systems. The conditions for the existence of a legal system are, that (i) there is a rule of recognition which is a SO at least among the group of officials S', and (ii) the other rules recognized by the rule of recognition are by and large either obeyed in S or enforced by S'. The other rules may not be SO's, not only because they are intentionally disregarded, but, for instance, because the norm subjects have not yet learned their content. But the rule of recognition is necessarily an SO because it cannot be derived from other parts of the system. Its existence is a social (or, as I would say, a conventional) fact. A rule is the RR of a system if there is a mutual belief among the members of the official class that it is the RR of the system and if they, in their official capacities, act as if it were the RR of the system. The RR of a system is, therefore, necessarily efficacious. This solves the supposed "textual contradiction" in Hart's account. Roscoe E. Hill (1970) and Philip Soper (1984, 172) have claimed that the notion of obligation presented in Chapter 5 of CL is "completely irrelevant" to Hart's picture of legal obligation. By this, they mean that legal obligations are not necessarily SO's. But, as we saw, an SO is not meant to be a general definition of "obligation".

The need of coordination explains the self–creating character of law. Suppose that in a group S there are certain rules which are generally followed, partly because they have coordinative functions, partly for other reasons. When things change, there arises a need in S to have further rules in order to cope with new situations. Various rules with different contents can work as possible solutions. Now the old, existing rules provide a salient solution *if they define some relatively unambiguous ways of creating new rules*. New rules are salient if they can be based on the pre–existing rules which are themselves salient. Thus, in a small and homogeneous S, there can be a simple rule of recognition of the form: "Whatever a general meeting of all the members of S accepts as a rule is a rule in S." That rule of recognition is still a social rule of obligation in the whole community, not a meta–rule in my sense.

In a larger and more complex S, a political division of labour develops. In order to establish coordination in S, authorities need common criteria for the rules they apply. Because the law–applying group S' is, as compared with the total group S, relatively small and well–defined, its law–applying activities can still be coordinated by mere SO:s. The rule of recognition under a political division of labour is based, not on general acceptance in S but on acceptance in the sub–group S'. The larger and more complex the community is, the more is there need for hierarchy and formal regulation even inside the official group. The political division of labour becomes more and more complex (as the modern development of public law shows). Ultimately, however, the existence of the system must be dependent on the existence of a conventional practice among the supreme interpreters and enforcers of law. Moreover, if the system is constitutional in the proper sense, at least some of the ultimate rules regulating the conduct of officials are not just sanctioned by the mutual criticism of officials. They provide reasons for citizens to react critically when the highest officials violate them. The core of the constitutional form of authority is that there are effective rules which constrain the power of the authorities, and that these rules are based not only the mutual control and self–control inside the official group, but also on control exercised by citizens.

We can now see how this theory is related to the earlier discussion on the ultimate foundations of legal systems (ch.6.). The rule of recognition has a status similar to that of the sovereign in the theories of Hobbes and Austin or of the basic norm in the theory of Kelsen. The rule of recognition stops the regress of justification. It is a rule which is not justified by a reference to the entire system (although its existence may have a moral justification), it just exists. There is a kind of analogy between the role of the criteria of validity in a legal system and the role of a truth–predicate in a Tarskian hierarchy of languages. The truth of the sentences of an object–language can be asserted only by using a predicate which is not a part of that language. Similarly, the validity of the norms of a system can be asserted only by using criteria of validity which are not parts of the system. The Hobbesian–Austinian system can be seen as a special case: in that system the rule of recognition simply says that whatever the sovereign decides is law and should be applied. Like Kelsen's Grundnorm or basic norm, RR has also a conceptual status which differs from the status of the other norms of the legal system in question.

The function of the rule of recognition was, according to Hart, to diminish the uncertainty of rule–application. Besides the rule of recognition, there are other meta–rules satisfying other functional needs. *Rules of change* empower individuals or groups in authoritative positions to introduce new primary rules for the conduct of the life of the population, and to eliminate old ones. They provide a remedy for the static quality of the original system (CL, 93). *Rules of adjudication* empower individuals to make authoritative determinations on the question of whether a primary rule has been broken. They make the working of the system more efficient (CL, 94). Thus, these rules provide, among other things, membership criteria for the officials' sub-group S', and determine the political division of labour inside it.

From Hart's descriptions of the role played by RR, one might infer that the difference between it and the Kelsenian *Grundnorm* is not great. Both can be seen as alternative ways of stopping the Hobbesian regress.

But the Hartian system of metanorms is not, or at least, need not be, based on the irreflexivity and asymmetry postulates shared by all theories discussed in ch. 6. As Suber says:

> rules of recognition must occasionally be changed and adjudicated, rules of change recognized and adjudicated and rules of adjudication recognized and changed. More to the present point, rules of recognition must be recognized, rules of change changed , and rules of adjudication adjudicated. (Suber 1990, 28)

Thus a modern legal system (unlike a primitive command–obedience system described by Hobbes and Austin) contains reflexive and symmetrical relationships. Most importantly: the metanorms define and regulate the normative powers of officials, but these norms exist only because the same officials accept, use and obey the very same norms. Neither is the relationship between the supreme norms (and authorities) and law–applying officials simply reversed, as is the case in J. Ch. Gray's version of Legal Realism. For the meta–norms do exist as practices which effectively limit the power of courts: they are elements of the legal system, not merely political realities standing behind it. Hart himself describes this reflexive nature of law in the following way:

> courts (are) exercising creative powers which settle the ultimate criteria by which the validity of the very laws, which confer upon their jurisdiction as judges must itself be tested. (CL, 148)

But here some have seen a problem in Hart's theory. If the rule of recognition is a practice among judges and other officials (S'), if all other rules are dependent on it, and if among these rules there are rules of adjudication determining who is a judge or an official, the different meta–rules do presuppose each other (MacCormick 1981, 109). Ladenson formulates the same argument in this way:

> On the one hand, he wants to analyze the concept of law in terms of the notions of rules of recognition; but on the other hand, he elucidates this latter notion primarily in terms of the concept of law. That is, Hart's approach to the issue of how to identify rules of recognition implies that they should be thought of as the rules that everyone in a given society, but particularly people who hold offices and positions *defined by law* ultimately appeals to in *legal* argument. (Ladenson 1980, 138–9)

This is not a question of the logic of norms. I do not see anything objectionable in rules which refer to each other: a legislature can establish a rule according to which a court has a power of constitutional review, while the court can declare that the legislature is constitutionally elected and its decisions, including the decision which established the powers of the court, are valid laws. The question is about the conditions for existence of legal systems. Here we have a feeling of *déja vu*. The problem is the same as has been discussed above in relation to other theories (see ch.6.), and also discussed by Hart himself in relation to the Realist theories (CL, 133). How should the officials be identified? Suppose that one social sub–group S' in a community S follows and upholds a rule of recognition RR while another sub–group S'' follows and upholds a different rule of recognition RR'. Both rules of recognition confer validity on rules which define the respective sub–groups as the sole guardians of law.

Ladenson's starting–point is correct. He starts from the fact of political authority which is independent of the existence of rules. But his theory about the nature of this authority is mistaken (cf. ch. 4.2. above). He equates authority with the existence of coercive power. There is another way of breaking the circle. Political authority is a conventional fact. It is based on the general recognition of the relevant population, and can exist independently of any authorizing rules (see ch. 4.1.). Its existence in a certain community can be historically explained by many factors, and among them are the traditions and practices of the community. But it does not necessarily base its authority on any pre–existing rules. It is there because it is accepted. According to this view, the existence of a political division of labour is more fundamental than the existence of a legal system.

This is the solution provided by MacCormick. He tries to break the circle by reading it in terms of the history of the system. MacCormick imagines a "primitive" society in which the elders have a judicial role. There is no power–conferring rule of adjudication saying that the elders have that power, but there might well be a rule of recognition saying which rules they have to use.

Several observations support this view. Firstly, authority relationships can exist without law, but not vice versa. Children learn first to obey authorities; the understanding of and compliance with general rules comes later. Secondly, ordinary people do not usually know the content of the constitution or of the essential rules of public law. Indeed, modern law is far too complex to be understood except by specialists. But ordinary people can generally recognize certain persons as legal authorities (as policemen, judges, M.P.'s or Heads of State). They have a conception of what these persons can or cannot do, and when and how far they should be obeyed. This identification of the authorities implies that there is a mutual belief in a specific property of being a legal authority which can be ascribed to some individuals. Thirdly, these authorities can sometimes establish their own authority without any pre–existing rule. A constitutional convention of a new nation can declare itself the supreme legislator without an appeal to any legal rule. A court can pronounce its own authority (on a concrete example, see Guest 1980, 170). These acts can win acceptance for various reasons. Acceptance does not, in these cases, imply anything like moral approval or tacit consent. Like the rule of a usurper on the throne, the acceptance can arise from the immediate need of coordination; some kind of order is better than none at all. Fourthly, the legally established authority of some officials can survive intact even when the metanorms which constitute the legal–political system change. Ultimately, the normative circle is broken by introducing the circular attitudes and beliefs into the theory. This is an innocent form of circularity, for the theory itself is not circular. It is a theory of a reflexive or circular phenomenon.

Hart himself recognizes the possibility of authoritative decisions not dependent on authorizing rules:

> One form of 'formalist' error may perhaps just be that of thinking that every step taken by a court is covered by some general rule conferring in advance the authority to take it, so that its creative powers are *always* a form of delegated legislative power. The truth may be that when courts settle previously unenvisaged questions concerning the most fundamental constitutional rules, they *get* their authority to decide them accepted after the questions have arisen and the decision has been given. Here all that succeeds is success. (CL, 149)

The structure of a modern legal system is, then, of the following form:

(i) individual norms can be traced back to the meta–rules;
(ii) the meta–rules support each other;
(iii) meta–rules are there because they are generally accepted, interpreted and enforced by the sub–group of official authorities;
(iv) official authorities are authorities because they are generally recognized as authorities by the entire community.
(v) this recognition is partly, but not totally, conditional to the official acceptance of a certain set of meta–rules.

In Hart's theory, there are no counterparts to the irreflexivity and asymmetry postulates essential for the theories of Hobbes, Austin, Kelsen and Ross. But what about the consistency postulate? As we saw, Hobbes, Austin and Kelsen supposed that every legal system is free of conflicts in the sense that either all commands or norms contained by it are practically compatible, or then, the system itself provides means of solving the apparent incompatibilities. From this it follows that every system is unified: there exists a single sovereign (Hobbes, Austin) or a single *Grundnorm* (Kelsen, Ross).

Hart's rule of recognition seems to have a similar status. But is it conceptually necessary for there to be only one RR in a system? What if both the group S' and the group S" following different rules of recognition actually possess an authoritative status in the community?

Firstly, let us suppose that there are several rules of recognition and one set of officials. The courts, for example, have to apply statutes and customary law. In such cases, there is normally a hierarchy of sources. Various rules of recognition, identifying different sources, can for theoretical purposes be unified into a single complex rule which says, e.g. that both statutes and custom are legitimate sources, but that in the case of a conflict the statutes override customs. The unity of the system is preserved. The idea of saliency provides an explanation of why law should have a systemic character (see chapters 2. and 5.) – a multiplicity of equally authoritative and potentially conflicting rules would make coordination among the official class, and consequently, among the people in general, more difficult. However, this does not require that all rules should be traced back to a single meta–rule. An individual rule can become binding just because officials and citizens start to treat it as binding. The unity perceived in a system by legal theorists can be more a less an artificial creation.

Secondly, let us suppose a situation in which two (or more) rules of recognition compete. This was the situation in the Soviet Union during the "war of laws" in 1989–91. The Supreme Soviets of individual republics refused to recognize the supremacy of the laws enacted by the central state, and the local officials applied them only selectively. In such a situation, the Hartian, the Kelsenian and the Hobbesian approaches agree: there is no single legal system. There are either several systems which overlap territorially, or, if the conflict is severe enough, no system at all.

Thirdly, there can be situations which fall between the extreme cases. Consider the relationship between the UK legal system and the system of the European Community as described by Malcolm Wood:

> Once constitutional perceptions are beyond the control of a small, homogenous UK elite, the very cohesiveness of the constitution begins to falter. This is most obvious in the largely unresolved tensions between the European Commission and court on the one hand, and UK officialdom on the other. In a sense, two rules of recognition apply, depending upon which set of official actions you are externally observing. (Wood 1988, 55)

I have no competence to assess the correctness of this description, but certainly it is at least empirically possible. Does this, as Wood says, "point to a key problem in the Hartian analysis"? For the traditional Hobbesian conception of a sovereign, the existence of such entities as the German Empire created unsolvable problems. Thus Pufendorf saw the Empire as "a chimera", because it seemed to have no recognizable sovereign: the fault was in the reality. Is the European integration a similar anomaly for the Hartian analysis?

Before answering this question, I should comment on the more extreme generalizations put forth by Wood. He claims that radical uncertainty concerning the content of the rule(s) of recognition also exists inside the official class. It occurs between junior and senior officials (pp. 55–6). Moreover "each institution in the state apparatus has, as its own internal imperative, the demands of holding and increasing its domain... Thus, the actions of senior officials can only be understood in the context of institutional imperatives, policies and power relations. Without a thorough understanding of these, the signals reaching the external observer may lead to a highly confused understanding of the rule/s of recognition" (p. 56).

What seems to be required is a return to comprehensive sociological or Realistic jurisprudence. It is no wonder that Wood's final description of the UK legal system is exactly similar to that given by the Realist Olivecrona: it is "a mass of unresolved conflicts and concepts" (p. 59). Thus the usefulness of a systemic notion of law is rejected. One possible answer would be to emphasize the differences between juristic and sociological viewpoints: the aim of juridical understanding is not to understand all the actions of officials but only to understand the strictly legal aspects – the reasons for actions provided by law, and the legal effects of those actions.

However, when accepting the factual nature of the ultimate rules of recognition, Hart's theory has already sinned against Kelsen's requirement of purity. The question put by Wood cannot be avoided. If a legal system is actually a mass of unresolved conflicts, if general laws and the actual behaviour of officials are highly incongruent, can we say that a rule of recognition exists? We must note that this is a problem for all non–Realist theories which presuppose some form of systemic unity. It is equally a problem for the Dworkinian theory of one right answer and for Lon Fuller's version of Natural Law in which consistency and predictability have a prominent place.

It seems, however, that if Wood's generalization is correct, his first argument, based on the uncertain relationship between the UK and European Community law, has no bite. That relationship can create special problems only if the British municipal system possesses, after all, some coherence. If the British system is just a mass of contradictions, why should it matter that its relationship to EC law is unclear, too? The coherence of a legal system is, unlike the logical consistency of a deductive system, a matter of degree. This becomes evident when we compare "normal" systems with the systems really in crisis. My intuition is that most legal systems are, if compared with the Soviet Union during its last crisis, still relatively coherent. For this very reason, the authority of international bodies like the European Community *do* create real problems. There do not exist an unlimited number of potentially conflicting formulations of the rule of recognition, but only some *relatively clear* competing alternatives (e.g. that British legislation is to be strictly submitted to the European system, or that the membership in the EC only modifies the content of the independent British system). The tension between the alternatives lasts as long as the underlying political conflict, but it is seen as a definite problem on both sides.

In contrast to what some authors seem to think, Hart does not describe a legal system as a system in the deductive sense, as a logically closed set of propositions. There can be conflicts inside a system, and as Martin Golding has remarked, conflicts need not cause any problems as long as they are not actualized. To take an example, the Finnish Constitution says unambiguously that the cabinet is nominated by the President but that it has to enjoy the confidence of Parliament. Sixty years after the enactment of the Constitution it finally became necessary to answer the question of whether the President can *dismiss* a cabinet which enjoys the confidence of Parliament. During all these years, the existence of a potential conflict at the heart of the very system was not recognized outside the circle of constitutional specialists.

But what happens when a conflict becomes relevant? Unlike e.g. Dworkin and Kelsen, Hart does not presuppose that every system determines a single right answer to any controversial question. If a legal system does not provide an answer, the outcome is determined by the interplay of power and chance. (According to an anecdote, when the Chancellor of Justice was asked to give an authoritative opinion in the Finnish case, he hastily glanced at a recent study on the Finnish Constitution, which happened to be written by a scholar who did not accept the President's power of dismissal. It became the official interpretation. One may wonder whether this interpretation would have been accepted if the incumbent President had not been seriously ill and unable to act.) The systemic nature of law does not mean that such dilemmas are impossible, nor does it imply that there always exists a pre-determined way of solving them. It means only that they are comparatively unusual and normally solved in a quick and relatively peaceful way.

Wood argues that this view presupposes a high degree of consensus inside the official class S':

> It is arguable that positive law can itself only be effective when there is social, political, economic, cultural and ethnic consensus within a population. In effect,

> the certainties demanded by positivism, and even in Hart's core theory, need a far higher level of social stability and consensus than is manifest in most societies. (p. 47)

The first sentence expresses an important truth. If there is *no* amount of consensus in a society, not even a consensus on the principle that the society in question should continue its existence, positive law cannot be effective. The society would either dissolve itself (like the Soviet Union) or collapse into a civil war (like Yugoslavia). A disagreement on the content of the rule of recognition – e.g. on the locus of the supreme norm–creating authority – can often be a decisive factor in such processes. The question is, how much consensus is needed, and what kind of consensus is needed? Here, my theory of social coordination as the basis of law can work as a complement to Hartian positivism. For all forms of social, ethnic, etc. dissensus are not equally fatal. One almost universally supposed function of law is to regulate such conflicts, and it is implausible to say that it can actually never fulfil that function. Multi–ethnic Switzerland is a very stable society. However, it has not always been that: during the nineteenth century there was continuous unrest, and even a civil war. One factor which has to appear in any explanation of Switzerland's present stability is its constitutional system, carefully tailored for a multicultural society.

Wood's criticism is interesting because most critics of Hart draw the opposite conclusion. They claim that Hart's theory is defective because it does not presuppose any moral acceptance or commitment, not even from the officials (see chapter 8.). The requirement of consensus is not a problem specific to Hart's theory. For example, the theory of Dworkin, especially in the version presented in his magnificient opus *Law's Empire*, presupposes a consensus, and it has been criticized by Joseph Raz precisely for that reason. The last chapters of my work are partly devoted to a discussion on the problem of consensus. But, returning to the original question of systemic unity: The problem arising from such special arrangements as the European Community seems to show that the answer is negative. In the integrated world where nation states are no longer the only claimants to the supreme political authority, a plausible version of the Hartian theory has to admit that there can be partially competing rules of recognition. The postulate of legal unity cannot be a logical requirement. Thus, none of the logical postulates essential for the positivistic tradition (and adopted by many non–positivists, see ch. 6.) is preserved in my version of the Hartian theory.

CHAPTER 8

EFFICACY AND OBLIGATION

8.1. Efficacy

In spite of their differences, most modern legal theories seem to accept a common necessary (but *not* sufficient) condition for the existence of a legal system (LS). A system of rules is an LS only if it is generally efficacious and performs certain social functions. There is, however, no agreement on the definition of efficacy or on the nature of relevant social functions.

Several theories of law contain an additional requirement. They require that a system, in order to be a legal system proper, has to satisfy some *moral* criteria. Such theories are usually collected together under the general title of Natural Law, although they need not to be naturalistic in the meta-ethical sense. There are important motives for formulating such theories. There is the need to relate descriptive legal theory to the normative theory of politics. There is also the need to answer to the perennial question: which are the limits of the obligations owed to the State? Although the latter question may be more important than any of the questions discussed in this book, I am not going to provide any definite answer.

Especially do the modern versions of Natural Law try to connect the required moral criteria with the more widely shared criteria of efficacy and/or functionality. In other words, they try to show that the correct account of the efficacy and/or functionality of legal systems has to refer to moral considerations. In order to assess this claim, we have to analyse the notions of efficacy and functionality. However, the criteria for the existence of legal systems are morally and politically important even if we do not accept a Natural Law framework. Consider the claim put forth by some Estonian Nationalists. According to this claim, the legal system of the old Republic of Estonia is still in force, and hence, all the institutions established during the Soviet rule in Estonia are non-legal and their legislative decisions are void. Consequently, the new constitution of the Republic of Estonia refers to the old constitution enacted in 1938 as the basis of its legitimacy, but not to the referendum on independence held under Soviet rule.

This claim has tremendous political consequences for all Estonians. The claim, as such, is not dependent on the question of whether the actual content of the rules laid down by the Soviet authorities is compatible with some moral criteria – e.g. by those seen as crucial in the various theories on Natural Law. From the claim, it follows that even good laws enacted by the Estonian Supreme Soviet are without legal force, unless they are explicitly or tacitly approved by the new Estonian state.

I have already established that the political division of labour, the differentiation of the population into a group of officials (S') and a group of citizens (S – which includes the officials acting in their non–official capacity) is essential for the existence of an LS. Again, most theories of law seem to agree that the existence of an official class, and the behaviour of that class, is relevant for something's being a legal system.

How should the notion of efficacy be defined? The relevant factors are the attitudes and the behaviour of the members of the groups. The most plausible possibilities are:

(1) Officials (the members of S') *conform* to the rules of the system.
(2) Officials *obey* the rules of the system.
(3) Officials *accept* the rules of the system.
(4) Officials *morally accept* the system.

(1') Citizens (the members of S) *conform* to the rules of the system.
(2') Citizens *obey* the rules of the system.
(3') Citizens *accept* the rules of the system.
(4') Citizens *morally accept* the system.

Some combination of these requirements defines the efficacy of a system. In both lists, the requirements are successively stronger: the earlier requirements are implied by the later ones. Ingram (1983, 488–9) ascribes the combination (2), (1') to Kelsen. He himself sees this combination as inadequate. Firstly, conformity is a weaker notion than obedience. It merely means that the behaviour of citizens is generally in accordance with the rules, not that the rules have any real effect on the behaviour. Then it is logically possible for a system to be merely epiphenomenal, perhaps not even known by the citizens. We would not call such a system "efficacious". Secondly, Ingram claims that the application of rules requires more than obedience on the officials' part. For the officials' behaviour constitutes a part of the system; therefore they cannot systematically disobey its rules. (Ingram 1983, 499)

Both of Ingram's points are basically correct: the second is correct in respect of the basic rules of a system (such as the rule of recognition). Any individual official could act against the basic rules. But if most officials systematically violate a rule purported to regulate their behaviour in their official capacities, the rule does not belong to the system. This is true simply because the basic rules are constituted by the official practices. For the same reasons the combination (2), (2') – which can be ascribed to Austin's theory of "habitual obedience" – is not sufficient either.

We have to admit that if a legal system is efficacious, officials have to accept its basic rules in some sense. This is a consequence of Hart's thesis that the basic rules of a system are social rules of obligation: they exist because and as far as they are followed. The question now is: does this acceptance amount to full moral approval of the basic rules?

Hart's own definition of efficacy combines requirements (3) and (2'). He rejects the moral approval requirement:

> Not only may vast numbers be coerced by laws which they do not regard as morally binding, but it is not even true that those who accept the system voluntarily, must conceive themselves as morally bound to do so, though the system will be most stable when they do so. In fact their allegiance to the system may be based on many different considerations: calculations of long-term interest; disinterested interest in others; an unreflecting inherited or traditional attitude; or merely the wish to do as others do. There is indeed no reason why those who accept the authority of the system should not examine their conscience and decide that, morally, they ought not to accept it, yet for a variety of reasons continue to do so. (CL 198–9)

From the citizens, all that Hart requires is general obedience:

> Only officials might accept and use the system's criteria of legal validity. The society in which this was so might be deplorably sheeplike; the sheep may end in the slaughterhouse. But there is little reason for thinking that it could not exist or for denying it the title of a legal system. (CL 114)

Many critics of Hart feel that the combination of (3) and (2') is too weak. They claim that the existence of a moral attitude must be included in the list of necessary conditions for the existence of a legal system. One point made by several critics is the following. If normative terms do not appear even within the scope of propositional attitudes, if there is even no belief in the moral legitimacy of the law, the whole idea of normativity is lost. Law can, after all, be reduced to complex patterns of behaviour maintained by the fear of sanctions. (See Finnis 1980, 11–18; MacCormick 1981, ch. 3.; Simmonds 1984, 99)

What most of the critics are opting for is replacing (3) by (4) (and perhaps (2') by either (3') or (4')). MacCormick (in MacCormick and Weinberger 1986, 132–3) argues that Hart himself should accept this modification. For, according to Hart, the basic rules of any LS must be social rules of obligation among officials. But it is a part of the definition of SO that they are considered to be socially important requirements (see definitions (SO 1) and (SO 2)). Therefore officials must believe that the basic rules have some social importance.

One author explicitly rejecting this critique is Rolf Sartorius (1987). He says:

> I shall even deny that officials in authority need have or need *believe that they have,* moral obligations to one another to act in accordance with the constitutional rules which they can be said to accept. My analysis is thus a thoroughly positivistic one. (Sartorius 1987, 43; emphasis mine)

I have already remarked that there is no reason to suppose that a "positivistic" (i.e. non–evaluative) description of the moral beliefs of other people is not possible. When we describe the attitudes prevailing among conservative white South Africans, or think of Aristotle's justification of slavery, we may correctly describe them as moral beliefs without committing ourselves to any kind of approval or acceptance. Requirement (4) does not imply that officials were right in their moral approval; but only such an implication would consist a threat to Hartian positivism.

It is obvious that (4) cannot be a categorical requirement for the existence of a legal system. For certainly there are in every LS *some* officials who are either critical or indifferent in respect of the basic rules of the system. They may still go along and *pretend* moral acceptance, for reasons mentioned by Hart. Hart's critics are, however, correct when insisting that law *claims* more. Law necessarily claims that the requirements it poses for its subjects are more than demands made by a cynical ruling class, or conditions of an armistice made between conflicting parties.

As a limiting case there is the possibility that all officials just pretend to approve the system. Then no official actually approves it, but most officials, believing that most officials approve it (or at least, that most officials believe that most officials approve it), continue to act as if they were approving the system. Then (4) is untrue. Should the critics say that in such a case there is no legal system? The question is theoretical, for it seems unlikely that such a system could provide sufficiently strong motives for compliance. Many theorists, from Hume to Hart, have claimed that no system can remain stable without some amount of voluntary, non–forced compliance. Although this is not a logical truth (see chapter 4.2.), it is a plausible empirical hypothesis. The fate of the Stalinist systems seems to confirm this. It seems that we can accept (4), or at least a modified form of it: in every legal system, most officials either believe in its moral value, or, having a higher order belief about the beliefs of other officials, at least pretend to believe in it.

For the reasons emphasized by Hart himself, the citizens' general attitude towards a modern legal system cannot be reduced to mere obedience. Many important rules of modern legal systems are not regulative or primary rules. They are not just commands directed to a passive population: they define the legal meaning of acts and confer powers. People do not just obey the law, they use it. Thus the combination (4), (3'), official moral acceptance combined with at least pragmatic acceptance among the people in general, is a more appropriate description of the efficacy of a modern system.

For D.C. Phillips, the combination of conditions (4) and (2') or (4) and (3') is not enough. According to him, a full moral approval from the citizens' side, (4'), is a necessary condition for the existence of an LS:

> For a system of laws to be legally valid, ordinary citizens, as well as legal officials, must take the internal point of view... A society's citizens can have an internal point toward the law only if they have a certain attitude toward the political system as a whole. Thus, they must first accept that an adequate justification is provided for the legitimate authority of the political system of

> which the law is a part. And the reasons people have for accepting the justified authority are largely moral, i.e., they concern rights, justice, the good, and the like. But Hart rejects the view that there is any *logical* connection between law and morality. (Phillips 1986, 269; emphasis in original)

Phillips claims further that accepting this suggestion would commit Hart to agreeing that "it is doubtful whether there was 'law' in Nazi Germany or whether there is today law in South Africa" (Phillips 1986, 269).

In the light of the quotations taken from CL, it is clear that Hart does not suppose that legal systems are necessarily accepted by relevant populations. It is also true that he emphasizes the conceptual difference between law and morality. But, contrary to what Phillips seem to think, we do not have to transgress the limits of positivism if we refuse to agree with Hart on these points. Phillips' makes the same mistake as Sartorius did. We may accept (4') and say that a system constitutes a legal system only if citizens believe that the system as a whole has a moral justification. This does not imply that the system really *has* a moral justification, only that it is believed to have one. The belief in morality does not make a system moral, neither is the condition that there is such a belief morally–laden.

A criticism similar to that presented by Phillips is also put forth by Anthony D'Amato (1984). D'Amato's argument takes the form of a story. Suppose that a parliament enacts a statute that requires parents to use brutal force against children and deprive children of any rights no matter how much pain is inflicted on them. The citizens of the country, outraged by this immoral decree, refuse to recognize the authority of parliament. They make a successful revolution. D'Amato claims that, contrary to Hart, the iniquitous statute need not be conceived as a valid law at all. By refusing to recognize the authority of parliament, the citizens denied its status as a legitimate source of the laws; therefore, decision–makers were not officials in the relevant sense. Consequently, the Hartian test of validity – something is law if it is recognized as such by officials – failed in this case. D'Amato continues:

> the example does suggest that in a clash between the legitimacy of officials and the legitimacy of one of their statutory commands, Hart errs in supposing that the formal validity of the statute will compel the public to recognize its status as "law" and the status of enacting officials as authoritative. Rather, the

> substantive iniquity of the statute could be so great as to dissolve in the public's mind the legitimacy of the statutes and of the leaders' claim to be "officials". (D'Amato 1984, 54)

What is needed, according to D'Amato, is a new theory of law. It

> would suggest a necessary relation between law and morality. It would insist that the popular acceptance of the legitimacy of officials' entitlement to make authoritative decisions is grounded on morality and not on a purely legal construct such as Hart's rule of recognition... Finally, in its broadest signification, a new theory might directly reverse the "might makes right" world view of both positivism and legal realism.(D'Amato 1984, 54–5)

The persuasiveness of the argument of D'Amato depends entirely on the moralistic content of his example. The statute enacted by parliament was evil indeed; and, as in all good educative tales, the forces of the Good carried the day. Unfortunately, not all revolutions are made by the forces of the Good. Suppose that a statute enacted by the parliament was intended to make all citizens equal before the law. The rebellious majority, however, believed in a racist moral theory; it could not recognize the members of an ethnic minority as equals. Therefore, it challenged the authority of parliament, made a revolution and established a new regime on a strictly racist basis. In this alternative story, too, the officials did lose their authority because they did not act according to the citizens' moral convictions. There was "a necessary relation between authority and morality" – between authority and the *shared, positive morality of the population*. The egalitarian "might" could not resist the racist "right".

It should be added that neither story is in contradiction to Hart's (or even Kelsen's or Austin's) requirements. For in both stories, the second condition of efficacy (2'), and consequently, of validity was not in force. The majorities refused to obey the laws of the system. Hart says that general obedience could be "sheeplike"; he never says that it always or even typically is like that. He does not say that the formal validity of a statute would compel people to accept it, but that even such apathetic acceptance is sufficient for the efficacy of a system.

Again, moral acceptance in a large population must necessarily be a matter of degree. A defender of condition (4') must admit that there can be a considerable number of dissenters in a system which nevertheless can be counted as a legal system. But then, we may get a paradoxical result. Although the popularity of the Nazi rule among German citizens was never democratically tested, the belief among the population that the regime was morally justified seems to have been quite common. Indeed, it is this wide acceptance of the system which makes the case so frightening. It is completely possible to imagine a Nazi–like system which is generally accepted as morally justified by most of its subjects. Condition (4') does not establish any logical connection between the concept of a legal system and critical morality. It says that there are limits for possible incongruity between an LS and the morality shared by the population living under that LS, but it does not pose any restrictions on the content of the shared morality.

Den Hartogh has remarked (in personal communication) that there have to be limits on moral diversity. We would call a system of beliefs "moral" only if they were in some sense similar to our own moral beliefs. From this, and from the condition (4'), it follows then that the content of a legal system cannot be whatsoever. There are necessary moral limits on the content of an LS.

This objection is correct as far as it goes. In order to be an instance of positive morality, a set of practices ought to play a certain psychological role in the lives of the members of the relevant community, and certain functional role in their society. It has, for example, to fulfil the Hartian requirement of Minimum content. There have to be rules regulating violence, protecting possessions, making commitments possible, etc. But these requirements do not pose such a connection between law and our own critical morality which would satisfy those who, like the modern natural lawyers, argue against the positivists' separation thesis. The positive morality of a society can be racist or sexist. It is still a set of moral practices in the descriptive sense, and an institutional system built on it can be a LS if it is efficacious and performs the general functions of law.

8.2. What is accepted?

As we saw, Phillips claims that "a society's citizens can have an internal point of view toward the law only if they have a certain attitude toward the political system as a whole". Similarly, T. M. Benditt says that

> ...to have an internal point of view toward at least certain laws logically requires that one has an internal point of view toward other laws and toward the system as a whole" (Benditt 1978, 107).

For both authors, the choice seems to be between a totally revolutionary attitude and loyal citizenship. Against this, it should be emphasized that the "acceptance of" and "obedience towards" a modern legal system does not mean just the entertaining of a single propositional belief. In a complex system, contracts are made and found valid or invalid, officials nominated and dismissed, votes counted, complaints examined, conflicts settled, organizations created, etc. according to rules. The same rules are taught, interpreted, justified, debated, criticized and invalidated. A legal system plays an important and complex role in the everyday lives of the citizens living under that system. Those parts of law which are important for a businessman are not the same as those which are important for a prison inmate; and the same person acting in the roles of a mother, a State official and an environmental activist has to deal with different parts of the law operating in different and sometimes conflicting ways. Consequently, the attitudes towards the system and towards its individual rules can be very complex and varied. If I accept the statutes of my university, does it logically require that I have to accept the legal system in which they ultimately belong as a whole? This sounds implausible.

Against the thesis endorsed by Phillips and Benditt it should also be recalled that substantial parts of law can survive intact when the system "as a whole" changes. The German BGB, enacted in 1898, has survived to our days; in the eastern parts of the present Germany it has survived through four revolutions. According to the systemic view shared by positivists like Austin, Kelsen and Hart and non–positivists like Dworkin, Phillips and Benditt, the validity of a particular subset of laws like the BGB ultimately presupposes the validity of the most fundamental rules of the LS it is a part of. But it does not follow that acceptance, even moral acceptance, of particular laws presupposes acceptance of the most fundamental rules. The particular laws can be accepted directly because they perform their coordinative functions. They can be seen to be good, useful and authoritative even when the system as a whole is rejected.

Consider the possible attitudes of those *not accepting* the system as a whole. They may continue, as the Palestinians did before the *intifada*, to obey laws for pragmatic reasons. They may comply, as the Estonians between 1989 and 1991, selectively while building grounds for their own independent political system. They may reject, like the moderate separatists in Canada and in the Western Europe, the most basic rules (e.g. the rights of the established parliaments to legislate over Scotland, Corsica or Quebec), while accepting the content of most laws enacted according to those unacceptable rules. In these cases, the acceptance of individual laws may still be moral in the sense that they are seen to perform their task in a morally tolerable way; there is no urgent need to change or break *those* laws.

Equally, the attitudes of those *accepting the system* may vary. An extreme case is exemplified by Dorr's Rebellion in Rhode Island in 1841, when constitutional recognition was asked for a local revolution. An extreme case of a different kind is a Mafia leader who ruthlessly breaks individual laws while accepting and actively supporting the system as a whole.

In a completely arbitrary "system" (like that of the Khmer Rouge in Kampuchea), or in a system disrupted by a total civil war, people cannot be said to accept a legal system, for the simple reason that there is no *system* to be accepted. If there is no definite set of relatively coherent and interconnected public rules which are generally enforced, the citizens cannot have any systematic attitude towards the law. But in less extreme cases a modern legal system, even a tyrannical one, provides other rational reasons than plain coercion to comply with important parts of it. Most essentially, it provides means for the citizens to coordinate their everyday activities. There are innumerable rules related to peoples' everyday life. They are followed, used and enforced in a routine-like way. Even revolutionaries and professional criminals comply with them when there are no important reasons not to do it. It is a characteristic property of a modern legal system that it provides many different reasons to use and obey its rules.

In some cultures, other, e.g. religious practices, can have a similar role. Consider how Evans-Prichard describes his acceptance of the Azande magic:

> I have often been asked whether, when I was among the Azande, I got to accept their ideas about witchcraft. This is a difficult question to answer. I suppose you can say I accepted them; I had no choice. (...) Azande were talking about

> witchcraft daily, both among themselves and to me; any communication was well–nigh impossible unless one took witchcraft for granted. (Cited in Mattick Jr. 1986, 44–5)

This kind of passive, pragmatic and nonpolitical acceptance is more important for the existence of a modern LS than fullblown political acceptance. Law is the magic of modern society; for most people for most of the time there is no choice but to accept substantial parts of it.

8.3. Obligation and the functionalist claim

The other generally accepted existence condition was that the system in question fulfils certain social functions. The efficacy condition excludes, for example, systems which are no longer in force (as the system of Imperial Russia), or systems which have not gained official acceptance (as a system drafted by a government in exile). The functional condition excludes systems which are not legal, e.g. religious or moral systems of rules. Again, there is very little agreement about the necessary functions of legal systems. Green (1987) distinguishes between *descriptive* and *normative* functionalist theories of law. For example, Marxist theories are descriptive functionalist theories. They claim that one of the functions of legal systems is to uphold the power of ruling classes. But almost all legal theories contain some functional claims. They say that the purpose of law is to solve disputes, or maintain peace, or maximize utility, etc. Note that the standard criticisms against functional explanations in social sciences are not necessarily relevant in this context. The functionality of law is not supposed to be independent of the intentions of the members of societies. Law can have functions for the same reason as a knife can have functions: it is designed so that it has them.

The distinction between normative and descriptive approaches is not easy to maintain. The basic idea in the normative approach seems to be this: The functionality of law makes it morally relevant; hence, the positivists' non–evaluative notion of law has to be refuted. The issue, however, is more complex. A positivist like Hart accepts the following condition:

(5) A system is a LS only if it performs functions $F_1,\ldots,F_n$.

In Hart's theory the functional requirements come from his Minimum Condition of Natural Law. Law must guarantee the biological survival of its subjects, and in order to do this, it must be able to create and maintain coordination between them (see ch. 7.1.). But survival certainly has a moral value. It is consistent with the positivist condition to accept the following proposition:

(6) It is prima facie morally better that a system performs functions $F_1,\ldots,F_n$ than that it does not perform them.

Therefore a positivist can agree that any legal system has at least some moral value, and that it has value because it performs its functions.

A normative functionalist needs something stronger than (6). For example:

(7) If a system performs functions $F_1,\ldots,F_n$, then the fact that some rule R belongs to that system is a prima facie moral reason for the subjects of the system to act according to R in relevant circumstances.

Now (7) is *much* stronger than (6). At most, (6) implies that the rules of an LS should be followed if violating them would hinder the system from performing its morally important functions, and if there is no moral reason which would override this. Of course, a positivist may admit many other reasons for complying with the law, but they do not follow from the mere existence of an LS.

It is important to see the difference between (6) and (7). (7), unlike (6), implies in conjunction with (5) that in every legal system there is a prima facie moral obligation to obey the law. Many authors use (6) as a basis to argue for the existence of such an obligation. For example, MacCormick (1973, 129–30) argues:

> However evil laws may be, that they are binding in the minimal sense mentioned, implies that they secure the existence of some sort of order in society. And on the whole order is morally preferable to disorder. The promotion of disorder is prima facie a moral wrong. This is not the place in which to enter into the debate about what considerations ought to be taken as overriding that prima facie obligation, though they are doubtless many and diverse. It is sufficient that we should observe how the obligatoriness of law is related to, and

> in some sense follows from, its binding force.

A similar thesis is defended by Peczenik:

> Each legal norm, regardless of its content, is thus morally justified in the following *weak* sense: it belongs to an order of the discussed kind and any such order is prima facie morally better than no such order at all. (Peczenik 1983, 28)

Let us take an example. In South Africa, a legal system seemed to exist even before the derogation of the apartheid laws. It fulfilled some basic functions of a legal system and it was efficacious. It secured the existence of an order which was deeply unjust, but nevertheless better than at least some conceivable lawless situations. (The strategy adopted by the ANC in the transition process seems to confirm this.) According to the argument of MacCormick and Peczenik, even the most oppressive laws intended to uphold white supremacy therefore possessed some kind of prima facie obligatoriness. If they were prima facie obligatory, this means that South Africans could violate them only in the light of other moral requirements which justified violation. I cannot agree. To me, it seems obvious that convenience, pleasure and profit could in many circumstances be sufficient justifications for breaking, say, the internal pass–laws. No overriding moral justification was needed. But then the apartheid laws could not be morally binding even prima facie.

A normative functionalist may respond by raising the threshold. He may demand stronger functional requirements for the existence of the legal system proper. Perhaps the South African system did not satisfy the more stringent requirements - hence it did not create a moral obligation to obey its individual laws because it was not a legal system.

This strategy is adopted by Benditt (1978). He defines the function of an LS as "resolution, or at least the regulation of conflict" (Benditt 1979, 103). But its ability to perform this function is dependent on an acceptance. The more a system gains acceptance, the more effective it is in performing its tasks. Thus, in order to function, a system must be acceptable to the people concerned:

> ...the function of a legal system is to regulate the conduct of the individuals to whom the rules of the system apply in such a way that the system itself can be accepted by those individuals, and hence that a system of rules is a legal system

> only if it can be accepted by most of the ordinary individuals to whom it applies. Note that it is not part of the concept of legal system that the system is actually accepted; people might refuse to accept a system and its rules for poor reasons. (Benditt 1978, 107–8)

The acceptance in question is *rational* acceptance: "a system of rules can be rationally accepted... only if there is some reason for appropriate sort of doing it" (Benditt 1978, 109). Appropriate reasons for accepting a legal system are that it is promoting justice, or the good of the people, or personal or social ideals (Benditt 1978, 109). Self–interest is not an appropriate reason.

From this it follows that Hart's sheeplike society in which the legal system enjoys only official acceptance "...is at best a limiting case of a legal system and perhaps ought not to be counted a legal system at all" (Benditt 1978, 105). The functional requirement in Benditt's theory seems to be much stronger than the Hobbesian requirement accepted by Hart and MacCormick that a legal system must be able to maintain a social order necessary for human survival. The structure of Benditt's argument is the following:

(B1) A system, x, is a legal system if and only if it fulfils the basic functions of a legal system.

(B2) If x does fulfil the basic functions of a legal system, then x is accepted by the relevant population.

(B3) If x is accepted by the relevant population then x is rationally acceptable.

(B4) If x is rationally acceptable then x promotes justice and the general good.

Then by recurrent applications of modus tollens:

(B5) If x does not promote justice and the general good, then x is not a legal system.

Has Benditt established a conceptual connection between moral criteria and the existence of an LS? I think not. The critical links in the chain are (B3) and (B4). Take (B3) first. What does Benditt mean by saying that something "can be rationally accepted"? In the passage cited, he denies that if something is acceptable, it is therefore accepted. For people can reject something for poor reasons. Why can't they *accept* something for poor reasons? If they can, (B3) does not hold.

What about (B4)? The problem is that people have different conceptions of justice and of the general good. If they have a wrong conception, they are still instrumentally rational in accepting a system which promotes justice and the good on their own terms. If any conception will do, there is no connection between the requirements of (true, correct) morality and the existence of a legal system. The argument only says that any legal system is concordant with the positive morality accepted by the majority of its subjects. On the other hand, if rational acceptability presupposes conformity with the correct conceptions of justice and the good, the list of legal systems might remain quite short.

The conclusion is that Benditt's version of normative functionalism is trapped in a dilemma which seems to be common to all theories of this variety. Either the functional–normative requirements are weak, and all or most systems which pass the positivist's non–normative test satisfy them. And hence the conclusions are unable to guide our moral judgements: we still have to make the distinctions between the legitimate and the non–legitimate, tyrannical and non–tyrannical systems. Or, the requirements are strong enough to rule out most systems that have ever existed. Hence there must still be room for descriptive analysis of various systems – and the normatively–laden distinction between legal and non–legal systems is not likely to be useful here: certainly the South African system was in many important senses similar to the European legal systems, although, according to some normatively–laden criteria, it would not qualify as a legal system. Furthermore, the normative criteria seem to establish a continuum between legal and non–legal systems. Equal political rights, for example, were introduced only gradually into the modern systems. In the nineteenth century, during the era of limited suffrage, most European systems were like the South African system in the sense that large portions of the population (women and the poor) were without political rights. If legally established political inequality were a sufficient condition for making a system non–legal, we should say that there were no legal systems in the world before the beginning of the twentieth century.

The conventionalist theory presented here is functionalistic. It supposes that one of the main functions of an LS is to maintain coordination among the members of the population living under that LS in socially important spheres of their lives. A system of rules which does not perform this task effectively cannot be an LS. One can try to interpret this functionalistic thesis in a normative way, by endorsing the following version of (7):

(7') If a system maintains socially important coordination in the population S, then the fact that some rule R belongs to that system is a prima facie moral reason for the members of S to act according to R in relevant circumstances.

A theory of this kind has been defended by William S. Boardman (1987). His argument is interesting, because his theory of law is strongly reminiscent of the theory I am presenting. Boardman argues that the coordinative function of laws and authorities provides an answer to the perennial question: How is it possible that the fact that doing A is required by a law or commanded by an authority can be a reason for a rational agent to do A? The conventionalist answer is that law provides independent reasons for action, if

(i) there is a coordination situation;
(ii) coordination is morally and/or prudentially important in that situation;
(iii) only law can maintain coordination in the situation.

This answer implies that we may have reasons to follow law even if law is morally imperfect. The realization of most important social values always requires coordination, and is almost always a matter of degree. Laws usually fall short of moral perfection, but we may still have moral reasons to comply with them.

However, the general obligation to obey law does not follow from these considerations. For the conditions (i)–(iii) do not always hold. Some laws are not intended to maintain coordination. A law which regulates private sexual behaviour has no coordinative effect. Some laws, although enacted for coordinative purposes, fail to perform their task and remain inefficacious. Suppose that the law requires us to drive on the right, but, for some or other reason, everybody continues to drive on the left. If the LS in which the law belongs remains generally efficacious, I am under a valid legal requirement to drive on the right. But there is not the slightest moral reason for me to drive on the right.

Neither does the condition (ii) always hold. Coordination is necessary for evil purposes, too. In order to pursue an apartheid policy, South African whites have to coordinate their conduct towards the non–white majority by laws. As I said, those laws are without any moral weight.

Lastly, it is not the only possible defect of a law that it is unjust. It can also be a bad law because it is impractical, capricious, or based on bad information. It may be possible that some private arrangements, although illegal, actually satisfy the purpose of the law in a better way. Then, law may not be the only way to maintain coordination, and condition (iii) does not hold.

Boardman is worried about the practical consequences of the view that there is no prima facie moral obligation to obey the law. He claims that it is "generally acknowledged in any case, that a citizen may not 'pick and choose' which legal reasons to obey on particular occasions" (Boardman, 1987, 555). I am not claiming (at least, not in this context) that there cannot be such an obligation in some legal systems. I am only claiming that the conventionalist version of the functionalist thesis cannot justify the general obligation to obey the law. By definition, even the most evil legal systems perform some socially important coordinative functions. This fact does not render any prima facie legitimation for injustices. As such, this view does not have any far–reaching practical consequences. It does not matter whether we say that the apartheid laws had no moral force at all, or that their prima facie obligatoriness was almost always overridden by other moral considerations. If even bad systems necessarily do some good, a conscientious citizen has to "pick and choose". Unlike the view that there is no moral obligation to obey the law, this opinion is neither new nor radical. For instance, Grotius said that a usurper's acts may be treated as binding, not because of any right possessed by him, but "in order to avoid the utter confusion which would result from the subversion of laws and suppression of courts"; at the same time, we have no obligation to obey such decisions of a usurper, which "have as their purpose to establish him in his unlawful possession" (Grotius,

1853, Bk.II,IV.xv.). We have no choice but to exercise our moral discretion.

The conclusion of my discussion is this: Every existing legal system has, due to its defining functions, some moral value. Because every general form of morality values those functions (especially those functions related to the survival of most members of the society), every existing legal system is at least minimally in agreement with the moral attitudes prevailing in the respective society. There exists a core which is common for all normative systems purporting to regulate the most essential aspects of the social life of human communities. There cannot, for example, a system which would be totally indifferent to the use of violence. It does not follow, however, that people are under an obligation to obey the rules of existing legal or moral systems; nor does it follow that critical morality is needed for assessing whether some possible system is an existing legal system or not.

CHAPTER 9

THE ROLE OF FORCE

9.1. The State and force

Max Weber defined the state as an organization which successfully maintained the monopoly of legitimate violence over certain territory. This definition, simple as it is, raises several problems. Firstly, it should be noted that it is at best the definition of the *modern* State. There have been organizations which are, perhaps anachronistically, called states by historians or anthropologists, but which did not satisfy the definition.

Secondly, the definition stresses the *legitimate* nature of the violence exercised by the State. It is not inconsistent with the possibility that there is a lot of illegitimate violence inside a State. Neither does it exclude the possibility that the State authorizes some other organizations or individuals to use violence in certain situations – for example, by recognizing the right to self–defence. The definition only requires that the State reserves for itself the right to determine when these private uses of violence are legitimate. Hence, according to the definition, an organization would count as a State even if it had no resources of coercion of its own, but could successfully exercise legitimate authority over the resources of others. The monopoly of the State would be reduced to its claim of authority. This sounds unintuitive. Surely, Weber's definition should be so read that the State actually possesses resources of its own to uphold its claim of monopoly. But a problem remains. Weber's notion of legitimacy is a descriptive one (cf. ch. 4.1.): something is legitimate if and only if it is generally believed to be legitimate by the relevant population, and if this recognition of legitimacy is reflected in their behaviour. Thus, if there are within a State sub–populations which recognize organizations other than the State as legitimate, and if these organizations can successfully maintain the monopoly of violence over a sub–territory claimed by them, aren't they *de facto* states? Is a rebellious movement a state if it actually controls a part of a country?

We should perhaps admit that here, as in many other areas of social theory, there are marginal cases as well as central cases. One amendment to Weber's formula might, however, be useful. An organization effectively controlling a territory should not be classified as a State just because it is recognized as legitimate: it is essential that its legitimacy *as a State* is recognized. Thus, the Allies' occupation forces in France had a temporary superior position in respect of the means of violence, and they were widely recognized as a legitimate power by the French, but they did not form the State organization in France, neither did France become a temporary part of the Great Britain or the USA during the occupation. On the other hand, the organization headed by the government in Vichy was a State, because it was (up to a point) recognized as a State by the relevant population.

The terms used here: 'violence', 'coercion', 'sanction', etc. are all notoriously problematic. Is violence always unjust? Is coercion a normative notion? And so on. I have no need to go deeper into this conceptual jungle. I will use the terms in an intuitive way, and my justification for this is that the claim made by the modern State is easily understandable. The modern State tries to maintain its monopoly over a certain source of power, namely the power arising from the possibility of limiting and changing individuals' options by using or threatening to use physical force against their persons. This is the core of Weber's definition. The important question is that of why the State claims this monopoly. Would it collapse without the monopoly? And if so, why? More precisely, what is the role of threat in legal systems? It should be noted that although one important element of the monopoly of the State is to provide sanctions against law–breaking, not all sanctions consist of violent threats, and not all threats or exercises of violence by the State are sanctions.

Obviously, the frequency of the actual exercise of violence or of explicit acts of threatening is not a good measure of the motivational importance of violence in a system. There may be almost no overtly violent acts or even threats if the population has "learned its lesson" so well that it never tries to challenge the State – and nevertheless the threat may be the only motive for obeying. Typically, our pre–theoretical picture of modern society is different. The modern constitutional system is not a tyranny. The motivational role of sanctions and other coercive measures seems to be only a limited one. The higher legal organs do generally respect the constitution, the officials execute the decisions of their superiors, and the ordinary citizens, more often than not, follow the law even when there is no policeman around. The fact that in some, but not in all, cases of disobedience there is some non–negligible probability of punishment does not usually play an important role in our practical reasoning. At the same time, we may still feel that if this conditional probability of suffering a punishment were removed, it would change our society in an essential way. It would not mean a sudden collapse of the society in the short run. Nevertheless, we tend to think that in the long run a modern, complex society is possible only inside the State's coercive framework. Hart's phrase, "voluntary cooperation in a coercive framework" seems to catch something essential. It is no accident, for example, that newly independent nations usually rush to establish at least a token army.

Sometimes violence is said to be the last remedy of the State; it is there but only 'ultimately' or 'in the last instance'. The intuitions we want to incorporate into a plausible explanation of the role of force and sanctions in a modern society are then the following:

(1) The enforcement monopoly claimed by the State seems to be necessary for the continual existence of a social order.
(2) It is also necessary for at least the most fundamental norms regulating the State organization to be respected for reasons other than fear of sanctions.
(3) In general, the direct motivational role of sanctions is less important in explaining general obedience to the law.

There are three main positions concerning the role of violence in societies. I will characterize them as the zero–sum, the consensualist and the Prisoners' Dilemma positions.

9.2. The Zero–Sum Position

The zero–sum or coercive view claims that society is necessarily maintained by coercion: threat is the main motive for all obedience. This position is held (in various degrees) by some anarchists and Marxists who emphasize the role of the State as the instrument of violence of the ruling classes. It is also held by some thinkers of an elitist persuasion, and perhaps by such right–wing philosophers as Carl Schmitt or Julian Freund, who claim that the latent possibility of violent conflict is behind all politics.

Here is a representative example of this position, from a thinker who is neither a revolutionary radical nor an authoritarian conservative:

> Society *means* that norms regulate human conduct; this regulation is guaranteed by the incentive or threat of sanctions; the possibility of imposing sanctions is the abstract core of all politics. (...) In the last analysis, established norms are nothing but ruling norms; i.e. norms defended by the sanctioning agencies of society and those who control them. (Dahrendorf 1970, 173–4)

In Dahrendorf's argument, the existence of society presupposes norms, the norms presuppose sanctions and the sanctions necessitate the existence of a specific group determining and applying these sanctions; this is, according to him, "the origin of human inequality" (cf. Ullmann–Margalit 1977, 134–8). A zero–sum theorist must suppose that there are latent conflicts of extreme intensity in every society, and nothing – short of the most extreme of all threats, the threat of physical harm – can hold this conflict in check. Either there is the great conflict between the ruling and the ruled classes (Marxists, anarchists, elitists), or there is, due to the wickedness of human nature, the continual possibility that individual passions will run rampant and destroy society. The latter seems to be the idea in Olivecrona's comment:

> This organized force is actually the backbone of our community as it stands. We cannot conceive a community – at least under modern conditions – which is not based on organized force. (...) The hidden reserves of hate, of lust for revenge, and of boundless egoism would break through in a destructive way if not held in check by the presence of force, immeasurably superior to that of any single individual or any private combination. (Olivecrona 1939, 136)

The claim that the organized force of the State is a causally necessary condition for the existence of a society does not, however, imply that the zero–sum view of society is correct. Organized removal of waste is a causally necessary condition, too. But we cannot plausibly say that "ultimately" it is just these cleansing–operations which keep societies together. As we shall see, threats of violent or other sanctions *may* be a necessary condition for general obedience without being an important motive for obedience. It is possible that people would not obey without sanctions, though at the same time their main motive is not the fear of sanctions.

The coercive position seems in part inconsistent with our everyday observations. People often obey without fear. Olivecrona tries to explain this in psychoanalytic terms: the fear motive is there, but we are usually able to hide it in the subconscious. But there is still a problem, visible in Dahrendorf's inference presented above. Even the agencies enforcing the norms are themselves governed by norms. If the existence of social norms implies the existence of sanctions and specific agents applying the sanctions, there is a regress. In modern societies, however, the power of the state agencies is ultimately limited by constitutional norms and conventions, which are not guaranteed by further sanctions. At least at that level, other motives must be operative. A coercivist may, like Austin, classify these norms just as rules of "positive morality", but even then they are effective morality. Thus it cannot be true that the mere existence of norms implies enforcement. This problem is equally present in some Marxist analyses. If individual members of a ruling class are motivated by their own egoistic interests, how can the State as the representative of their collective interests ever emerge?

So it seems that a zero–sum theorist must admit that there are other motives for obedience which are important, at least among the ruling subpopulation of any society. As Alf Ross remarks:

> Ultimately there must be norms for the exercise of force which are not themselves upheld by force but are followed in fearless allegiance. (Ross 1958, 57)

9.3. The Consensualist Position

A consensualist starts from the observation that there must be a lot of non–forced obedience in any society at least under normal conditions. Actually, Olivecrona's description of the State power as "immeasurably superior" (in respect of the ability to use force) to any "private combination" is normally incorrect. The combined force of the majority of citizens would usually overwhelm the power of the police or armed forces. The State would generally be helpless even against the determined resistance or disobedience of a sufficiently large minority.

Thus a consensualist supposes that there must be a fundamental consensus in any society on at least those basic values on which the most basic norms are based. The possibility of using force presupposes obedience and acceptance, rather than the other way round:

> The obedience rests on a common will. Force is necessary to prevent violations, but force is possible only because there is a fundamental agreement. Enforcement is the exception, agreement the rule. (MacIver 1947, 230)

What is important in this position is that the supposed consensus is a consensus on *values*: societies are not seen only as mutually beneficial arrangements between self–interested agents. As Talcott Parsons, one of the most important proponents of this view, comments

> A relatively established 'politically organized community' is clearly 'a moral community' to some degree, its members sharing common norms, values and culture – which is to say that I start with a view that repudiates the idea that any political system that rests *entirely* on self–interest, force, or a combination of them, can be stable over a considerable period of time. (Parsons 1967, 265)

The claim put forth by Parsons looks like an empirical proposition. However, on closer analysis, it may turn out to be tautology. If the members of some community refrain from harming each other over "a considerable period of time" (how long is that?), should we conclude that there must be a consensus on some values? Would a consensus on the value of co–existence itself be enough? If we make inferences about people's values by studying their behaviour (as we do), the absence of conflict seems itself to be evidence for the existence of a value consensus.

What would be an empirical measure for the degree of value consensus (for obviously it is a matter of degree)? A measure of the relative *similarity* of values won't do. For many wars and civil strifes have been fought between religious or dynastic factions having essentially similar values. There are obvious reasons why similarity of values cannot be a sufficient condition for the existence of a stable community. Firstly, some shared values can themselves prescribe a violent solution for disputes (e.g. a feudal–warrior morality). Secondly, peoples' actions are not determined only by values (or, more generally, by ends) but also by factual beliefs. These beliefs include beliefs about the values and beliefs of other people. Group A may share some values with B without knowing it, or A may believe that B has some beliefs which make it act against A's values. The existence of common values does not imply that those sharing the values are able to coordinate their actions in order to realize them.

9.4. The Prisoners' Dilemma Position

There is a persistent theme in the classical theories of the Social Contract: Although a political system is necessarily coercive by its nature, it is generally rational to accept it. The Social Contract is described as a self–limiting act, by which people unanimously and voluntarily confer the right to use force on a political organization.

Thomas Hobbes' familiar story about the contract arising from a state of nature is a good example of a theory of this kind. According to Hobbes, people are mainly self–interested. They have interests in scarce resources (derivable from their dominant interest in self–preservation which is the essential precondition of satisfaction of any other interests), and these interests are often in conflict. Conflicts of interests can lead to fighting, and because all humans are equally vulnerable, no one can be sure of his own victory. Knowing this, people are likely to try to defend themselves by pre–emptive attacks. This creates mutual insecurity and reinforces the motive to attack, and the life in the state of nature remains solitary, poor, nasty, brutish and short. Thus the individuals living in this miserable state have a common interest to create peace. But because of the ever–present possibility of conflicts, peace is possible only if there is an external agency, the mighty Leviathan, which can guarantee peace by using its superior force. When Leviathan has been created, people are at its mercy: it is not and cannot be controlled by anything.

The traditional interpretation of the story made Hobbes a zero–sum theorist without qualification: it was simply supposed that the Hobbesian men were evil by nature. The problem of the traditional interpretation was that it made the emergence of the Leviathan completely inexplicable. If humans were wicked through and through, how could they ever reach an agreement on anything?

The development of game theory has lead to a new interpretation. The original story seems to have many characteristics typical of the

Prisoners' Dilemma game. A PD–structure seems to explain how an arrangement, like the Leviathan, can be mutually beneficial and yet is maintainable only by the threat of sanctions. As individuals in Hobbes' state of nature, players in a PD–game are caught in a trap made by themselves. They could improve their position by respecting a mutually agreed rule of conduct, but they could not be expected to do so without the intervention of an external force. This interpretation of Hobbes has recently became a commonplace. However, I have my doubts; a third possible reading is presented in chapter 9.5.

The subject of this chapter is the basic idea – Hobbesian or not – that the PD–structure explains the role of organized force in societies. Some classical theories of social contract certainly suggest this reading. Consider, for example, the theory of Cesare Beccaria:

> Laws are the conditions by which independent and isolated men, tired of living in a constant state of war and of enjoying freedom made useless by uncertainty of keeping it, unite in society. They sacrifice a portion of this liberty in order to enjoy the remainder in security and tranquillity. The sum of all these portions of liberty sacrificed for the good of everyone constitutes the sovereignty of a nation, and the sovereign is the legitimate depository and administrator. The mere formation of this deposit, however, was not sufficient; it had to be defended against the private usurpations of each particular individual, for everyone always seeks to withdraw not only his own share of liberty from the common store, but to expropriate the portions of other men besides. Tangible motives were required sufficient to dissuade the despotic spirit of each man from plunging the laws of society back into original chaos. These tangible motives are the punishments established for lawbreakers. (Cesare Beccaria 1986, 7)

Thus, the PD–view can be more aptly called the Beccarian view of society. This view appears in its most developed form in the several books written by James Buchanan (Buchanan 1975; Buchanan 1986; Buchanan and Brennan 1985).

According to Buchanan, the existence of a society where rules of conduct are generally respected is a pure public good in the economic sense of the term (on public goods, cf. ch. 3.). The problem of optimal production of a public good is usually modelled as a PD–situation.

In their book, Buchanan and Brennan (1985, ch 3) start their argument from a basic premise:

(1) Individuals can adequately be described as rational self–interested

agents (in the public as well as the private or economic spheres of life).

What is important here is the supposition of methodological symmetry: individuals following social norms or acting in public roles are simply *homines economici*, and there is no reason to suppose that their behaviour is more other–regarding than at the market–place.

As in the original Hobbesian setting, scarcity is a reason for conflicts. When interests conflict, "each would find it advantageous to invest effort, 'a bad' in order to secure the goods" (Buchanan 1975, 24). In the condition of scarcity, this leads into a sub–optimal "arms–race" between individuals trying to defend their possessions and to exploit the others. Therefore:

(2) The interest conflicts in the condition of scarcity are usually PD's.

(3) PD's can be solved only by establishing fixed rules which define the rights of individuals to scarce goods. (Buchanan 1975, ch. 4)

Because individuals are self–interested, they cannot be expected to comply voluntarily with the rules in a PD–situation. An additional motive is needed:

(4) The mutual compliance of rules can be created only by using sanctions against non–compliance.

Sanctions are, by definition, consequences which are likely to reduce the utility of acts of non–compliance (Buchanan 1975, 67). However, a working system of sanctions *is itself a public good*, and consequently, a new PD arises. The purpose of sanctions in the original PD is to create a general deterrence against violations of rules: that is in the interests of all. At the same time each individual has an interest in avoiding the costs of law–enforcement (Buchanan 1975, ch. 8). This may be called a second–order PD. The possibility of second–order PD's makes decentralized sanction systems unreliable. An example of this (not discussed by Buchanan) is the general inefficiency of international sanction policy adopted by the UN , or by the League of Nations before it. For example, in an interview in *The Economist* (9. 7. 1986), Prime Minister Thatcher justified her own reluctance to apply economic sanctions prescribed by the UN against South Africa by the claim that "economic sanctions never work". Given the charitable interpretation that she really would have preferred change in South Africa, her comment was a typical self–fulfilling prediction in a second–order PD. Sanctions can work only if they are generally applied; but if everybody believes that they will not be generally applied, that becomes a reason not to apply them.

If the second–order PD is as serious as the corresponding first–order problem, the Leviathan becomes necessary. (There is, however, a problem in the explanatory use of PD's. How is the PD–structure supposed to explain both the fact that there are sanctions at the municipal level and the fact that they are absent at the international level? If sanctions are functional, why are they sometimes there and sometimes not there? This is also a problem in Hobbes' original theory, first noticed by de Maistre.)

(5) There should be an external agent which enforces the rules of cooperation.

Now comes the point at which Buchanan and Hobbes part. For Buchanan notices that the Leviathan, when vested with absolute power, has no motive for respecting any pre–established rules. Because of (1), the Leviathan must be a self–interested agent. Hence it is likely to enforce those and only those rules of cooperation which work for its own interests. This is the same problem which caused troubles for zero–sum theorists. According to Buchanan, an ideal law–enforcing agency should act in a purely mechanical way:

> Ideally some wholly impersonal mechanism, a robot that could do nothing but follow automatized instructions, might be selected. Failing this, resort to third party adjudication produces a 'government' of the ideal type in practicality. (Buchanan 1975, 95)

The best possible approximation of this ideal of mechanical enforcement is an external agency which is strictly constrained by second–order or constitutional rules:

> Individuals may be willing to turn over the enforcement task to an external agent, but with the proviso that this agent will carry out the enforcement task only to the limits preferred by the participants. (Buchanan 1975, 132)

Therefore:

(6) There should be rules constraining the actions of the enforcement agency.

There are two problems in this PD–theory of law and State. The first problem is related to the creation of the enforcement agency, the Leviathan. The creation of the Leviathan is itself a collective action which is dependent on individual efforts. Given the self–interest postulate (1), every individual sees the situation only from the point of his own self–interest. If the Leviathan is likely to emerge in any case, an individual has no incentive to contribute to its formation. If it is not likely to emerge, he again has no reason to contribute, for it is unlikely that his contribution would be the decisive one. The formation of the enforcing agency is itself a PD–situation, and because it is the first collective action, no further enforcer can be called in to the rescue (see Braybrooke 1976).

But suppose that individuals somehow succeed in creating the enforcement agency. Because of (4), the agency is likely to ignore any rule intended to constrain its activities if the rules are not enforced by sanctions. But that would lead into an infinite regress making "a new Soveraign; and again for the same reason a third, to punish the second; and so continually without end" (Hobbes). The only remaining possibility is that the individuals themselves act as guardians of their own rights, and, if necessary, start resisting an enforcement agency which transgresses its constitutional limits. This would create a deterrence against abuses of power by the Leviathan. But organized resistance against abuses of power is itself a collective action and creates a new PD. Every citizen would benefit if the power of the Leviathan were constrained, but every individual is also under a temptation to become a free rider and to let the others do the (possibly dangerous) job. And certainly the Leviathan itself has no interest in helping individuals overcome *this* problem.

Buchanan and Brennan notice this problem when they recommend their "constitutional reform" (which, for them, means that the State activities should be constrained by the prescriptions of free market ideology):

> To hold out hope for reform in the basic rules describing the sociopolitical

> game, we must introduce elements that violate the self-interest postulate. (Buchanan and Brennan 1985, 146)

This is a surprising concession. After criticizing and even ridiculing political theories which build on the belief that individuals in their public roles act in "the general interest" rather than in their own narrow interests, after making "methodological symmetry" of economic and political action as their basic postulate, the authors actually reject (1) and put their hope on the constitutional reformers' ability to act in the common interest. But this concession is not enough. Continual *adherence* to a reformed constitution presupposes that the non-selfish motives must be continually operative. The reform seems to be pointless if the Leviathan cannot be made to follow the reformed constitution. Buchanan and Brennan, as many other free-market theorists, believe that the modern welfare-state has opened the way for a completely controlled society. Unlike some of their fellow libertarians, they do not blame collectivistic ideologies for this. The force behind this development is self-interest which propels the continual growth in the power of governments and bureaucracies. But if this is true, their recommendation for a more limited State cannot be offered as a *remedy* for the problem. If there are no countervailing powers for political self-interest, it is impossible to halt the process at any preferred level. The Leviathan will break or erode the reformed constitution.

On the other hand, if there are non-selfish motives which can constrain the Leviathan, there is no a priori reason why it cannot be constrained at any desired level. If a constitutional minimal State can be made stable, why not a constitutional redistributive or productive State? Or, alternatively, why aren't the balancing non-selfish motives which make the constitutional reform possible operative already in the state of nature? Then there would be no need for the Leviathan at all.

Buchanan claims that anarchy is sub-optimal, but the State, when established, has an in-built tendency to extend its power. This is in accordance with Hobbes' original theory, but it seems that Hobbes was more consistent. For him, the choice was between the state of nature and absolute power.

It is worth noticing that a similar problem also haunts other theories of the minimal State. For example, Robert Nozick describes the most extensive morally justified political organization as an enforcement agency with a local monopoly. The only justified task of this agency is to enforce the pre-existing natural rights of its "customers", the people living under its jurisdiction. Nozick, however, does not provide a reason why an organization with a local monopoly of force would limit its activities only to this task. The argument cannot be that all individuals necessarily respect natural rights; the enforcement agency was established as a guardian of these rights. Moreover, it is not clear that the agency has a duty to limit its activities at that level. The agencies compete with each other, but because they possess (justly) a monopoly of enforcement "services" over their territories, the "customers'" only choice is either to stay under the jurisdiction of an agency or move out into the jurisdiction of another agency. Now it is the cost of "exiting", of moving out (or perhaps of changing the system or establishing a new) which determines the "price" demanded by the agencies from their "customers" ("price" is not a monetary price but the total amount of the extra burdens on a "customer"). Economically rational enforcement agencies will set a monopoly price which is slightly lower for their "customers" than the total costs of moving out.

There is no reason why this monopoly profit demanded by the enforcement agencies should be unjust in Nozickian terms. For monopoly profit as such does not constitute an injustice. It is unjust only if the "customers" fall under the "Lockean proviso" – they are, in respect of rights violations, worse off than in the state of nature. The burdens set by an agency should be compared with the right violations appearing in the state of nature. This logic seems to be inescapable, for enforcement of rights is, for Nozick, just one commodity provided by private entrepreneurs, and there is no reason why they would not have a motivation or right to utilize their monopoly position, as in the case imagined by Nozick, of the man who has invented a drug vital for human life.

Hobbes' story in the *Leviathan* can therefore be seen as a limiting case of Nozick's theory. There, the state of nature is so deplorable that rational individuals are willing to pay for the enforcement agency any monopoly price it asks (short of their lives) in order to get protection.

9.5. Conventionalism and force

The basic problem of the PD–approach to law and State is that, in spite of the mixed–motive nature of the game, there is no motivational element for players to follow cooperative rules. A PD–game is a "dilemma" precisely because if (i) players are rational in the narrow sense, (ii) their preferences form a PD–structure the players necessarily end in non–cooperation. The game can be transformed by punishing non–cooperation, but, in spite of the mutual beneficiality of such an arrangement, the punishment is still the only motive for cooperating. A zero–sum game could be transformed in a similar way; in both cases the induced pattern of behaviour would collapse at the moment the threat of sanctions is removed.

Thus, the PD–approach is unable to explain Ross' observation that at least some norms must be "followed in fearless allegiance", or Hart's claim that "what reason demands is *voluntary* cooperation in a *coercive* system" (CL, 193). The PD–approach shows why collective reason demands cooperation and it also shows why coercion is nevertheless needed to produce this cooperation. But it cannot show how cooperation can nevertheless be voluntary.

My main idea, that conventions have an important role in legal systems, seems to offer a solution. Conventionalism supposes that at least in respect of some important legal duties, the underlying configuration of preferences and interests is more adequately described as a coordination game. Most importantly, legal institutions, when trying to establish a coherent interpretation of legal norms, and the main political actors, when following the constitution, are typically in coordination situations. The ultimate norms of the system are respected because the relevant actors share a common interest in finding some stable solution which is not too ineffective and is compatible with their values. The existing practices satisfy these requirements at least to some degree and they constitute a salient solution simply because they happen to be there already. The supposed coordination is then based on a consensus, but it is a consensus on the instrumental value of certain procedures rather than on substantial moral values.

According to this view, many norms are followed because they are mutually beneficial. But if this is true, the role of sanctions and the State as the enforcer of norms remains unexplained. This problem is illustrated by the exchange of arguments between Chaim Gans and

Edna Ullmann–Margalit in the Israel Law Review (1983). Gans defends the coordination approach. His presentation of the position is worthy of a lengthy quotation:

> It is necessary that (at least to some extent) these instructions are obeyed and expected to be obeyed. Given some facts about human nature, i.e. that 'all are tempted at times to prefer their own immediate interests' and that many are ready to use force to advance these interests, and given that these facts are known to almost everyone, the mutual expectations that instructions of the co–ordinator are being obeyed, if many of these are incompatible with people's immediate interests, will be very weak indeed. We must distinguish here between two points. First, on the whole, if a given co–ordinator is not known to be the most forceful and there are others who are known to use their force, the salience and/or efficiency of that suggested co–ordinator will be in jeopardy. The monopolization of force by law is thus vital for its co–ordinative functioning, functioning which makes the acts specified by the law dutiful. Second, and in particular, if artificial motivation is not created so that preferring one's own immediate interests in breaking the law is in high danger of ending against one's own interests, then again the mutual expectations that others obey the law is in jeopardy. Since people's expectations with regard to their fellows' behaviour are guided by what they know about their fellows, and since it is common knowledge that all are tempted at times to prefer their own interests, the expectations that they will obey the co–ordinators' instructions are weak. Sanctions are therefore required not only as 'the normal motive of obedience', nor only 'as a guarantee that those who would voluntarily obey shall not be sacrified to those who would not', but also as an incentive for expectations that the law will be obeyed, an incentive necessary for the law's functioning as a co–ordinator. (Gans 1983, 345)

The coordinative notion of law is in accordance with the general picture of institutions drawn earlier in this work. Although law certainly performs many other functions, one of its main functions is to coordinate activities, as Gans says. The role of sanctions in law, however, is unclear in this picture. Gans makes an interesting attempt to show how sanctions can further general obedience even if they do not provide the major motive for obedience. People's behaviour in interaction situations is partly dependent on their expectations of the behaviour of *others*. The existence of sanctions reinforces expectations that the others will follow the rules, for even if they were occasionally tempted to do otherwise, they have to weigh the gains of law–breaking against the displeasures of punishment.

However, Edna Ullman–Margalit is right when remarking that if the underlying interaction situation is a coordination game, as Gans supposes, there cannot be any real temptation to follow 'one's own interests' rather than obey the instructions of a coordinator. The only problem with which the players are faced in a coordination game is the coordinated choice between alternative equilibria. When one alternative is chosen and its special status has became a mutual belief, there is no need to enforce the rule which defines its specific status by sanctions. According to Ullman–Margalit, the situation described by Gans in the passage cited must be a PD–situation:

> In situations of this type the arrival of the State, which constitutes a solution, does require something like coordination among the people involved, but this solution is far from equilibrial, let alone a co–ordination equlibrium. Indeed, this state may well be jeopardized along the lines described by Gans, and hence may well stand in the need of being fortified by force and sanctions.
>
> So it seems as if there is a prima facie case for analyzing the legal system – any legal system – in terms of a solution to a generalized Prisoners' Dilemma type problem rather than as producing states of co–ordination equilibria (Ullman–Margalit 1983, 354)

But we cannot plausibly interpret the situation described by Gans as an instance of PD. For Gans, the belief that the others will obey the law in their turn is a reason for an individual agent obeying. In a PD, however, such a belief is a reason for *not* obeying. If the situation actually is a PD, sanctions cannot have the indirect role reserved for them in Gans' description. In spite of the fact that there is a cooperative aspect both in coordination games and in PD–games, in the conditions of complete information the ruling motive in the games of the latter type is to cheat. It can be overridden only by introducing a new motive which transforms the game. As we have already seen, the paradoxical aspect of PD's is just that the Pareto–optimal nature of the outcome following from mutual cooperation is not motivationally sufficient. Even if it were rational to obey voluntarily, people will not do so.

So an unspecified reference to the law's coordinative nature leaves the role of punishment and force in general open. The dilemma is this: either the situation is a coordinative one and there is no reason for punishments, or it is a PD and punishments provide the only operative motive for compliance. In the discussion between Gans and

Ullman–Margalit, only one variable of the game is focused on: the preferences of the players. Two other variables, namely the rationality of the players and their epistemic situation (their beliefs concerning beliefs, preferences, or rationality) are left out of consideration. Now, it wouldn't be of much help to change the game by supposing that the players in the game fail to cooperate without sanctions because they are irrational. For if that were true, would the introduction of sanctions improve the situation? People who are irrational, in the sense that they act against their preferences, will be likely to break the rules in spite of the sanctions.

A more promising line might be to consider different kinds of epistemic situations (cf. ch.2). If a game is played under the conditions of perfect information, everybody knows everybody's preferences, everybody knows that everybody knows everybody's preferences, etc. The only source of uncertainty in a game can be that the preferences of the players do not determine a single solution, and a coordinator is therefore needed. Some of the basic intuitions of Gans can perhaps be divined by relaxing the postulate of perfect information. Surprisingly, Hobbes made this move when he tried, in the preface to *De Cive*, to defend himself against the accusation that he had painted a picture of human nature in too dark colours:

> But this, that men are evill by nature, followes not from this principle; for though the wicked were fewer than the righteous, yet because we cannot distinguish them, there is a necessity of suspecting, heeding, anticipating, subjugating, self–defending, ever incident to the most honest, and fairest condition'd...

The standard PD–interpretation of Hobbes' state of nature has no room for this uncertainty. There is no uncertainty in a pure PD–situation: everybody will play non–cooperatively, and everybody knows that. In recurrent PD's, the players can learn to "keep the Covenants" if they do not expect only a limited numbers of games, and if they do not discount future gains too heavily. But then again the Leviathan with its sword becomes superfluous.

A "righteous" person – let's call her Ms. X – in Hobbes' description is one who prefers to follow rules and keep the peace on condition that the others will do that, too. She has no independent motive to play non–cooperatively. X wants to follow the rules of mutual respect for moral reasons, or due to her altruism, or perhaps just because she sees this as a reasonable thing to do. But she does not want to be a sucker. Since ending up as the only cooperator would mean considerable losses, she is willing to cooperate if and only if there are sufficient guarantees that the others will be willing to cooperate too. X's preference ordering is the following:

(a) mutual cooperation
(b) unilateral non–cooperation from X's side
(c) mutual non–cooperation
(d) unilateral cooperation from X's side.

A "wicked" person, Y, may be one of those who "seeks vainglory". He may have an inherent need to break the rules, or he may have acted out of his personal or group interests. His ordering can be, for example, that of a player in a PD–situation:

(a) unilateral non–cooperation from Y's side
(b) mutual cooperation
(c) mutual non–cooperation
(d) unilateral cooperation from Y's side.

Now suppose that the players are not in a state of perfect information in respect of each others' preferences. Especially suppose that righteous X believes she is playing against a wicked opponent, or she believes that she is playing against a righteous opponent who believes that she is a wicked, or... Suppose that X does not have the means of checking Y's beliefs. Under these conditions, X plays safe and will not cooperate. In a general case, under conditions of imperfect information the players are likely to coordinate less often than under perfect information. This might be true *even when there are actually no wicked players in the game*. Uncertainty, or the lack of a mutual belief is enough.

Now when sanctions are introduced, this uncertainty diminishes. The righteous player knows now that if her opposite numbers are not willing to follow the rules of cooperation voluntarily, they will do so because they are afraid of sanctions. The intuitions of Gans about the State as law–enforcer are preserved. The situation is basically a cooperative one – an Assurance Game. Sanctions are necessary in order to create cooperation, but mainly as "an incentive for expectations that the law will be obeyed" rather than as "the normal motive of obedience". What we get is, ideally, "voluntary cooperation in a coercive system".

This model catches the "dilemma of mankind" as described in Hobbes' *De Cive*. In chapters I.4. and III.27. Hobbes explicitly denies that all individuals are similarly motivated in the state of nature. For some "the will to hurt ariseth from Vain Glory", for "the other, from the necessity of defending himselfe". However, their *overt* behaviour is similar, for observing the laws of reason would "procure... a more certain quick destruction, and the keepers of the Law become a meer prey to the breakers of it". There are, then, two types of possible preference orderings in the state of nature. What they are?

Firstly, no one "esteems a war of all against all" (DC I.13.). Mutual non–cooperation is therefore worse than mutual cooperation in everybody's preferences.

Secondly, everyone is afraid of death and wants his or her own good. Thus, unilateral cooperation of one's own is the worst alternative for every individual. For the same reason, unilateral noncooperation is always better than mutual noncooperation.

The remaining question is, that of how the individuals evaluate mutual cooperation as compared with unilateral non–cooperation of their own? If, as Hobbes admits, there may differences in the motivations of individuals they must be found here. Those motivated by "Vain glory" prefer their own unilateral non–cooperation; they are PD–players. Those who want to follow the laws of reason are AG–players. But because they cannot recognize other AG–players, there is no behavioural difference between the types. Individuals belonging to either type do not cooperate in the state of nature and do cooperate in the commonwealth, although for different reasons. If we want to explicate Hobbes' problem in game theoretical terms, this is, I think, the only possible model compatible with the description of the problem in *De Cive*. (The version which appears in the *Leviathan* may be a different story.)

Several interesting consequences can be derived from this model. The difficulties of coordination are heavily dependent on the nature of the situation. In large, anonymous groups with a heterogeneous and changing population there is usually more uncertainty, and coordination consequently tends to be more difficult. Very small amount of original uncertainty can have an epidemic effect in such a group. A small bunch of terrorists or a lonely murderer can create panic in a law–abiding community. This is the most effective weapon of modern terrorism: its limited ability to use actual violence (as compared with the resources available for the modern states) is compensated for by its ability to spread uncertainty in societies.

If an enforcement agency in a society is generally known to be ineffective or non–existent, uncertainty and the resulting general non–coordination may reinforce itself. The international security dilemma can be interpreted from this perspective. Nations participating in the international arms–race do not *necessarily* have hostile intentions. They do not necessarily – as in a PD or a zero–sum –game – see "victory" or hegemony as their most preferred end. Their problem is that they have no means of either convincing themselves that the others are not playing a PD or a zero–sum –game, or proving to the others their own intentions. Their individual moves in the game are often susceptible of different interpretations. For example, a purely defensive weapon system can be interpreted as an attempt to protect a country against a second strike inflicted by its victim in an offensive war. Similarly, carrying fire arms for protection or establishing a private militia for protecting a political or ethnic group can be interpreted as offensive moves. A violent conflict in which both sides are motivated only by self–defence is possible. Such a conflict has an AG–structure: the best possible outcome for both parties is peaceful co–existence, not domination. What is lacking is mutual belief in this. It is interesting that some new studies in International Politics stress the roles of uncertainty and misperception at the expense of the traditional motives of domination and power struggle.

All this is in accordance with my conventionalist view. If sanctions or force were the main motive for rule–following, the rules themselves would not need to be conventional. We have a rational reason to act according to this motive even if we do not believe that rules are generally followed. In my model, superior force is needed to create the mutual belief which is necessary for the maintenance of a cooperative pattern of actions. It is then a causal condition for the existence of certain rules. Thus, the theory also explains the intuitions we have about the role of force in modern societies.

This explains why there can be legal rules (constitutional rules, etc.) which are effective without being enforced by sanctions. The sub–population of officials following these constitutional rules is smaller, and many of its acts are public. An official decision–maker playing the game of the wicked in respect of the rules cannot easily conceal his activities and avoid criticism. For this reason, publicity and openness are essential components of constitutionalism.

Because of the limited motivational role of law–enforcement, the presence of enforcement agencies is less dominating in society than it could be. No police force is able, in the long run, to control a society in which (i) people do not want to obey voluntarily, (ii) are able to coordinate their actions, and (iii) believe that the police are not able to control them. In my model, the needed amount of force potential is that which is sufficient to assure the law–abiding majority that the rules are generally followed. It is likely to be smaller than the amount needed to work as a deterrent against everybody's willingness to break rules.

This last point can serve as a basis for an interesting analogy. In chapter 2. I tried to link monetary institutions with AG's. The State – or its monetary institutions – tries to maintain cooperation in the money game by committing itself to a stabilizing policy. Thus a central bank works as a supreme enforcing agency: by creating a mutual belief that it is ready to accept certain objects at a determined value it maintains the general belief that these objects are valuable and can be trusted.

A central bank, however, is not able to cover all the paper notes in circulation. Its functioning is based on the belief that only a limited number of claims is made at a time. Similarly, the State as the enforcer of rules is committed to following the policy of applying sanctions consistently against violators – but people know that its resources are limited. The State is bound to uphold the belief in its own ability to maintain continual adherence to the rules by applying sanctions against violations, and therefore it also has an incentive not to "inflate" the requirements it imposes on its citizens. Knowing this, the citizens may be more willing to obey. A purely coercive regime – discussed in ch. 4.2. – is like a State that prints money unrestrictedly. In both cases, a loss of credibility is bound to appear.

This analogy between banking and law enforcement is developed in the sociological essays of Talcott Parsons (1967, chapters 9 and 10) and in a work by Karl W. Deutsch (1966). Deutsch's presentation of the analogy is especially illuminating:

> Governments, like banks, base their operation on the fact that the popular expectations favorable to them – that one ought to leave one's money in the bank and that one ought to obey the law and the police – are highly coordinated, so that most individuals most of the time can count on everybody else to do as they do; while opposite expectations – that one should withdraw money, or break the law – are usually quite uncoordinated, so that no individual could count on bringing down a bank or a government by starting a concerted run on the first or concerted revolution against the second. (Deutsch 1966, 121)

This analogy is made more precise if we suppose that the underlying game is a similar one: an Assurance Game with imperfect information. While I rejected Parsons' consensual solution to Hobbes' problem. I can nevertheless accept his (and Deutsch's) view of the role of sanctions. Some critics of Parsons (e.g. Barnes 1989, 19) have complained that the money analogy is unilluminative because our understanding of the role of money in social systems is no better than our understanding of power. If my analysis of money in ch. 3. is correct, the analogy has a more firm basis. In his strongly critical article on the money – power analogy, David Baldwin (1971) nevertheless admits that it performs a valuable service by "calling our attention to the importance of expectations and the linkages between them and the political process" (p. 608). My explication is intended to highlight just that linkage.

The model is less vulnerable to the criticism of the PD–model of the State. Because conflicts are supposed to arise from a lack of mutual beliefs of a certain type, rather than from the lack of motivation, it is more plausible to suppose that the external enforcing agency could be constrained by rules which are not themselves enforced by formal sanctions. Assuming Buchanan's postulate of methodological symmetry, an enforcement agency is, prima facie, likely to be motivated in the same way as other agents in society. But because the model is based on the supposition that most agents are, or at least may be, under suitable conditions, willing to follow the rules, there is no need to revive Buchanan's *bete noire*: the idea that the use of public power, unlike individual action or the actions of interest groups, is generally directed by a "common interest" defined in a non–individualistic way.

In chapter 5. I tried to show why rational agents would, in certain circumstances, commit themselves to obedience on condition that they have good reasons for believing that the commanding authority is generally impartial. In this chapter, we have seen why rational agents could accept a system of authoritative enforcement. But not only are the citizens rational when limiting their own autonomy. Just because of the conditionality of this acceptance, it may be rational for an authority to bind itself by rules of impartiality. Many ideas included into the theories of constitutionalism and the rule of law, such as equality, predictability, publicity, consistency, legality, etc. are instrumentally useful for this.

CHAPTER 10

CONCLUSIONS

Our common world is largely determined by institutions. They define what we are – what our position is in relation to other people. They define the meaning of our actions and of the products of our actions.

Given this, an individualistic programme of social theory seems to be barred by insurmountable obstacles. Methodological individualism tries to explain the workings of institutions by referring to the properties of individuals. But, although "inside" institutions there are just individuals, the socially relevant descriptions of these individuals and of their actions necessarily refer back to the institutions we want to explain.

On other hand, these individuals – we – are agents in the sense that a great part of our behaviour can be correctly understood only by admitting that it emerges from choice and deliberation, not only from the workings of blind social forces and structures. But if we accept agency as a basic and irreducible aspect of the human existence, we are also committed to accepting that individuals do matter.

The theory of conventional facts presented in chapter 1. was an attempt to reconcile these two sides of the human condition. We cannot get rid of the institutional properties of individuals, but we can analyse these as functional aspects of such individual belief– and action–complexes which refer to these properties. Through institutions we, collectively, define what we, distributively, are and what our actions mean.

Conventionalism is an attempt to explain the nature of institutions in individualistic terms – without denying that individual actions and attitudes can often be explained by referring back to these institutions. It does not deny that a correct description of the relevant attitudes and actions may require the use of institutional terms. The circle is not a vicious one in so far as the institutional terms appear only inside the scope of attitudinal or intentional operators. It might be claimed that this form of individualism is too watered down to be counted as a form of methodological individualism proper. Against this claim I have no defence; the reader is free to invent a new label for my theory if he or she feels that necessary.

In chapter 2., this kind of theory was connected with elementary games. In effect, this connects the conventionalist theory with the most influential individualistic theory – the theory of rational choice. However, certain assumptions of the rational choice paradigm are actually inconsistent with the notion of rational agency. To put the argument in a nutshell: any plausible theory of rational agency implies the possibility of a real choice. The most common versions of rational choice theory assume that perfect foreknowledge is possible – and, as I tried to show, perfect foreknowledge excludes real choice. The idea presented (although not fully developed) in this work was that institutions work as a supplement for perfect foreknowledge in coordinative interaction situations. One underlying theme of this work is that uncertainty is a basic and all–pervasive fact of our lives. The most important cause of uncertainty is the necessary unpredictability of human action.

Conventionalism asserts that the existence of the basic building blocks of our social world is partially dependent on our belief that they exist. In a sense, this is a form of subjectivism. This subjectivism is, however, substantially unrelated to the two other forms of subjectivism common in modern philosophical discussion. Firstly, conventionalism neither implies nor is implied by the theory that our knowledge of the world is always a product of the human subject. A conventional fact is "subjective", i.e. dependent on the beliefs of human subjects. But the fact that the relevant subjects have these beliefs is an "objective" fact – in other words, it is as subjective or objective as any fact about our external world. If all facts are ultimately "subjective", conventional facts are doubly so.

Secondly, conventionalism does not imply *moral* conventionalism. This point is emphasized in the discussion on "positive" and "critical" morality in chapters 7.2. and 8. The critical test of the conventionality of a fact is whether an agent who knows that a belief in a fact is not generally shared in his community can still meaningfully believe in it. If not, the fact is a conventional fact. Thus I cannot meaningfully believe that something is money without believing that the others in the relevant community share my belief. Obviously our moral beliefs do not have this property. I can meaningfully hold a moral belief while knowing that the others do not share it. In this sense, morality is not conventional.

The difference between law and morality lies here. Legal facts are necessarily grounded on shared beliefs about these facts. I elaborated this idea in chapters 7. and 8. where I try to present a conventionalist reinterpretation of H.L.A. Hart's classical theory. By using the conventionalist machinery, I try to show how the theory can, in this reconstructed form, be defended against some criticisms. I also try to link the theory to some earlier theories on the foundations of legal systems (presented in ch. 6.). The basic idea is that authority, which is one source of social power (ch. 4.), can be conceived in a conventionalist way (ch. 5.). In modern legal systems, legal authority is vested in a special class of officials – this is what I call the political division of labour (ch. 7.4.). Hart's meta–rules (most importantly, the rules of recognition) exist conventionally in the subcommunity of officials. These rules explain how other rules can exist as parts of a legal system, even when they are not accepted or even understood by the entire community. In modern societies, law necessarily has a systemic nature. However, this does not mean that a legal system is a system in the logical sense, nor does it imply that a legal system necessarily has the hierarchical structure presupposed by the earlier theories of law.

All this seems to imply an acceptance of the theory vaguely called "legal positivism", and consequently taking a stance against "natural law" –theories which are commonly considered as the main opponent of positivism. Although I have not argued the point, I think that this opposition is based on a partial misunderstanding. If by "natural law" we simply mean the thesis that there is a necessary connection between descriptive legal judgements and critical moral judgements, I indeed reject it (ch. 8.). But if by "natural law" we mean a wider theory of justice and human good which guides our critical moral judgements on legal practices – and this is how the classical theorists from the Stoics to the nineteenth–century writers used the term – there is no reason why I could not include such a theory in my conventionalist framework.

In the chapters on authority, several conceptions of authority were discussed. Both substantive and formal (or rule–based) conceptions were found inadequate. The alternative, a conventionalist conception, is not a novelty: the classical theories of Hobbes, Hume, Weber, Simon and Hart are but versions of it. One of the advantages of a theory of this kind is that it is able to answer the challenge of the philosophical anarchism that speaks against all conceptions of authority. Fundamentally, the problem of authority is a problem about the justifiability of certain forms of practical reasoning. What is being asked is why the fact that a certain rule or a decision issued by someone claiming authority can ever be relevant in a deliberation which purports to answer the question: what should we do? Although there can be specific justifications for the use of authoritative rules and decisions in particular contexts, the most general rationale behind authorities is that they can sustain coordination among human beings.

After trying to separate law from morality, I also tried to deal with the question of the role of force and sanctions in legal systems (chapter 9.) and to link this to the more general "Hobbesian question": how is a social order possible? I try to sail between the extremities: between the idea that law and the State can be reduced to the use of organized coercion, and the idea that they presuppose a substantial consensus on basic ends and values. As I claimed in chapter 5., political authorities are generally useful because of their coordinative role. Political authority as a source of power should be clearly distinguished from political coercion (ch. 4.2.). But the legal authorities, while having authority, also exercise coercion. Indeed, the systematic use of organized force seems to be a necessary condition for the existence of a legal system. I try to solve this dilemma by using the Assurance Game (introduced in chapter 2.) as a model of interaction. In that game, sanctions can have a role even when they are not needed as a means of deterrence against anybody. The game seems to provide a conceptual solution to a perennial paradox: why do people voluntarily and unanimously put themselves under coercive arrangements.

In the theories which belong to the liberal mainstream, institutions, especially legal institutions, are seen as valuable mainly because they protect individuals against the unjust interventions of other individuals. By establishing a system of mutual constraints they establish a sphere of personal freedom for every individual living under them. This kind of system is needed mainly because there is a permanent scarcity of resources and goods available for individuals. The conventionalist theory developed here differs from this mainstream conception, although the difference may be more a matter of degree. Firstly, conventionalism stresses that institutions are useful not only because they provide mutual protection, but because they enable us to do new things, by coordinating our activities and by making it possible to create new institutional meanings by the means of old ones. Secondly, this kind of coordination is needed even in a world of abundance and/or perfect benevolence, for even there individuals are still agents who make their choices separately, without a pre–established harmony. Consequently, they are always less than perfectly informed, and for this reason their collective actions can always fail.

It may be claimed that the picture painted in chapter 9. on the role of force and sanctions in legal systems is too idyllic. The model supposes well–meaning but suspicious individuals who are brought into cooperation by a neutral and benevolent State. The real picture of the world is grimmer, characterized by conflict and oppression. My answer is that even in such a world there is a lot of voluntary cooperation, and that coercion alone cannot explain the persistence of social institutions.

This work is mainly about the descriptive metaphysics of the social world. However, some normatively relevant points are made at the end of chapters 5. and 9. Like many contract theorists (e.g. Hobbes, Kant or Rawls) I try to establish a link between morality and rationality. My claim is, however, a modest one. I try to show that agents facing recurrent coordination problems can rationally accept an authority which bases its decisions on comprehensiveness, impartiality and relevancy. These principles are also a part of modern constitutional morality: they are exemplified in such moral ideals as the fairness of trials, the impartial hearing of all parties, the neutrality of voting systems, publicity in legislation, etc. The idea is that in the modern conditions (characterized partially by Hart's Minimum Conditions of Natural Law) these ideals are also instrumentally valuable, whatever our ultimate values might be. Thus, I think that a case can be made for modern constitutionalism. It has been reassuring to note that when writing this work, constitutionalist ideals seem to be gaining more and more acceptance in the former socialist countries as well as in the Third World, and the reasons for this acceptance seem to be rational–instrumental as well as moral. Perhaps the constitutional form of political authority does enjoy an evolutionary advantage in the modern world. Finally, I should like to make a wider plea. I do believe that a stronger normative theory of our social obligations, including political obligations, could be developed by using a conventionalist account as a starting point. An important attempt in that direction was recently made by Jeremy Waldron in his article in *Philosophy and*

Public Affairs ('Special Ties and Natural Duties', vol. 22, 1993, pp. 3–30). Partially following Waldron, I suggest that we, as human beings, have positive duties to realize certain general values, for example justice, the well–being of humans and of our natural environment. These values can be founded on our basic nature, although the duties to realize them cannot be derived from natural facts in the strictly logical sense. The realization of these values is necessarily a social matter – some of the most important requirements of critical morality are addressed to us collectively rather than individually. It requires cooperation and coordination between individuals and between groups. Especially in modern conditions, this coordination may require very complex forms. Consequently, there are positive duties to establish and support those institutions which are instrumental in the realization of the most basic values, including some institutions vested with political authority. To develop such a theory might be intellectually more challenging and practically more important than the task of description adopted in this book. It should be able to explain, not only our intuitions concerning the traditional problem of allegiance towards the State, but also the 'political obligations' we might have towards smaller political units and towards the developing international authorities. It should also be able to reconcile these potentially incompatible demands. Thus conventionalism might provide a basis not only for describing the social world we inhabit, but also for criticizing and justifying particular institutions.

BIBLIOGRAPHY

Aarnio, A., (1984) 'On the Validity, Efficacy and Acceptability of Legal Norms', in W. Krawietz, T. Mayer–Maly and O. Weinberger (eds.) *Objektivisierung des Rechtsdenkens. Gedächtnisschrift für Ilmar Tammelo*, Berlin: Duncker & Humblot.

Aristotle (1934) *The Nicomachean Ethics*, tr. E. Rackham, London: Heinemann

Austin, J., (1954) *The Province of Jurisprudence Determined and The Uses of the Study of Jurisprudence*, ed. H.L.A. Hart, London: Weidenfeld and Nicolson, [1832, 1863].

Bach, K., (1975) 'Analytical Social Philosophy – Basic Concepts', *Journal for Theory of Social Behaviour 5.*, 189–214.

Baldwin, D. A., (1971) 'Money and Power', *The Journal of Politics 33.*, 578–614.

Barry, B. (ed.), (1976) *Power and Political Theory*, London: Wiley.

Barnes, B., (1989) *The Nature of Power*, Cambridge: Polity Press.

Beccaria, C., (1986) *On Crimes and Punishments*, tr. D. Young, Indianapolis: Hackett, [1764].

Beetham, D., (1991) *The Legitimation of Power*, Basingstoke: Macmillan.

Bell, R., Edwards, D.V. and Wagner R.H. (eds.), (1969) *Political Power. A Reader in Theory and Research*, New York: Free Press.

Benditt, T., (1978) *Law as Rule and Principle*, Hassocks: Harvester Press.

Bendix, R., (1977) *Max Weber. An Intellectual Portrait*, Berkeley: University of California Press.

Bierstedt, N., (1963) *The Social Order*, New York: McGraw - Hill.

Boardman, W.S., (1987) 'Coordination and the Moral Obligation to Obey the Law', *Ethics 97.*, 546–57.

Bobbio, N., (1965) 'Law and Force', *The Monist 49.*, 321–34.

Bobbio, N., (1971) 'Nouvelles réflexions sur les normes primaires et secondaires', in *La regle de droit*, Travaux du Centre National de Recherches de Logique, Bruxelles.

Braybrooke, D., (1976) 'The Insoluble Problem of the Social Contract', *Dialogue 15.*, 3–37.

de Bruin, G. (1987) 'Economic Theory of Bureaucracy and Public Godd Allocation' in J.E. Lane (ed.) *Bureaucracy and public Choice*. London: SAGE, 33–62

Buchanan, J., (1975) *The Limits of Liberty. Between Anarchy and Leviathan*, Chicago: University of Chicago Press.

Buchanan, J., (1986) *Liberty, Market and the State*, Brighton: Wheatsheaf Books.

Buchanan, J. and Brennan, G., (1985) *The Reason of Rules*, Cambridge: Cambridge University Press.

Clark, H.H. and Carlson, T.B., (1982) 'Speech Acts and Hearer's Beliefs', in N.V. Smith (ed.) *Mutual Knowledge*, London: Academic Press, 1–36.

Dahrendorf, R., (1970) *Essays in the Theory of Society*, London: Routledge & Kegan Paul.

Davis, L.H., (1977) 'Prisoners, Paradox, and Rationality', *American Philosophical Quarterly 14.*, 319–27.

Davis, L.H., (1985) 'Is Symmetry Argument Valid?', in R. Campbell and L. Sowden (eds.) *Paradoxes of Rationality and Cooperation*, Vancouver: University of British Colombia Press.

D'Agostino, F. (1986) *Chomsky's System of Ideas*, Oxford: Clarendon Press.

D'Amato, A., (1984) *Jurisprudence. A Descriptive and Normative Analysis of Law*, Dordrecht: Martinus Nijhoff.

Deutsch, K.W., (1966) *The Nerves of Government*, New York: Free Press.

Dickie, G., (1984) *The Art Circle. A theory of art*, New York: Haven.

Dornbusch, R. and Fisher, S., (1978) *Macroeconomics*, New York: McGraw - Hill.

Downie, R.S., (1971) *Roles and Values*, London: Methuen.

Dworkin, R. (1978) *Taking Rights Seriously*, London: Duckworth.

Durkheim, É., (1927) *Les règles de la méthode sociologique*, Paris: Librairie Félix Alcan, [1895]

Easton, D., (1979) *A Systems Analysis of Political Life*, Chicago: Chicago University Press.

Eckhoff, T. and Sundby, N.K., (1975) 'The Notion of Basic Norm(s) in Jurisprudence', *Scandinavian Studies in Law 19.* 123–51.

Ellis, H.S., (1934) *German Monetary Theory 1905–1933*, Cambridge (Mass.): Harvard University Press.

Filmer, R., (1949) *Patriarcha and Other Political Works*, ed. P. Laslett, Oxford: Blackwell, [1652–80].

Finnis, J., (1980) *Natural Law and Natural Rights*, Oxford: Clarendon Press.

Finnis, J., (1984) 'The Authority of Law in the Predicament of Contemporary Social Theory', *Notre Dame Journal of Law, Ethics and Public Policy 1.*, 115–37.

Flathman, R., (1980) *The Practice of Political Authority*, Chicago: University of Chicago Press.

Flodin, M., (1986) *On Valid Law and Valid Moral Norms*, Dissertation, University of Lund.

Freund, J., (1965) *L'Essence du politique*, Paris: Éditions Sirey.

Galtung, J., (1977) *Methodology and Ideology. Theory and Methods of Social Research. Vol. 1.*, Copenhagen: Christian Ejlers.

Gans, C. (1983) 'The Normativity of Law and its Co-ordinative Function', *Israel Law Review 16.*, 333–49.

Gilbert, M., (1989) 'Rationality and Salience', *Philosophical Studies 57.*, 61–78.

Grafstein, R., (1981) 'The Failure of Weber's Conception of Legitimacy: Its Causes and Implications', *The Journal of Politics 43.* 456–72.

Green, L., (1985) *The Authority of the State*, Oxford: Clarendon Press 1988.

Green, L., (1987) 'The Political Content of Legal Theory', *Philosophy of the Social Sciences 17.*, 1–20.

Grotius, H., (1853) *The Rights of War and Peace*, ed. W. Whewell, Cambridge: Cambridge University Press, [1625].

Guest, S. (1980) 'Revolution and the Position of the Judiciary', *Public Law*, 168–83.

Habermas, J., (1984) *The Theory of Communicative Action. Vol 1: Reason and the Rationalization of Society*, Tr. T. McCarthy, London: Heinemann.

Hacker, P.M.S., (1977) 'Hart's Philosophy of Law', in P.M.S. Hacker and J. Raz (eds.) *Law, Morality and Society. Essays in Honour of H.L.A. Hart*, Oxford: Clarendon Press, 1–25 .

Hart, H.L.A., (1961) *The Concept of Law*, Oxford: Clarendon Press.

Heal, J., (1978) 'Common Knowledge', *Philosophical Quarterly 28.*, 116–131.

Hill, R.E., (1970) 'Legal Validity and Legal Obligation', *The Yale Law Journal 80.*,

Heidegger, M. (1959), *An Introduction to Metaphysics*, tr. R. Manheim, New Haven: Yale University Press.

Hobbes, T., (1972) *Man and Citizen*, ed. B. Gert, New York: Humanities Press, [1642, 1658].

Hobbes, T., (1973) *Leviathan*, London: Dent (Everyman's Library), [1651].

Homans, G., (1950) *The Human Group*, New York: Harcourt, Brace & World.

Hunton, P., (1986) *A Treatise on Monarchy*, in *Divine Right and Democracy*, ed D. Wootton, Harmondsworth: Penguin, [1643].

Hutchinson, T. W., (1977) *Knowledge and Ignorance in Economics*, Oxford: Basil Blackwell.

Ingram, P. (1983) 'Effectiveness', *Archiv für Rechts- und Sozialphilosophie 69.*, 484–504.

James, W. (1979) 'The Will to Believe', in *The Works of William James: The Will to Believe and Other Essays*, Cambridege (Mass.): Harvard University Press.

Jarvie, I. C., (1972) *Concepts and Society*, London: Routledge and Kegan Paul.

Jellinek, G., (1921) *Allegemeine Staatslehre*, Berlin: Julius Springer, [1900].

Kant, I., (1965) *The Metaphysical Elements of Justice*, tr. J. Ladd, Indianapolis: Bobbs-Merrill, [1797].

Kant, I., (1977) *Kant's Political Writings*, ed. H. Reiss, Cambridge: Cambridge University Press.

Kelsen, H., (1911) *Hauptprobleme der Staatsrechtslehre*, Tübingen: J.C.B. Mohr.

Kelsen, H., (1949) *General Theory of Law and State*, tr. A. Wedberg, Cambridge (Mass.): Harvard University Press.

Kelsen, H., (1957) *What is Justice? Collected Essays*, Berkeley.

Kelsen, H., (1970) *The Pure Theory of Law*, Berkeley: University of California Press.

Krabbe, H., (1930) *The Modern Idea of the State*, tr. G. H. Sabine and W. J. Shepard, New York: Appleton.

Kreps, D.M. et al. (1982) 'Rational Cooperation in the Finitely Repeated Prisoners' Dilemma', Journal of Economic Theory 27., 245–52

Lacan, J. (1966) *Ecrits*, Paris: Editions du Seuil.

Ladenson, R., (1980) 'In defense of a Hobbesian Conception of Law', *Philosophy and Public Affairs 9.*, 134–59.

Lagerspetz, E., (1988) 'Reflexive Predictions and Strategic Actions', *Social Science Information 27.*, 307–20.

Leibniz, G.W. (1981) *Political Writings of Leibniz*, tr. and ed. P.Riley, Cambridge: Cambridge University Press

Lewis, D., (1969) *Convention*, Cambridge (Mass.): Harvard University Press.

Locke, J., (1960) *Two Treatises of Civil Government*, London: Dent, [1690].

Lucas, J.R., (1966) *The Principles of Politics*, Oxford: Clarendon Press.

Luhmann, N., (1980) 'Selbstlegitimation des Staates', ARSP Beiheft 15. 65–83.

Lyons, D., (1984) *Ethics and the Rule of Law*, Cambridge: Cambridge University Press.

van Maarseveen, H. and van der Tang, G., (1978) *Written Constitutions*, New York: Oceana.

MacCormick, N., (1973) 'Legal Obligation and the Imperative Fallacy', in A.W.B. Simpson (ed.) *Oxford Essays in Jurisprudence, Second Series*, Oxford: Clarendon Press, 100–130.

MacCormick, N., (1981) *H.L.A. Hart*, London: Edward Arnold.

MacCormick, N., (1987) 'Comment', in R. Gavison (ed.) *Issues in Contemporary Legal Philosophy. The Influence of H.L.A. Hart*, Oxford: Clarendon Press.

MacCormick, N. and Weinberger, O., (1986) *An Institutional Theory of Law*, Dordrecht: Reidel.

MacIver, R., (1947) *The Modern State*, Oxford: Clarendon Press.

McMahon, C., (1987) 'Autonomy and Authority', *Philosophy and Public Affairs 16.*, 303–28.

MacPherson, T., (1970) *Social Philosophy*, London: van Nostrand.

Martin, M., (1987) *The Legal Philosophy of H.L.A. Hart*, Philadelphia: Temple University Press.

Mattick, P. Jr., (1986) *Social Knowledge*, New York: M.E. Sharpe.

Mayo, B., (1986) *The Philosophy of Right and Wrong*, New York: Routledge and Kegan Paul.

Menger, C., (1963) *Problems of Economics and Sociology*, tr. F.J. Nock, Urbana: University of Illinois Press, [1883].

Miller, S., (1991) 'Co–ordination, Salience and Rationality' *The Southern Journal of Philosophy 29.*, 359–370.

Monroe, A.E., (1923) *Monetary Theory before Adam Smith*, Cambridge (Mass.): Harvard University Press.

Morawetz, T., (1980) *The Philosophy of Law*, New York: MacMillan.

Moulakis, A. (ed.), (1986) *Legitimacy/Legitimité*, Berlin: Walter de Gruyter.

Munzer, S., (1972) *Legal Validity*, The Hague: Martinus Nijhoff.

Nelson, W. N., (1980) *On Justifying Democracy*, London: Routldege & Kegan Paul.

Nozick, R., (1974) *Anarchy, State and Utopia*, New York: Basic Books.

Olivecrona, K., (1939) *Law as a Fact. (First edition)*, London: Oxford University Press.

Olivecrona, K., (1957) *The Problem of the Monetary Unit*, New York: MacMillan.

Parfit, D., (1984) *Reasons and Persons*, Oxford: Oxford University Press.

Parker, H., (1965) *Observations upon Some of His Majesties Late answers and Expressions* in W. Haller (ed.), *Tracts on Liberty in the Puritan Revolution*, New York: Otagon Books, [1642].

Parsons, T., (1967) *Sociological Theory and Modern Society*, New York: Free Press.

Peczenik, A., (1983) *The Basis of Legal Justification*, Lund.

Peczenik, A., (1989) *On Law and Reason*, Dordrecht: Kluwer.

Phillips, D.C., (1986) *Toward a Just Social Order*, Princeton: Princeton University Press.

Postema, G.J., (1982) 'Coordination and Convention at the Foundations of Law', *Journal of Legal Studies 11.*, 165–203.

Rawls, J., (1971) *A Theory of Justice*, Oxford: Oxford University Press.

Raz, J., (1983) *The Authority of Law*, Oxford: Oxford University Press.

Raz, J., (1985) 'Authority and Justification', *Philosophy and Public Affairs 14.*, 3–22.

Ross, A., (1958) *On Law and Justice*, London: Stevens.

Ross, A., (1969) 'On Self–Reference and a Puzzle in Constitutional Law', *Mind 78.*, 1–24.

Rousseau, J.–J., (1973) *The Social Contract and the Discourses* tr. and ed. G. D. H. Cole, London: Dent.

Ruben, D.–H., (1985) *The Metaphysics of the Social World*, London: Routledge & Kegan Paul.

Sahlins, M., (1974) *Stone Age Economics*, London: Tavistock Publications.

Sanders, J.T. (1983) 'Political Authority', *The Monist 66.* 545–556.

Sartorius, R., (1981) 'Political Authority and Political Obligation', *Virginia Law Review 67.*, 3–17.

Sartorius, R., (1987) 'Positivism and the Foundations of Legal Authority', in R. Gavison (ed.) *Issues in Contemporary Legal Philosophy. The Influence of H.L.A. Hart*, Oxford: Clarendon Press, 43–61.

Schotter, A., (1985) *Free Market Economics*, New York: St Martin's Press.

Schutz, A. (1967) *The Phenomenology of the Social World*, tr. G. Walsh and F. Lehnert, Northwestern University Press.

Searle, J., (1974) *Speech Acts*, Cambridge: Cambridge University Press.

Searle, J. (1991) 'Intentionalistic Explanations in the Social Sciences', *Philosophy of Social Sciences 21.*, 332–344.

Segerberg, K., (1979) 'Epistemic Considerations in Game Theory', *Theory and Decision 11.*, 363–373.

Seton–Watson, H. (1977) *Nations and States*, Boulder: Westwood Press.

Simmonds, N.E., (1984a) *The Decline of Juridical Reason*, Manchester: Manchester University Press.

Simmonds, N.E., (1984b) 'The Nature of Propositions of Law', *Rechtstheorie 15.*, 96–108.

Simon, H., (1957) *Administrative Behavior*, New York: MacMilllan.

Soper, P., (1984) *A Theory of Law*, Cambridge (Mass.): Harvard University Press.

Spencer, M.E., (1970) 'Weber on Legitimate Norms and Authority', *The British Journal of Sociology 21.*, 123–34.

Stankiewicz, W.J. (ed), (1969) *In Defense of Sovereignty*, New York: Oxford University Press.

Steiner, H., (1978) 'Can Social Contract be Signed by an Invisible Hand?', in P. Birnbaum, J. Lively and G. Parry (eds.) *Democracy, Consensus and Social Conflict*, London: SAGE Publications, 293–316.

Stonier, A.S. and Hague, D.C., (1973) *A Textbook of Economic Theory*, London: Longman.

Suber, P., (1990) *The Paradox of Self–Amendment*, New York: Peter Lang.

Tallqvist, J.V., (1920) *Merkantilistiska banksedelteorier*, Åbo: Acta Academiae Aboensis.

Taylor, R. (1983) 'The Basis of political Authority', *Monist 66.*, 457–71.

Thurow, L. C. (1983) *Dangerous Currents*, Oxford: Oxford University Press.

Timasheff, N., (1974) *An Introduction to the Sociology of Law*, Westport: Greenwood Publishers, [1939].

Tuomela, R., (1984) *A Theory of Social Action*, Dordrecht: Reidel.

Ullmann–Margalit, E., (1977) *The Emergence of Norms*, Oxford: Clarendon Press.

Ullmann–Margalit, E., (1983) 'Is Law a Coordinative Authority?', *Israel Law Review 16.*, 350–55.

Warnock, G.J., (1971) *The Object of Morality*, London: Methuen.

Watkins, J., (1974) 'Comment: Self–Interest and Morality', in S. Körner (ed.) *Practical Reason*, Oxford: Blackwell.

Watkins, J., (1985) 'Second Thoughts on Self–Interest and Morality', in R. Campbell and L. Sowden (eds.) *Paradoxes of Rationality and Cooperation*, Vancouver: University of British Colombia Press, 59–74.

Weber, M., (1978) *Economy and Society: An Outline of Interpretive Sociology*, ed. by G. Roth and C. Wittich, Berkeley: University of California Press [1920].

Winch, P., (1967) 'Authority', in A. Quinton (ed.) *Political Philosophy*, Oxford: Oxford University Press, 83–111.

Wolff, R.P., (1969) 'On Violence', *Journal of Philosophy 66.*, 601–16.

Wolff, R.P., (1976) *In Defense of Anarchism. 2nd ed.*, New York: Harper & Row.

Wolff, R.P., (1977) 'Reply to Professors Prithcard and Smith', *Journal of Value Inquiry* 7., 303–6.

Wood, M. (1988) 'Rule, Rules, and Law', in P. Leith and P. Ingram (eds.) *The Jurisprudence of Orthodoxy*, London: Routledge and Kegan Paul.

INDEX OF NAMES

Law and Philosophy Library

1. E. Bulygin, J.-L. Gardies and I. Niiniluoto (eds.): *Man, Law and Modern Forms of Life*. With an Introduction by M.D. Bayles. 1985 ISBN 90-277-1869-5
2. W. Sadurski: *Giving Desert Its Due*. Social Justice and Legal Theory. 1985 ISBN 90-277-1941-1
3. N. MacCormick and O. Weinberger: *An Institutional Theory of Law*. New Approaches to Legal Positivism. 1986 ISBN 90-277-2079-7
4. A. Aarnio: *The Rational as Reasonable*. A Treatise on Legal Justification. 1987 ISBN 90-277-2276-5
5. M.D. Bayles: *Principles of Law*. A Normative Analysis. 1987 ISBN 90-277-2412-1; Pb: 90-277-2413-X
6. A. Soeteman: *Logic in Law*. Remarks on Logic and Rationality in Normative Reasoning, Especially in Law. 1989 ISBN 0-7923-0042-4
7. C.T. Sistare: *Responsibility and Criminal Liability*. 1989 ISBN 0-7923-0396-2
8. A. Peczenik: *On Law and Reason*. 1989 ISBN 0-7923-0444-6
9. W. Sadurski: *Moral Pluralism and Legal Neutrality*. 1990 ISBN 0-7923-0565-5
10. M.D. Bayles: *Procedural Justice*. Allocating to Individuals. 1990 ISBN 0-7923-0567-1
11. P. Nerhot (ed.): *Law, Interpretation and Reality*. Essays in Epistemology, Hermeneutics and Jurisprudence. 1990 ISBN 0-7923-0593-0
12. A.W. Norrie: *Law, Ideology and Punishment*. Retrieval and Critique of the Liberal Ideal of Criminal Justice. 1991 ISBN 0-7923-1013-6
13. P. Nerhot (ed.): *Legal Knowledge and Analogy*. Fragments of Legal Epistemology, Hermeneutics and Linguistics. 1991 ISBN 0-7923-1065-9
14. O. Weinberger: *Law, Institution and Legal Politics*. Fundamental Problems of Legal Theory and Social Philosophy. 1991 ISBN 0-7923-1143-4
15. J. Wróblewski: *The Judicial Application of Law*. Edited by Z. Bańkowski and N. MacCormick. 1992 ISBN 0-7923-1569-3
16. T. Wilhelmsson: *Critical Studies in Private Law*. A Treatise on Need-Rational Principles in Modern Law. 1992 ISBN 0-7923-1659-2
17. M.D. Bayles: *Hart's Legal Philosophy*. An Examination. 1992 ISBN 0-7923-1981-8
18. D.W.P. Ruiter: *Institutional Legal Facts*. Legal Powers and their Effects. 1993 ISBN 0-7923-2441-2
19. J. Schonsheck: *On Criminalization*. An Essay in the Philosophy of the Criminal Law. 1994 ISBN 0-7923-2663-6
20. R.P. Malloy and J. Evensky (eds.): *Adam Smith and the Philosophy of Law and Economics*. 1994 ISBN 0-7923-2796-9
21. Z. Bankowski, I. White and U. Hahn (eds.): *Informatics and the Foundations of Legal Reasoning*. Forthcoming.
22. E. Lagerspetz: *The Opposite Mirrors*. An Essay on the Conventionalist Theory of Institutions. 1995 ISBN 0-7923-3325-X

KLUWER ACADEMIC PUBLISHERS – DORDRECHT / BOSTON / LONDON